China's Rural Labor Migration and Its Economic Development

Series on Chinese Economics Research*
(ISSN: 2251-1644)

Series Editor: Fan Gang *(Peking University, China)*

Published:

Vol. 20: *China's Rural Labor Migration and Its Economic Development*
by Liu Xiaoguang

Vol. 19: *Environmental Economics Research and China's Green Development Strategy*
by Zhang Youguo
translated by Xu Hao, Xie Linlin

Vol. 18: *The Transformation of China's Economic Development: Perspectives of Sino–US Economists*
by Yang Wandong, Zhang Jianjun, Huang Shudong and Zhu Andong

Vol. 17: *Income Distribution and China's Economic "New Normal"*
by Wan Haiyuan and Li Shi

Vol. 16: *Research on Efficiency and Fairness of Resources Allocation by China's Governmental Administration*
by Sheng Hong and Qian Pu

Vol. 15: *Industrial Overcapacity and Duplicate Construction in China: Reasons and Solutions*
by Li Ping, Jiang Feitao and Cao Jianhai

Vol. 14: *Reforging the Central Bank: The Top-Level Design of the Chinese Financial System in the New Normal*
by Deng Haiqing and Chen Xi

Vol. 13: *Social Integration of Rural-Urban Migrants in China: Current Status, Determinants and Consequences*
by Yue Zhongshan, Li Shuzhuo and Marcus W Feldman

Vol. 12: *Game: The Segmentation, Implementation and Protection of Land Rights in China*
by Zhang Shuguang

*For the complete list of volumes in this series, please visit
www.worldscientific.com/series/scer

Series on Chinese Economics Research – Vol. 20

China's Rural Labor Migration and Its Economic Development

LIU Xiaoguang

Renmin University of China, China

中国社会科学出版社
CHINA SOCIAL SCIENCES PRESS

 World Scientific

Published by

World Scientific Publishing Co. Pte. Ltd.

5 Toh Tuck Link, Singapore 596224

USA office: 27 Warren Street, Suite 401-402, Hackensack, NJ 07601

UK office: 57 Shelton Street, Covent Garden, London WC2H 9HE

Library of Congress Cataloging-in-Publication Data

Names: Liu, Xiaoguang (Associate professor), author.

Title: China's rural labor migration and its economic development / Liu Xiaoguang,
Renmin University of China, China.

Description: Hackensack, NJ : World Scientific, [2020] | Series: Series on Chinese economics
research, 2251-1644 ; vol. 20 | Includes bibliographical references and index.

Identifiers: LCCN 2019057616 | ISBN 9789811208584 (hardcover) |
ISBN 9789811208591 (ebook)

Subjects: LCSH: Labor market--China. | Migrant labor--China. | Rural-urban migration--China. |
Economic development--China.

Classification: LCC HD5830.A6 L5865 2020 | DDC 331.5/440951--dc23

LC record available at https://lccn.loc.gov/2019057616

British Library Cataloguing-in-Publication Data

A catalogue record for this book is available from the British Library.

Sponsored by B&R Book Program

农业劳动力转移与中国经济发展
Originally published in Chinese by China Social Sciences Press
Copyright © China Social Sciences Press, 2017

For any available supplementary material, please visit
https://www.worldscientific.com/worldscibooks/10.1142/11507#t=suppl

Desk Editors: Aanand Jayaraman/Lixi Dong

Typeset by Stallion Press
Email: enquiries@stallionpress.com

Foreword

In less than 40 years of reform and opening-up, China's economy has changed dramatically, with more than a 200-fold increase in the nominal GDP and even more than a 30-fold increase in the real GDP after the exception of the price factor. Throughout the history of mankind, China's economy has grown at an unprecedented rate, eclipsing numerous ingenious growth theories. In 2016, China became the world's second largest economy with a GDP of nearly RMB 75 trillion, but its growth rate still ranked first in the world, making a great impression on many economists.

In the miracle of China's economic growth, the great changes on the labor market undoubtedly play a vital role. Compared with the previous vigorous market-oriented reform of state-owned enterprise (SOE) employees, China's agricultural labor force has a larger scale of transfer, a longer duration and a more far-reaching impact, but it has not been duly valued and studied. In 2016, the total number of migrant workers exceeded 280 million, accounting for 36.3% of the total number of the population with employment and 68.1% of the urban population with employment in China. It is really a "very large but special" group. To a large extent, it can be said that the academic community has just a relatively superficial understanding of the role of the group in China's economic development, and knows little about the social benefits that the group enjoys in cities. More importantly, much of the academic research assumes or believes, to varying degrees, that they just provide an element of cheap labor for the industrial development of urban sectors. Such wrong recognition is especially prevalent in reality. Even faced with the continuous slowdown in the transfer of agricultural labor in recent years, many cities are still reluctant to make the basic benefits of citizens that the group deserves accessible to the group. One of the reasons is no doubt the serious underestimation of the group's role in and contribution to urban development, regardless of any considerations.

This book aims to clarify the role of the transfer of agricultural labor in China's economic development rather than the labor element provided to the urban sectors. The continuous large-scale transfer of agricultural labor to cities changes the fundamental characteristics of China's labor market, profoundly affects China's investments, savings, technological progress and economic cycle fluctuation, and more importantly, plays an important and special role in the rapid development of non-agricultural industries. To illustrate it, this book first systematically presents the three most important characteristics of China's economic development, involving China's investment, savings and economic growth, and respectively summarizes them as the riddle of China's rising return on capital, the riddle of China's rising rate of saving and the riddle of "Okun's law" not applicable to China. Solving these issues is the key to understanding China's model of economic development. This book comprehensively explains the three riddles of development from the perspective of the transfer of agricultural labor through theoretical and empirical analysis. One of the important practical implications of this book is that the impact of the current slowdown or even stagnation in the transfer of agricultural labor on China's economy is not only marginal but also directional. If it is expected to maintain fast economic growth, it is absolutely a sensible choice to put more effort into promoting the transfer of agricultural labor at both the national and urban levels. It is not only out of fairness but also for the development of the city itself to give due recognition to the contributions of migrant workers to urban construction.

Liu Xiaoguang
Research Building of Renmin University of China
January 2017

Preface

Since the reform and opening-up in 1978, China has achieved remarkable progress in economic development. By 2014, the average annual GDP growth rate was nearly 10% and the total GDP increased 28-fold, a miracle in the history of world economic development. However, with the outbreak of the global financial crisis, China's economic growth has gradually declined, from a peak of 14.2% in 2007 to 6.9% in 2015, arousing widespread concern about the sustainability of China's rapid economic growth, especially the controversial imbalance in its economic structure caused by high investment and high savings. Fortunately, China's job market still seems to be in good shape without being significantly affected in the context of the economic downturn. How to understand China's economic development, economic structural imbalance and recent labor market performance becomes a major concern for academics and policymakers.

A review of China's economic developmental experience in recent decades reveals the following three basic characteristics. First, since the reform and opening-up, China has maintained an extremely high rate of investment, 39.4% per year on average, nearly 50% in recent years, which is almost twice the world average. For a long time, however, China's return on capital has shown a sustained upward trend rather than a downward trend. Second, since the reform and opening-up, China's national rate of saving has been rising steadily; especially in the 21st century, it has risen faster, from 37.6% in 2000 to 52.6% in 2010, and it fell to 49.5% in 2014. Third, no significant inverse relationship exists between China's GDP growth rate and the existing data for the unemployment rate described by "Okun's law", which seems to indicate a lack of necessary correlation between China's macroeconomic cycle and the changes in the labor market. These three characteristics involve China's investments, savings, economic growth and labor market, so that they are the key to understanding China's model of economic development. They can be summarized as the riddle of China's rising return on capital, the riddle of China's rising saving rate and the riddle of the "Okun's law" not applicable to China.

The aforementioned three basic characteristics or riddles of China's economic development can be understood from different perspectives. This book attempts to make an analysis from the transfer of agricultural labor to gain some preliminary understanding of China's model of economic development. Before the reform and opening-up, China implemented a strict household registration system to control the flow of farmers into cities, thus forming a separated urban–rural labor market. However, since the reform and opening-up, China has gradually relaxed the restrictions on the flow of farmers in policy. The agricultural labor force has been shifting to non-agricultural sectors at an annual rate of 8 million for more than 30 years. The year 2014 witnessed the fact that the peasant workers with a number of 270 million accounted for more than 50% of the total number of employed people in non-agricultural sectors, and the number of migrant workers accounted for more than 60% of the total number of peasant workers. The continuous large-scale transfer of agricultural labor has not only completely changed the fundamental characteristics and the efficiency of the configuration of China's labor market but has also profoundly affected China's investments, savings, technological progress, urban–rural income distribution and macroeconomic fluctuations, and more importantly, it has played a vital role in the rapid development of urban sectors.

Thus, this book first of all combines the theory of the development of a dual economy and the theory of endogenous growth to analyze the three basic characteristics of China's economic development from the perspective of the transfer of agricultural labor on the basis of an overview of the basic picture of the transfer of agricultural labor. This book argues that the key in the understanding of China's high amount of investment and high amount of savings is to understand China's capital return and productivity improvement, and further to understand the backup technological progress and continuous mass transfer of agricultural labor. The transfer of agricultural labor in turn contributes to the unique pattern of the relationship between China's labor market and the macroeconomic cycle. Finally, this book proposes some policy suggestions for China to develop macro policies and developmental strategies based on the results of the research. The book consists of the following six chapters.

The first chapter gives an introduction, which states the research background and ideas of analysis of this book. Considering the three basic characteristics of China's economic development, this paper further brings forward the three riddles to understand China's economic development, namely, the riddle of China's rising return on capital, the riddle of China's rising rate of saving and the riddle of the "Okun's law" that is not applicable to China. On this basis, the author proposes the idea of research to interpret and analyze these aspects from the perspective of the transfer of agricultural labor.

The second chapter specially introduces the situation of the transfer of China's agricultural laborers, and discusses the general situation and the driving factors of the transfer of agricultural labor, and the supporting role of the improvement of agricultural productivity in China's economic transformation. The description of the general situation of the transfer of agricultural labor helps to understand the past, the *status quo* and the prospect of the transfer of agricultural labor. Analysis suggests that the driving factors of the transfer of agricultural labor are the improvement of the urban–rural income gap and the level of infrastructures, the increase in the economy and the return on capital, and the development of private sectors in China, and the existing biased factors such as financial development and public spending on education are unfavorable for the transfer of agricultural labor. With an analysis of the evolutionary trend of China's agricultural labor productivity in the context of the transfer of agricultural labor, this book investigates the supporting roles of the improvement of the efficiency of agricultural production in China's economic transformation.

Since the reform and opening-up, great progress has been achieved in the efficiency of China's agricultural production, which can even be regarded as an agricultural revolution. It not only addresses the problem of the security of China's food but also plays a fundamental role in supporting the contemporary economic transformation.

The third chapter solves the riddle of China's rising return on capital through theoretical and empirical analysis. The structural transformation of China's economy is re-examined from an endogenous perspective, and an expanded model of a dual economy is constructed based on the emphasis on the transfer of agricultural labor and the effect of technology spillover in order to explain the coexistence of the high investment rate and the rising rate of capital return in China. The expanded model relaxes the hypothesis of unit elasticity of the "knowledge spillover model" on the effect of technology spillover to indicate the strong and weak conditions for an economy of different stages to maintain or increase its return on capital. The theoretical research shows that the requirement on the effect of technology spillover is turned from a strong condition to a weak condition for the transfer of labor to realize rising return on capital, and besides, the combination of the transfer of labor and technology spillover is the key to explaining the rising capital return in China. The empirical analysis reveals that the effect of China's technology spillover meets the weak condition and backs up the rising return on capital in conjunction with the continuous transfer of the labor force.

The fourth chapter analyzes the riddle of China's rising rate of saving. A general model of equilibrium is established to analyze the residents' decisions regarding consumption and savings, and divides the total rate of saving into the rate of saving of urban residents, the rate of saving of migrant workers and that of farmers. The migrant workers have a higher tendency toward marginal saving than farmers and urban residents, thanks to the difference of levels of social security and income. In the course of the continuous transfer of agricultural labor to non-agricultural sectors, the population of migrant workers has been expanding with the capital accumulation of non-agricultural sectors, and their behavior regarding a high degree of saving has also contributed to the rise of the rate of household saving and that of national saving.

The fifth chapter analyzes the transfer of agricultural labor and the short-term fluctuations in China's macroeconomy. In light of the empirical observation of the relationship between China's macroeconomic cycle and the transformation of its labor market, this chapter proposes the concept of Okun's law in a broad sense, which introduces the factor of the transfer of agricultural labor, and explains why Okun's law is not applicable to China by virtue of the empirical data of China. The application form of Okun's law in a broad sense is associated with the stage of economic development. Okun's model, which only includes the variable of unemployment rate, is applicable to the developed countries that have completed their transfer of labor, and Okun's relationship applicable to more economies in transition is supposed to include the variable of the transfer of agricultural labor. China's unique institutional environment leads to a lack of a significant link between the rate of urban unemployment and the macro-cyclical change. This chapter also uses the transnational panel data to preliminarily test the generalized Okun's law.

The sixth chapter summarizes the main research conclusions, presents the policy suggestions, and points out the shortcomings of this study and the future direction of in-depth study. The research conclusions and policy suggestions involved the following aspects. First, China's rising return on capital and sustained rapid economic growth in recent years, on the one hand, get benefits from the effect of technology spillover in the process of investment and production, and on the other hand, are supported by the transfer of agricultural labor. Therefore, it is still necessary to actively implement the policies favorable for transfer of agricultural labor, give full play to the combined effect of the transfer of labor and technology spillover in the improvement of return on capital, and maintain rapid economic growth. At the same time, we should formulate and implement the policies favorable for technological innovation, raise the level of the effect of technology spillover, and make preparations for meeting the strong condition of return on capital in the future. Second, reducing the urban–rural gap in social medical security is an effective measure to improve the level of consumption and reduce the rate of saving. Improving the level of social medical security enjoyed by rural residents through the establishment of a unified social medical security system can boost the consumption of farmers, especially migrant workers, and decrease the rate of household saving, thus helping to reduce the national rate of saving. Third, in addition to the changes in the indicators of the unemployment rate, more attention should be paid to the cyclical changes in the transfer of agricultural labor in the event of formulation of any employment policy. In China's period of transition, the transfer of labor force constitutes a basic variable connecting the macroeconomic cycle and the fluctuation of the labor market, which shields urban employment from macroeconomic volatility, coupled with the household registration and labor employment system and policies. The strong convertibility of migrant workers between non-agricultural employment and agricultural employment absorbs the impact of macroeconomic fluctuations on the labor market to a great extent, and reduces the sensitivity of the indicators of the unemployment rate to macroeconomic fluctuations. Fourth, China now is still witnessing the huge transferable agricultural labor force, and the potential "transformation dividend" will continue to exert an enormous growth effect for a long term. So, it is optimistic that China can successfully get out of the medium income trap in the future, and the key is to develop a reasonable incentive policy to promote the transfer of agricultural labor and the construction of new urbanization.

About the Author

Mr. Liu Xiaoguang is currently an Associate Professor of National Academy of Development and Strategy, and the Director of China Centre for Government Debt Research in Renmin University of China (RUC). He received a PhD of Economics from Peking University, and was a Visiting Scholar at New York University and University of Chicago. He served as a Part-time Economist at the International Monetary Fund, as well as a Consultant for the Asian Development Bank. Liu's study focusses on Macro Finance, International Economics and the Labor Market, on which he has published more than 20 academic papers and 4 monographs. He has been consistently engaged in compiling the Keynote Presentation of *China Macroeconomic Forum*, a quarterly forum hosted by RUC since 2006. Based on his outstanding work, Liu has been awarded *Liu Shibai Economics Prize, Outstanding Scientific Research Award of Renmin University of China, China's Think Tank Academic Achievement Award and National Excellent Doctoral Dissertation of Economics.*

About the Translator

Zhang Zhen holds a Ph.D. in philosophy. Her main research interest lies in systems philosophy and social philosophy. She has published papers in several Chinese core journals such as *Studies in Dialectics of Natural*, and has translated into Chinese and published Dee Hock's book *One from Many: VISA and the Rise of Chaordic Organization.*

Acknowledgments

Since the time when I was a graduate student, I have been paying close attention to and studying the transfer of agricultural labor and economic development in China. This book, as a further refinement and improvement of my doctoral dissertation research, can be said to have absorbed the essence of my research findings during my studies at Peking University. After in-depth consideration and polishing during my teaching at Renmin University of China, the book was finally published.

For the compilation of this book, I would first like to extend my sincere gratitude to many teachers and friends during my studies at the National School of Development, Peking University, such as Song Guoqing, Lin Yifu, Yao Yang, Zhang Fan, Fan Gang, Huang Yiping, Alfred Schipke, Alberto Pozzolo, Xu Jianguo, Zhang Bin, Zeng Gang, Lu Ming, Zhang Yuan, Chen Binkai, Lin Wei-ji, Chen Jianqi, Li Yuan-fang, Li Xin, Li Lixing, Yan Ping, Wang Min, Zhao Bo, Luo Zhi, Xie Peichu, Gouqin, Ma Guangrong, Jia Xu, Wang Jian, Zhang Jieping, Zhang Xun, Zhao Yue Shen Guangjun, Zhou Guangsu, Wang Yaqi, Li Shuangshuang, Jiang Zhixiao, Zhou Junan, Eu Xingxing, Yang Yewei and Qiu Muyuan.

Besides, I would like to thank the many colleagues during my teaching experience at the National Academy of Development and Strategy, RUC, such as Hu Naiwu, Yang Ruilong, Liu Fengliang, Mao Zhenhua, Yang Guangbin, Guojie, Radar, Yanyan, Nie Huihua, Wang Jinbin, Zheng

Xinye, Chen Yanbin, Zheng Chaoyu, Wang Lili, Wu Cong, Zhang Jie, Luo Laijun, Taoran, Li Yong, Yu Chunhai, Yinheng, Ding Shouhai, Fan Zhiyong, Yu Ze, Sun Wenkai, Wang Xiaosong, Liu Ruiming, Feng Junxin, Yu Yihua, Xia Xiao Hua, Liu Xiaolu, Zhao Yong, Chen Zhanming, Songlu, Liu Kai and Lin Xuelin.

I would also like to thank the National Academy of Development and Strategy for funding, all my colleagues for their strong support and Wang Cheng, editor of the China Social Sciences Press, and his colleagues, for their meticulous editing and proofreading.

Last but not least, I would like to express my special thanks to my supervisor, professor Lu Feng, who guided me to complete my doctoral dissertation and embark on the right academic path with his rigorous scholarship and generous manner; professor Liu Yuanchun, who encouraged me to deepen my research and compile it into a book, and brought me to the ideal path of serving my country through scientific research with his lofty patriotism of governing and benefiting the people. Besides, special thanks are given to the members of my family for their quiet support, as they always give me strength and allow me to march forward regardless of the hardships.

Liu Xiaoguang
Research Building of Renmin University of China
January 2017

Contents

Chapter 1

Introduction

I. Characteristics of China's Economy

Since the reform and opening-up in 1978, China's economic development has achieved a remarkable feat, with a real GDP growth rate of nearly 10% on average in the past 36 years, and a 28-fold increase in the total GDP in 2014 from 1978 (see Figure 1.1). The total GDP measured in US dollars at a market exchange rate exceeded $10 trillion, and its share of the global economy rose from only 1.9% in 1980 to 13.4% in 2014, and if measured in purchasing power parity, that share rose from 2.3% in 1980 to 16.3% in 2014.[1] In terms of all indicators, China's economic development in the past nearly 40 years is a miracle in the history of world economic development.[2] However, since the outbreak of the global financial

---

[1] The data come from the World Economic Outlook Database compiled by the International Monetary Fund.

[2] The details are as follows: Since the reform and opening-up, the level of income of both urban and rural residents in China has been constantly improved. The per capita disposable income of urban residents and the per capita net income of rural residents amounted to only RMB 343 and RMB 134 in 1978, and reached up to RMB 28,844 and RMB 9,892 in 2014, with an increase of 83 times and 73 times from 1978 in nominal terms, respectively. Based on the international poverty line of less than $1.25 of expenditure per person per day, the number of people living in absolute poverty in China fell from 835 million in 1981 to 68 million in 2013. By the end of 2014, the number of people participating in the

1

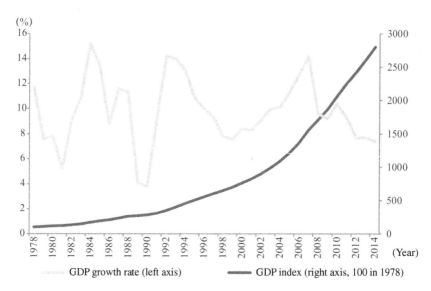

Figure 1.1.   China's GDP growth rate and GDP index (1978–2014).

Source: *China Statistical Yearbook* prepared by the National Bureau of Statistics.

crisis, China's economic growth rate has gradually declined, from the peak of 14.2% in 2007 to 6.9% in 2015, with a decrease in the growth rate by half. Most forecasting agencies have lowered China's growth forecast to about 6% in the coming years.[3] Besides, the general concerns about China's economy are the economic structure imbalance and the sustainability arising from high investment and high savings rate. Fortunately, China's job market still seems to be in good shape without being significantly affected in the context of the economic downturn. How to understand China's economic development, economic structural imbalance and recent labor market performance becomes a major concern for academics and policymakers.

---

basic endowment insurance for urban workers reached 341 million nationwide, the number of people participating in the basic endowment insurance for urban and rural residents reached 501 million and the number of people participating in the basic medical insurance reached 598 million.

[3]For example, the International Monetary Fund (2015) cut its forecast for China's growth rate in 2015 and 2016 to 6.8% and 6.3%, respectively.

A review of China's economic developmental experience in recent decades reveals the following three basic characteristics. First, since the reform and opening-up, China has maintained an extremely high rate of investment, 39.4% per year on average, nearly 50% in recent years, which is almost twice the world average. For a long time, however, China's return on capital has shown a sustained upward trend rather than a downward trend. Second, since the reform and opening-up, China's national savings rate has been rising steadily; especially in recent years, it has risen faster from 37.6% in 2000 to 52.6% in 2010, and fallen to 49.5% in 2014. Third, no significant inverse relationship exists between China's GDP growth rate and the existing data for the unemployment rate described by Okun's law, which seems to indicate a lack of a necessary correlation between China's macroeconomic cycle and the changes in the labor market. These three characteristics involve China's investments, savings, economic growth and labor market, so that they are the key to an understanding of China's model of economic development.

Considering the key characteristics of China's economic growth, it is apparent that the key to an understanding of China's model of economic development is to understand China's high amount of investments, high savings rate and its labor market, while the key to an understanding of China's high amount of investments and high savings rate is to understand China's high capital return and improvement in productivity, and then to understand China's technological progress and continuous large-scale transfer of agricultural labor. The transfer of agricultural labor in turn forms a unique pattern of the relationship between China's labor market and the macroeconomic cycle. To highlight their importance, this book summarizes the three basic characteristics as the riddle of China's rising return on capital, the riddle of China's rising savings rate and the riddle of Okun's law that is not applicable to China. In the following sections, we will introduce the three basic characteristics or the riddles of development in detail to further present the research ideas of this book.

1. *The riddle of China's rising return on capital*

The most striking thing is that China has maintained a high rate of investment in the context of the rapid growth of China's economy.

The calculation based on the data released by the National Bureau of Statistics showed that China's investment rate was never lower than 30% from 1980 to 2014, averaging 39.4%. In the 21st century, China's investment rate has risen further, close to 50% recently, far higher than that of other countries in the world and almost twice the world average (see Figure 1.2). China's high amount of investments has not only supported the rapid economic growth but has also aroused widespread concerns about the economic structural imbalance and sustainability. Therefore, it is more worthwhile to further study and analyze why China can maintain such a high rate of investment for a long term. In the world, the problem facing most countries is always an insufficient amount of investments rather than the high rate of investment. In other words, it is not easy to keep such a high rate of investment in the long run, and even in the presence of favorable policies, it is almost impossible to achieve it without economic fundamentals.

For this reason, it is necessary to deeply analyze the capital return in China. The study shows that such a high rate of investment in China has not led to a decline in the capital return; on the contrary, much empirical evidence provided by scholars in recent years shows that, since the middle and late 1990s, China's return on capital has been on the rise for a long time, as reported earlier by the World Bank.[4] The results of the estimation of China's return on capital by Bai, Hsieh and Qian based on the national income data suggest that China's return on capital has been maintained at a high level of more than 20% throughout the period of reform and opening-up, and also has been on the rise in recent years.[5] In view of the results of the calculation of capital returns and of capital stock data in the financial accounts in industrial enterprises, the Research Group of the CCER China Economic Observer demonstrates that China's return on capital presents a feature of first falling then rising, and the nine series of indicators show a sustained trend of growth after the end of the last century. By calculating the rate of return on industrial capital, Shu Yuan, Zhang Li and Xu Xianxiang also point out that the rate of capital return in

---

[4]The World Bank (WB) China Office: *China Quarterly Update*, May 2006.
[5]Bai, C., C. Hsieh and Y. Qian: The Return to Capital in China, *Brookings Papers on Economic Activity*, 2006 (2), pp. 61–88.

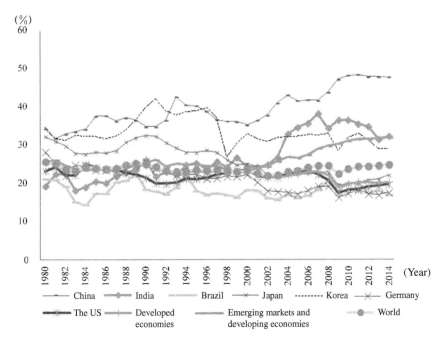

Figure 1.2. Comparison of investment rates between China and the world's major economies (1980–2014).

Note: Investment rate, known as capital formation rate, refers to the percentage of total capital formation in GDP.

Source: World Economic Outlook Database compiled by the International Monetary Fund.

China has increased significantly over the past decade.[6] From the perspective of vintage capital theory, Fang Wenquan re-estimates the capital return in China, and adjusts the rate of capital return downward by 3%–5% by virtue of the revised depreciation rate, but the overall change remains upward.[7] Based on the calibration of statistical caliber and the method of calculation, Zhang Xun and Xu Jianguo match the different measurement methods of capital return in China, and further conclude that

---

[6] Shu Yuan, Zhang Li and Xu Xianxiang: An Analysis of the Chinese Industrial Capital Return and Allocation Efficiency: Calculation and Decomposition, *Economic Review*, 2010 (1), pp. 28–36.

[7] Fang Wenquan: China's Capital Returns: A Re-estimation from the Perspective of the Vintage Capital Model, *China Economic Quarterly*, 2012 (11) (2), pp. 159–178..

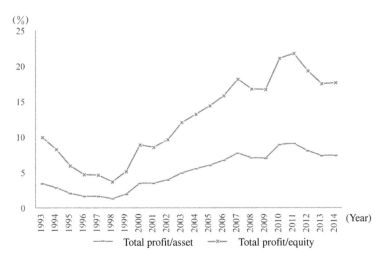

Figure 1.3.   Return on industrial capital in China (1993–2014).

Note: The two kinds of Chinese industrial capital returns from 1993 to 2012 are calculated according to the method of Lu *et al.* (2008). In this method, the total profit is the amount of profit without a deduction of enterprise income tax, which is a measurement index of capital return; asset and equity (net assets) are two measurement indexes of capital stock with different calibers.

Source: Compilation of the Statistical Data of China's Industrial Transportation and Energy for 50 Years and The China Statistical Yearbook over the years.

the total return on capital has risen steadily from 1998, but dropped in 2009; however, the return on industrial capital still presents an upward trend, for instance, the return on industrial fixed assets was up to 27.8% in 2012.[8] The upward trend of China's return on capital is clearly shown in the report data in Figure 1.3.

So, how can we understand the phenomenon of the coexistence of a high rate of investment and a rising capital return in China? This phenomenon is not only inconsistent with the law of diminishing marginal capital returns but also significantly different from the international developmental experience. Solving this riddle is undoubtedly the key to understanding China's model of economic development.

---

[8]Zhang Xun and Xu Jianguo: Re-measurement of China's Return on Capital, *The Journal of World Economy*, 2014 (8), pp. 5–25.

2. *The riddle of China's rising savings rate*

China's national savings rate has been rising steadily, and especially in the 21st century, it has risen faster from 37.6% in 2000 to 52.6% in 2010, and recently fallen to 49.5% in 2014 (see Figure 1.4). China's high savings support not only its high investment from the capital supply side but also greatly contribute to the imbalance of the country's economic structure. On the one hand, the imbalance of the low consumption–high savings structure starts to emerge; on the other hand, the storage–investment difference is expanding, resulting in an external imbalance.[9] Greenspan even argues that a high savings rate in developing countries has led to the long-term low interest rate and been the fundamental cause of the housing bubble and the global financial crisis of the past two decades.[10] Therefore, it is particularly important to explain the reasons for China's high national savings rate and thus develop the idea of alleviating structural imbalances.

To understand the root cause of the rising rate of national savings, it is necessary to decompose the structure of national savings. According to departments, national savings can be divided into resident savings, enterprise savings and government savings. Figure 1.5 shows the proportion of those three types of savings in the national savings since 2000. In 2009, the three types of savings accounted for 48.3%, 41.9% and 9.8% of national savings, respectively, clearly showing the dominant position of residents and enterprises in the national savings. In recent years, the savings rate of residents (residents' savings rate) and the savings rate of enterprises both have shown an upward trend to jointly raise the overall national savings rate. Therefore, the discussion of resident savings and enterprise savings is conducive to understanding the national savings rate. Fan Gang and Lu Yan explain why the enterprise savings rate has been rising in recent years.[11] Through study, they believe that China is still in

---

[9]Fan Gang and Lv Yan: Economic Development and National Savings Expansion: Extended by the Lewis Dual Economy Model, *Economic Research Journal*, 2013 (3), pp. 19–29.

[10]Greenspan, A.: The Fed Didn't Cause the Housing Bubble, *The Wall Street Journal*, 2009 (11), p. 15.

[11]Fan Gang and Lv Yan: Economic Developing Stage and National Saving Expansion: Extend by the Lewis'Dual Economy Model, *Economic Research Journal*, 2013 (3), pp. 19–29.

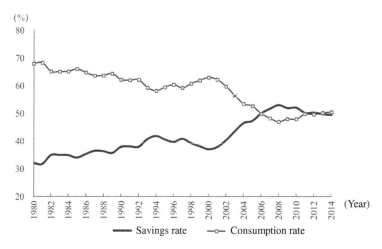

Figure 1.4.   China's national consumption rate and savings rate (1980–2014).

Note: The consumption rate is the proportion of consumption expenditure in the GDP with an expenditure-based GDP accounting; savings rate = 1 – consumption rate.
Source: China Statistical Yearbook.

the dual economy state before the Lewis turning point, and the existence of a surplus labor force puts the labor force in a weak position in the game of labor and capital, further leading to a slow increase in wages; with the reform of the system and the opening-up of the market, the efficiency of the production of enterprises has greatly improved, but capital occupies more of this part of the value. With the expansion of the capital scale, profits will accumulate at a higher rate and eventually form large-scale enterprise savings.

China's resident savings rate also keeps rising from 31.1% in 2000 to 40.4% in 2009 (Figure 1.6). In spite of a slight decrease in recent years, the proportion of resident savings is still large and will further increase under the guidance of the policy of "increasing the disposable income of residents", which will play a significant role in determining the trend of the national savings rate in the future. In addition, according to the international comparative study of Blanchard and Giavazzi, the savings rate of Chinese enterprises and of the Chinese government are not exceptional in transnational comparisons, and the high savings rate in China is

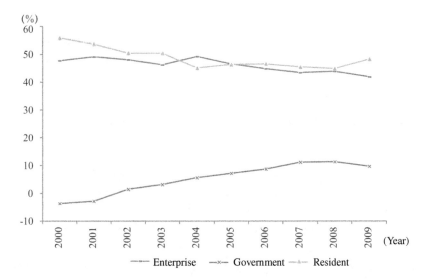

Figure 1.5.   Proportion of three-sector savings in national savings (2000–2009).
Source: 2001–2010 Fund Flow Statement in *The China Statistical Yearbook*.

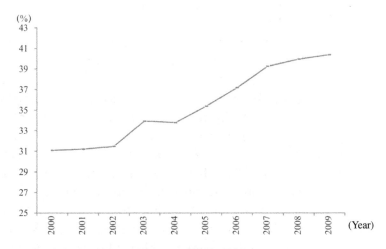

Figure 1.6.   China's resident savings rate (2000–2009).
Source: 2001–2010 Fund Flow Statement in *The China Statistical Yearbook*.

still closely associated with a high resident savings rate.[12] Thus, it is necessary to focus on the reasons for the rise of the resident savings rate in China in recent years, and further explore the trend of the national savings rate.

3. The riddle of "Okun's Law" not being applicable to China

In recent years, China's job market has maintained a good condition without being significantly affected in the context of the economic downturn. For example, the registered urban unemployment rate was about 4% and the surveyed unemployment rate was about 5% in 2014, almost unchanged from 2013. Moreover, China's economic performance since the reform and opening-up suggests that, as for the market of China's labor force and its macroeconomic fluctuations, a significant inverse relationship has not been established between the GDP growth rate and the unemployment data, as inferred by the standard model of Okun's law. This seems to show that China's macroeconomic cycle lacks a due correlation with the changes in the labor market, or the model of Okun's law is not applicable to the Chinese empirical data.

Okun's law, as a standard model of modern macroeconomics textbooks, is essentially used to analyze the relationship between a country's macroeconomic cycle and the labor market changes, and its specific form is to reveal the stable negative relationship between a country's unemployment rate and actual output. Figure 1.7 shows the annual data of the changes in the US unemployment rate and the economic growth rate from 1948 to 2013, indicating that the Okun relationship was roughly established. In the late 1970s, China began to implement the reform and opening-up policy and gradually set up an institutional framework for the market, with an annual growth rate of nearly 10% achieved over the past 30 years. The intensification of the market-oriented reform led to an increase in the unemployment pressure in China in the late 1990s, which prompted the government to give importance to the objectives of the

---

[12]Blanchard, O. and F. Giavazzi: Rebalancing Growth in China: A Three-Handed Approach, *China & World Economy*, 2006 (14) (4), pp. 1–20.

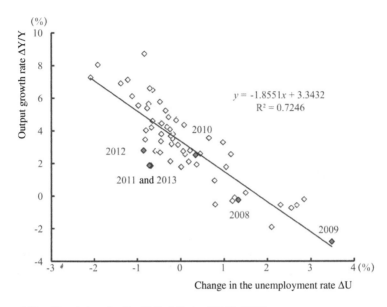

Figure 1.7. Okun's law for the United States (1948–2013).

Source: The Bureau of Economic Analysis (BEA) and the Bureau of Labor Statistics (BLS).

employment policy. Quite a lot of the literature has focused on the relationship between Okun's law model and the Chinese data in academic circles. Surprisingly, as shown in Figure 1.8, there is no significant inverse relationship between China's GDP growth rate and the official unemployment rate as described by Okun's law, which is in sharp contrast with the situation in the United States.

Researchers have investigated the applicability of Okun's law in China from different aspects. Some scholars have discovered that there is no significant relationship between the change in the rate of registered urban unemployment and the economic growth rate in China, and that the real GDP growth rate and the change in the rate of unemployment vary greatly from the assumed form of Okun's law.[13] Yin Bibo and Zhou Jianjun also pointed out that the negative relationship between China's economic

---

[13] Jiang Wei and Liu Shicheng: The Okun Model and China's Empirical Data (1978–2004), *Statistics and Decision*, 2005 (24), pp. 7–9; Li Han and Pu Xiaohong: An Analysis of the Applicability of Okun's Law in China, *Commercial Research*, 2009 (6), pp. 21–22.

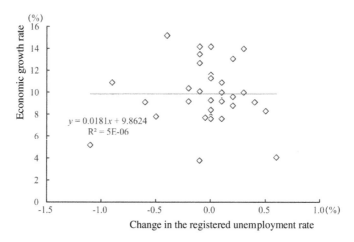

Figure 1.8.   Changes in China's GDP growth rate and unemployment rate (1979–2012).
Note: The data come from the *China Statistical Yearbook* over the years, estimated by the author.

growth rate and the growth rate of employed people proves the inapplicability of Okun's law in China.[14] Fang Fuqian and Sun Yongjun tested the five versions of the empirical form of Okun's law, such as difference, gap, asymmetry, etc., and found out that none of them is applicable to the Chinese situation.[15] By calculating the Okun equation in the expansion period and the recession period, Lin Xiumei found that the coefficient of the rate of unemployment on the growth rate is very small, and only when the value of the deviation trend of the growth rate is about 20 percentage points was the change in the rate of unemployment about 1 percentage point, reflecting the fact that the expansion stage coefficient is a plus sign and is inconsistent with the theoretical hypothesis.[16] The results of the calculation of the Okun equation of the three industries by Zou Wei based on the data of the three industries show that a significant Okun

[14]Yin Bibo and Zhou Jianjun: China's High Economic Growth and Low Employment: Empirical Study of Okun's Law in China, *Finance & Economics*, 2010 (1), pp. 56–61.

[15]Fang Fuqian and Sun Yongjun: Applicability Test of Okun's Law in China, *Economics Information*, 2010 (12), pp. 20–25.

[16]Lin Xiumei and Wang Lei: A Study of the Non-linear Dynamic Correlation between Economic Growth and Unemployment Rate — Reconsideration of Okun's Law, *The Journal of Quantitative Economics*, 2006 (1), pp. 64–73.

relationship exists between the primary and secondary industries, and the positive Okun coefficient estimation sign of the tertiary industry deviates from the predicted meaning of Okun's law.[17]

The above basic empirical facts and the results of the research on the relationship between the unemployment rate and the macroeconomic fluctuation indicate that it is "unacclimatized" to directly apply the existing model of Okun's law to China. So what is the root cause of this phenomenon? What is the real form of China's Okun relationship? The answers are undoubtedly of great theoretical and practical significance for judging China's current employment situation and for formulating labor market policies.

II. The Understanding of China's Economy from the Perspective of the Transfer of Agricultural Labor

The three basic characteristics or riddles of China's economic development can be understood from different perspectives. Based on the empirical observation of China's economic transformation, it is clear that behind China's high investment, high savings rate and high capital return, a common supporting factor is the continuous large-scale transfer of agricultural labor. What's more, the short-term change in the transfer of agricultural labor relative to its long-term trend is also a key variable that reflects the relationship between the labor market and the macroeconomic cycle, eventually forming a unique form of correlation between China's labor market and the fluctuation of the macroeconomic cycle. Therefore, this book attempts to analyze the three riddles of China's economic development from the transfer of agricultural labor so as to gain some understanding of China's economic developmental model.

The track of the reform and development of China's labor market shows that the large-scale transfer of agricultural labor has not only brought about profound changes to China's labor market but has also

---

[17]Zou Wei and Hu Xuan: The Deviation of China's Economy against Okun's Law and the Study of Unemployment, *The Journal of World Economy*, 2003 (6), pp. 40–47+80.

greatly boosted economic growth and the improvement of the efficiency of production. Before the reform and opening-up, China implemented a strict household registration system to tightly control the flow of farmers into cities, thus forming a separated urban–rural labor market. Since the reform and opening-up, China has gradually relaxed the restrictions on the movement of farmers in policy to adapt to the rapid development of non-agricultural sectors. The agricultural labor force has been shifting to non-agricultural sectors at an annual rate of 8 million for more than 30 years. In 2014, the number of migrant workers reached 274 million, accounting for more than half of the employed population in non-agricultural sectors.

The continuous large-scale transfer of agricultural labor has not only completely changed the fundamental characteristics and efficiency of the configuration of China's labor market but has also profoundly affected China's investments, savings, technological progress, urban–rural income distribution and macroeconomic fluctuations, and more importantly, it has played a vital role in the rapid development of urban sectors. Research shows that the transfer of agricultural labor is closely associated with the improvement of China's total factor productivity,[18] the rapid development and exports of the manufacturing industry,[19] the high savings rate and the high investment rate,[20] the change in the pattern of income distribution[21] and other important macroeconomic characteristic phenomena. Du Yang *et al.* discovered through their latest research that the flow of the labor force from rural areas to urban areas is conducive to expanding the size of the labor market and improving the total factor productivity of the urban economy.

---

[18] Hu Yongtai: China's Total Factor Productivity: The First Role of the Re-allocation of the Agricultural Labor Force, *Economic Research Journal*, 1998 (3), pp. 33–41.

[19] Young, A.: Gold into Base Metals: The Growth of Productivity in the People's Republic of China during the Reform Period, *Journal of Political Economy*, 2003 (111), 1220–1261.

[20] Li Yang and Yin Jianfeng: High Savings, High Investments, and China's Economic Growth in the Process of Labor Transfer, *Economic Research Journal*, 2005 (2), pp. 4–15+25.

[21] Li Daokui, Liu Linlin and Wang Hongling: The U Curve of Labor Share in the GDP during Economic Development, *Economic Research Journal*, 2009 (1), pp. 71–83.

The net benefits brought by the flow of labor are still considerable, despite the negative impacts on the capital–output ratio and working hours.

Furthermore, the empirical observation of the special correlation between China's labor market and fluctuations in the macroeconomic cycle reveals that, for such a transitional economy as China's, the short-term change in the transfer of agricultural labor relative to its long-term trend is also a key variable reflecting the relationship between the labor market and the macroeconomic cycle. As shown in Figure 1.9, against the background of employment transformation in China, the agricultural labor force presents a downward trend; however, the amount of decrease in a given year is significantly related to the macro-cyclical changes measured by the growth rate of the GDP. In the years of rapid macroeconomic growth, the number of employed people in the primary industry decreased more rapidly, and *vice versa*. Therefore, to understand the relationship between China's labor market and the changes in the macroeconomic cycle during the period of transition, it is necessary to make a break-through in limitations of the standard Okun model by using the

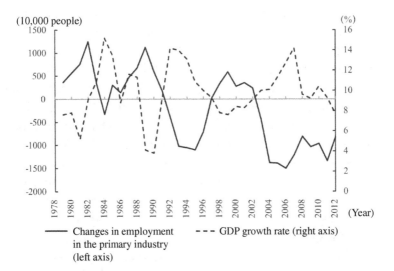

Figure 1.9. Employment change in China's primary industry and the growth rate of the GDP (1978–2012).

Note: The data come from the *China Statistical Yearbook* over the years, estimated by the author.

unemployment rate to express labor market changes, and appropriately introduce the variables of the transfer of agricultural labor to construct a generalized model of Okun's law. Compared with the generalized Okun model, the standard Okun model is only applicable to the special cases of developed countries. To explore the riddle of the inapplicability of Okun's law to China, we may go beyond the basic assumptions of the standard model and find a more general way to connect the labor market and macroeconomic fluctuations of economies in different stages of development.

Therefore, this study aims to explain the three basic characteristics of China's economic development from the perspective of the transfer of agricultural labor to further understand China's economy in several aspects. It first combines the theory of the development of a dual economy and the theory of endogenous growth to analyze the three basic characteristics of China's economic development from the perspective of the transfer of agricultural labor. This book argues that the key to get an understanding of China's high investment and high savings is to understand China's capital return and the improvement in its productivity, and further to understand the backup technological progress and continuous mass transfer of agricultural labor. The transfer of agricultural labor in turn contributes to the unique pattern of the relationship between China's labor market and the macroeconomic cycle.

A potential contribution of this study is to supplement the existing literature on China's mechanism of economic development. China's mechanism of economic development has been expounded from different perspectives, leading to an in-depth understanding and a summarization of the experience of China's economy. For instance, in the article "Growing Like China" published by Song *et al.* in the *American Economic Review*, the model of economic transformation involving two types of enterprises is constructed to explain that under the assumption of exogenous technological progress, the return on capital of the two types of enterprises remains unchanged, while the total return on capital increases due to the combination effect in the process of state-owned enterprises out of the market by private enterprises with relatively high productivity. The article explains China's economic growth well, especially the part regarding economic transformation, and emphasizes the improvement of economic efficiency brought about by the flow of factors within the non-agricultural sectors. However, in the process of China's economic development, the improvement of the efficiency of production brought about by the flow of labor factors from the agricultural sectors to the non-agricultural sectors, represented by the transfer of agricultural labor, is equally important. Besides, human capital is improved through "learning by doing" in the process of investment and production, and the embedded technological progress relevant to fixed assets is utilized to achieve endogenous technological progress and the transfer of agricultural labor, thus exerting a profound impact on China's macroeconomic growth model. This book attempts to better understand the specific mechanism of China's rapid economic growth from these new perspectives, and also expects that the results of this study can provide policy suggestions for China in formulating its national strategy of development.

Chapter 2

Overview of the Transfer of Agricultural Labor

I. The Evolution of the Transfer of Agricultural Labor

Before the reform and opening-up, China had implemented a stringent household registration system to strictly control the flow of farmers into cities, resulting in a separated urban–rural labor market. However, China has gradually relaxed the restrictions on the movement of farmers in policy since the reform and opening-up. The agricultural labor force has been shifting to the non-agricultural sector at an annual rate of 8 million for more than 30 years. In 2014, the number of migrant workers reached 274 million. Figure 2.1 shows the scale of the transfer of agricultural labor and the proportion of migrant workers in the total labor force, fully revealing that the transfer of agricultural labor has greatly backed up the development of China's non-agricultural sector at least in terms of labor supply. Data show that migrant workers accounted for an average of 42.7% of the employed population in the non-agricultural sector from 1985 to 2014, and the ratio has been on the rise, especially from 33.6% in 1990 to 50.1% in 2006 and to 50.9% in 2013.

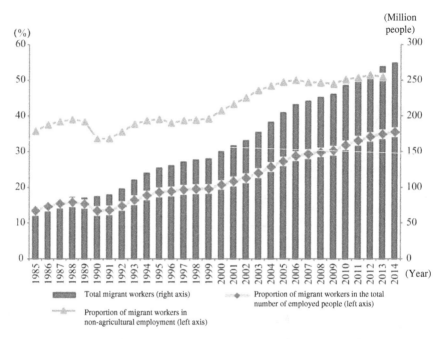

Figure 2.1.   The total number of migrant workers in China and their proportion in the total number of the employed population (1985–2014).

Source: The data for the period 2008–2014 were extracted from the *National Monitoring Survey Report on Migrant Workers* by the National Bureau of Statistics over the years; for the data regarding the period 1985–2007, see Lu Feng: *Reflection on Economic Catch-up by a Large Country — An Understanding of China's Open Macro Economy (2003–2013)* (Volume 1), Peking University Press, 2014, Edition 1.[1]

Besides, the transfer of agricultural labor has also been constantly strengthened, and it has experienced a gradual process from rural non-agricultural sectors to small towns and township enterprises, and finally

---

[1]Data description: The total number of migrant workers in 1978–2006 was the sum of the employed people in industry, construction, transportation, warehousing, post and telecommunications, wholesale and retail catering and other industries under rural employment sectors through the "rural non-agricultural employment" set forth in the *Agricultural Statistics Data of 60 Years in New China* (edited by the Ministry of Agriculture, China Agricultural Press, 2009). The data about the total number of migrant workers in 2008–2014 were extracted from the *National Monitoring Survey Report on Migrant Workers* over the years. The data for 2007 were the linear average of the previous year and the next year.

trans-provincial areas.[2] Due to the shift from local employment to migrant employment, the transfer of agricultural labor expands at a deeper level and on a wider scope. For instance, the outgoing country workers only accounted for 12% of the group of migrant workers in 1985; this ratio rose to 63%–64% around 2002, and then remained mostly stable.[3] Figure 2.2 also clearly shows this development. Therefore, both at the industrial level and at the spatial level, the allocation efficiency of China's labor resources continues to improve.

The continuous large-scale transfer of agricultural labor has not only completely changed the fundamental characteristics and the efficiency of the configuration of China's labor market but also profoundly affected China's investment, savings, technological progress, urban–rural income distribution and macroeconomic fluctuations, and more importantly, it has played a vital role in the rapid development of urban sectors. Research shows that the transfer of agricultural labor is closely associated with the improvement of China's total factor productivity,[4] the rapid development and exportation of the manufacturing industry,[5] the high savings rate and the high rate of investment,[6] the change in the pattern of income distribution[7] and other important macroeconomic characteristic phenomena. Du Yang *et al.* discovered through their latest research that the flow of the labor force from rural areas to urban areas is conducive to expanding the size of the labor market and improving the total factor productivity of

---

[2]Cai Fang: Growth and Structural Changes in Employment in Transitional China, *Economic Research Journal*, 2007 (7), pp. 5–15+23.

[3]Lu Feng: Wage Trends among Chinese Migrant Workers: 1979–2010, *Social Sciences in China*, 2012 (7), pp. 48–68+205. In recent years, the latest development shows the signs of migrant workers returning to their hometowns, and the proportion of local migrant workers in the newly transferred labor force has recovered slightly.

[4]Hu Yongtai: China's Total Factor Productivity: First Role of the Re-allocation of the Agricultural Labor Force, *Economic Research Journal*, 1998 (3), pp. 33–41.

[5]Young, A.: Gold into Base Metals: Productivity Growth in the People's Republic of China during the Reform Period, *Journal of Political Economy*, 2003 (111): 1220–1261.

[6]Li Yang, Yin Jianfeng: High Savings, High Investment, and China's Economic Growth in the Process of Labor Transfer, *Economic Research Journal*, 2005 (2), pp. 4–15+25.

[7]Li Daokui, Liu Linlin, and Wang Hongling: The U Curve of Labor Share in the GDP during Economic Development, *Economic Research Journal*, 2009 (1), pp. 71–83.

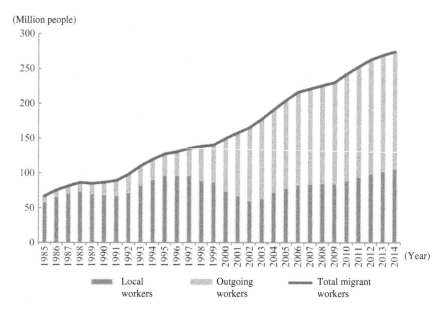

Figure 2.2.   The transfer of China's agricultural labor (1985–2014).

Source: The data for the period 2008–2014 were extracted from the *National Monitoring Survey Report on Migrant Workers* by the National Bureau of Statistics over the years; for the data regarding the period 1985–2007, see Lu Feng: *Reflection on the Economic Catch-up by a Large Country — An Understanding of China's Open Macro Economy (2003–2013)* (Volume 1), Peking University Press, 2014, Edition 1.[8]

the urban economy. The net benefits brought by the flow of labor are still considerable, despite the negative impacts on the capital–output ratio and working hours.[9]

---

[8]Du Yang, Cai Fang, Qu Xiaobo, and Cheng Jie: Sustain the China Miracle: Reaping the Dividends from Hukou Reforms, *Economic Research Journal*, 2014 (8), pp. 4–13+78.

[9]Data description: There are three indicators in the figure, namely, the total number of migrant workers, the number of outgoing country workers and the number of local non-agricultural laborers, as detailed in the following sections. (I) Source of the data about the total number of migrant workers: The total number of migrant workers during the period 1978–2006 was the sum of the employed people in industry, construction, transportation, warehousing, post and telecommunications, wholesale and retail catering and other industries under rural employment sectors through the "rural non-agricultural employment" set forth in the *Agricultural Statistics Data of 60 Years in New China* (edited by the Ministry of Agriculture, China Agricultural Press, 2009). The data about the total number of migrant workers during the period 2008–2014 were extracted from the *National*

In the future, there is still a lot of room for the further transfer of agricultural labor in China. Similar to the extensive international experience, the proportion of China's agricultural labor force has fallen since the reform and opening-up. Over the past 30 years and more, the proportion of the agricultural labor force has decreased by an average of more than 1 percentage point annually, from over 70% on the eve of the reform to about 31.4% in 2013. The international experience reveals that the proportion of the agricultural labor force in developed countries usually drops to less than 10% (see Figure 2.3) with the improvement of the level of economic development. Over the past century, for instance, the average proportion of the agricultural labor force in Organisation for Economic Co-operation and Development (OECD) countries has declined from 53% to about 10% today. Lu Feng and Yang Yewei speculate that the proportion

---

Monitoring Survey Report on Migrant Workers over the years. The data for the year 2007 were the linear average of the previous year and the next year. (II) Source of the data about the number of outgoing country workers: The data regarding the number of outgoing country workers in 2005 and before came from the *China Rural Statistical Yearbook* (2006) and the China rural household survey data, cited from Sheng Laiyun: *Flow or Migration — An Economy Analysis of the Process of the Flow of China's Rural Labor*, Shanghai Far East Publishers, 2008. The data regarding migrant workers in 2006 came from the National Rural Migrant Laborers Continued to Increase in 2006, in: *The World of Survey and Research*, 2007 (4). The data about the number of outgoing country workers from 2008 to 2014 came from the *National Monitoring Survey Report on Migrant Workers* over the years. As defined in the *National Monitoring Survey Report on Migrant Workers*, the local migrant workers refer to the workers who have worked in the non-agricultural sector within the township for more than six months, which is the same as the definition of local non-agricultural employment by Sheng Laiyun. Therefore, the data regarding the local migrant workers in the *National Monitoring Survey Report on Migrant Workers* enjoys the same statistical caliber as that of Sheng Laiyun, with consistent statistical caliber in the previous year and the following year. The data for the year 2007 were lacking and thus taken as linear average of 2 years before and after 2007. (III) Source of the data about the number of local non-agricultural workers: In 2006 (including 2006), the number of local non-agricultural workers was equal to the above balance of estimated "total number of migrant workers" minus "the number of outgoing country workers". The data of local non-agricultural workers from 2008 to 2014 were extracted from the *National Monitoring Survey Report on Migrant Workers* over the years, with the corresponding indicator of the local migrant workers. The data for the year 2007 were missing and thus taken as a linear average of 2 years before and after 2007.

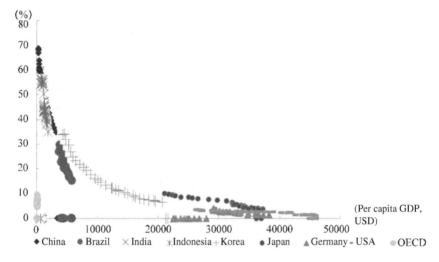

Figure 2.3.   The level of economic development of each country and the proportion of agricultural labor force.

Source: World Bank WDI Database.

of China's agricultural labor force will decline to 13.6% in 2030, indicating the great potential for the transfer of China's agricultural labor force in the next 20 years.[10] Du Yang *et al.* also call for comprehensively intensifying the reform of the household registration system, to further promote labor mobility and "sustain the China Miracle by reaping the dividends from Hukou reforms".[11]

II. Driving Factors for the Transfer of Agricultural Labor

Fresh and valuable materials have been provided by the practical experience of economic development and labor transfer during the period of China's reform and opening-up to understand the relationship between

---

[10]Lu Feng, Yang Yewei: Measurement of Factors behind the Decline of the Agricultural Labor Share in the Total Labor Force of China (1990–2030), *Chinese Journal of Population Science*, 2012 (4), pp. 15–26+113.

[11]Du Yang, Cai Fang, Qu Xiaobo, and Cheng Jie: Sustain the China Miracle: Reaping the Dividends from Hukou Reforms, *Economic Research Journal*, 2014 (8), pp. 4–13+78.

economic transformation and labor transfer discovered by developmental economics. The group of the large-scale transfer of laborers constitutes an important supporting force for China's economic growth, which helps expand the size of the labor market and increase the total factor productivity of the urban economy. The key to the long-term rapid growth of the Chinese economy will still lie in the continued transfer of surplus labor, which will bring about obvious benefits to China's economic development in the next few years.[12]

After more than 30 years of rapid economic growth, China's economy has entered a critical stage of optimization of the economic growth rate and structural adjustment. On the one hand, China still has a lot of agricultural labor force to be transferred because the existing agricultural labor force accounts for more than 30%. On the other hand, a "labor shortage" has occurred frequently in the developed provinces along the east coast in recent years. Many enterprises face a labor shortage, despite the rapid rise in labor wages. Labor shortage has been an important factor in the declining international competitiveness of Chinese enterprises. In this context, how to promote the continued transfer of the surplus agricultural labor force is an important issue to be addressed urgently.

To solve this practical problem, it is theoretically necessary to further clarify the determinants of labor transfer. In the past 30 years or so, why has the rural labor force shifted on a large scale and shown the extremely obvious characteristics of spatial agglomeration? What are the major factors that have affected this process and made it a turning point? How does the difference between urban and rural productivity form and act on the transfer of labor? In addition to the differences in productivity between urban and rural sectors, are there more specific factors that affect the transfer of labor in China? Only when these general and special factors are clarified can we truly grasp the internal laws of the historical process of the transfer of labor in China to bring forward pertinent suggestions and measures for the further promotion of the transfer of labor and for the reform of the labor factor market and economic growth in the next stage.

---

[12]Li Yang, Yin Jianfeng: High Savings, High Investments, and China's Economic Growth in the Process of Labor Transfer, *Economic Research Journal*, 2005 (2), pp. 4–15+25; Du Yang, Cai Fang, Qu Xiaobo, and Cheng Jie: Sustain the China Miracle: Reaping the Dividends from Hukou Reforms, *Economic Research Journal*, 2014 (8), pp. 4–13+78.

Therefore, this section focuses on the driving factors of the transfer of agricultural labor by means of a theoretical and empirical analysis. Due to limitations of space, the theoretical analysis is limited and can be found in the "Appendix B: Driving Factors and Spillover Effects of the Transfer of Agricultural Labor". The processes and results of the empirical analysis are described in the following sections.

1. *Econometric model, regression variables and data description*

This section shows the empirical analysis of the determinants of the transfer of agricultural labor by the use of the panel data of China's provinces and regions. Before the regression analysis, it is necessary to briefly introduce the methods of measuring to be used. In view of the fact that the core variables examined are likely to be affected by spatial correlation, the spatial econometric model is used for the regression analysis. The research by Xu Haiping and Wang Yuelong reveals that a significant autocorrelation exists in the urban–rural income gap in China's provinces, municipalities and autonomous regions in terms of spatial distribution, and the studies by Luo Yongmin and Zhang Guangnan also indicate that infrastructure has spatial spillover effects.[13] A spatial correlation may be derived from the system of economic variables under consideration or from the spatial correlation of the terms of error. Therefore, depending on the source of the effect of spatial correlation, the model of spatial measurement can be divided into the spatial autoregressive model (SAR) and the spatial error model (SEM). By reference to the practices in the above literature, both SAR and SEM models are used for analysis in this section to overcome the influence of potential spatial correlation and carry out maximum likelihood estimation. The same is also true for the setting of

---

[13] Xu Haiping, Wang Yuelong: China's Urban–Rural Income Gap and Total Factor Productivity: Spatial Econometric Analysis Based on Provincial Data, *Journal of Financial Research*, 2010 (10), pp. 54–67; Luo Yongmin: An Analysis of the Economic Effects of the Urban–Rural Gaps of Infrastructures in China — Based on the Spatial Econometric Model with Panel Data, *Chinese Rural Economy*, 2010 (3), pp. 62–74+88; Zhang Guangnan, Hong Guozhi, and Chen Guanghan: Infrastructure, Spatial Spillover and Manufacture Cost, *China Economic Quarterly*, 2013 (1), pp. 285–304.

a spatial weight matrix. The weight coefficient of adjacent provinces is set as 1, and the weight coefficient of non-adjacent provinces is set as 0.[14] The weight matrix is standardized in the specific measurement estimation. For purposes of comparison, the regression results under the two models are reported symmetrically in each table.

The following sample interval analyzed in this section is from 1992 to 2010 out of the main considerations: (1) It is an ideal research interval because it is generally believed that China's reform and opening-up has entered a new stage, and the economic system of a comprehensive market has gradually been established after Deng Xiaoping's southern talks in 1992.[15] (2) Because of strict governmental control over labor mobility, the real climax of the transfer of labor did not begin until after Deng Xiaoping's southern talks in 1992, though the transfer of agricultural labor in China started in the early stages of reform and opening-up. In fact, since 1992, the government's attitude toward the transfer of labor has also changed from "allowed" to "encouraged".[16] Therefore, this section uses China's provincial panel data regarding the period 1992–2010 for quantitative analysis to examine the driving factors of the transfer of agricultural labor.

The explained variable is the transfer of agricultural labor, and the key explanatory variables include the urban–rural income gap, the growth rate of the GDP, the level of infrastructure, total factor productivity and agricultural labor productivity (measured by the ratio of the total agricultural machinery power to the population employed in agriculture). In addition, a series of important variables are also introduced, including the degree of openness (measured by the ratio of the foreign direct investment (FDI) and the total volume of exports and imports to the GDP), the proportion of the total output of state-owned enterprises (measured by the proportion

---

[14]Luo Yongmin: An Analysis of the Economic Effects of the Urban–Rural Gaps of Infrastructures in China — Based on the Spatial Econometric Model with Panel Data, *Chinese Rural Economy*, 2010 (3), pp. 62–74+88. Guangdong and Hainan are considered as adjacent provinces in this section.

[15]Song Z., K. Storesletten, and F. Zilibotti: Growing Like China, *American Economic Review*, 2011 (101): 196–233.

[16]Huang, P., F. N. Pieke: China Migration Country Study, Paper Presented at the Conference on Migration, Development and Pro-poor Policy Choices in Asia, Dhaka, 003.

of state-owned and state-owned holding units in the value of the total output of the industrial sector), the scale and efficiency of financial development (using the ratio of total loans to GDP as an indicator of the scale of financial development, and the ratio of total loans to total deposits as a proxy variable for financial efficiency[17]) and the level of public education expenditure (measured by the public education expenditure per capita). In addition to these influence variables, the impact of other potential factors is also further considered, including the urban unemployment rate (measured by the registered urban unemployment rate and the surveyed urban unemployment rate estimated using urban household survey data), return on capital (measured by the ratio of the total profits of industrial enterprises to the net value of fixed assets of industrial enterprises) and the level of inflation (measured by consumer price indicator (CPI)). Theoretically, all these factors may affect the transfer of labor, so a regression analysis should be carried out to investigate the impact, with the following details.

(1) *Key variables*

(i) The transfer of agricultural labor

The number of rural employees and the number of employees in the rural primary industry in various provinces and regions from 1978 to 2008 can be found in the *Compilation of Agricultural Statistics Data of 60 Years in New China* (the Compilation). These two groups of data measure the distribution of employment of the rural registered labor force in agricultural and non-agricultural sectors. The Compilation "directly collects and calculates the employees who have lived outside the household for more than half a year, but whose income is linked to the family economy in the statistical caliber of rural population and rural employees used in relevant proportions". Therefore, it is possible to accurately measure the number of

---

[17]Yao Yaojun: Financial Development, Urbanization and Urban–Rural Income Gap in China — Co-integration Analysis and Granger Causality Test, *China Rural Survey*, 2005 (2), pp. 2–8+80; Ye Zhiqiang, Chen Xiding, and Zhang Shunming, Can Financial Development Reduce the Urban-Rural Income Gap? — Evidence from China, *Journal of Financial Research*, 2011 (2), pp. 42–56, and other existing literature.

members of the agricultural labor force who have transferred by subtracting the number of employees in the rural primary industry from the number of rural employees. In addition, the provincial and regional data with the same statistical calibers in the Compilation for 2009 and 2010 can be found in the *China Statistical Yearbook*, which facilitates the extension of the data regarding the transfer of labor to 2010.[18] Based on this, the indicator of the transfer of agricultural labor is constructed to reflect that transfer.

The amount of the transfer of agricultural labor$_t$ = transfer of agricultural labor$_t$ − transfer of agricultural labor$_{t-1}$, where, the transfer of agricultural labor$_t$ = the number of rural employees$_t$ − the number of employees in the rural primary industry$_{t-1}$.

Considering the complexity of the issue of the transfer of China's labor force, it is necessary to carefully select and extract the information about the transfer of labor from multiple sets of data according to the needs of research. The data from the 2010 national census contain detailed information on population migration in the provinces and regions, but a certain discrepancy exists between the data on migration and the data regarding the transfer of employment, and the data are only cross-sectional data for 2010. In case of the individual effects of the provinces and regions beyond control, it is difficult to fully verify the exact relationship between infrastructure and the transfer of labor. The data from the second national agricultural census exclude the rural workers who have lived outside for half a year, significantly underestimating the number of rural employees and the transfer of labor.

(ii) Urban–rural income gap

The urban–rural income gap is one of the key explanatory variables in this section, as well as one of the main drivers of the transfer of agricultural

---

[18]Under the data caliber used in this section, the number of those involved in the national transfer of labor in 2008, 2009 and 2010 was 236.62 million, 245.34 million and 255.49 million, respectively. According to the *2011 National Monitoring Survey Report on Migrant Workers of the National Bureau of Statistics*, the total number of national migrant workers was 225.42 million, 229.78 million and 242.23 million, respectively, in the past 3 years. The two groups of data are relatively close, which can support the credibility of the data.

labor according to the theory of developmental economics. In this chapter, the urban–rural income gap is measured by the difference between the per capita disposable income of urban residents and the per capita net income of rural residents where the per capita disposable income of urban residents and the per capita net income of rural residents are adjusted based on the CPI of various provinces and regions in 2000.

(iii) Level of infrastructure

First, the indicator of highway density is constructed using the ratio of the highway mileage of Chinese provinces and regions to the area of provinces and regions to be used as the main measurement indicator of the level of infrastructure. The data of highway mileage and land area in all provinces and regions were taken from the *China Statistical Yearbook*. The village roads were taken into account to calculate the highway mileage after 2006, causing an inconsistent caliber of statistics. Considering basically no impact on the transfer of the urban and rural labor force by village roads, the mileage of village roads is excluded from the highway mileage of the period 2006–2010 to calculate the highway density as the key measurement variable of the level of infrastructure. Specifically, in order to adjust the caliber, some data about village road mileage from 2006 to 2010 are first found from statistical yearbooks, traffic yearbooks and the official websites of the transportation departments of various provinces and regions and then excluded. The remaining data were estimated approximately by the average ratio of the village road data at the start and end of the period to the highway mileage data containing village roads. In addition, this chapter also examines the impact of the level of communications infrastructure on the transfer of agricultural labor and selects the ratio of the number of mobile phones and public telephones to the number of rural employees as the measurement indicator of the level of infrastructure.

(iv) Total factor productivity

Total factor productivity represents the difference in productivity that cannot be explained by the enterprise's own factor inputs, such as the technical level, organizational efficiency and operating environment. In general, an increase in total factor productivity tends to raise the marginal productivity, thereby increasing the demand for labor and promoting the transfer of agricultural labor. Concerning the estimation of total factor productivity at the provincial level, a method of fixed effect for Solow residuals and a Generalized Method of Moment (GMM) estimation method of Arellano and Bover are provided in the literature.[19] The method of fixed effect for Solow residuals may encounter two problems, namely, Simultaneity Bias, and Selectivity and Attrition Bias. The GMM method, especially the systematic GMM method, can solve the regression problem of macro variables to a large extent by introducing the level of the endogenous variable and the differential lag term as instrumental variables.[20] Therefore, the systematic method of GMM estimation is adopted to estimate the total factor productivity of provinces and regions by use of the industrial sector GDP, the net value of fixed assets of industrial enterprises above the designated size and the industrial enterprise labor panel data of 31 provinces, municipalities and autonomous regions in China from 1978 to 2010.

(v) Agricultural labor productivity

On the one hand, an increase in the productivity of agricultural labor has raised the output of the unit agricultural labor and the income of rural residents and weakened the driving forces of the transfer of agricultural labor. On the other hand, an increase in the output of agricultural products has enabled the agricultural labor to be released from industrial sectors and prompted its transfer. The total mechanical power of agricultural labor (the ratio of the total agricultural machinery power to the population employed in agriculture) is selected to measure the productivity of agricultural labor, as analyzed in the subsequent sections.

(2) *Important variables*

Other important variables selected in this section include the degree of openness, the proportion of state-owned enterprises, the level of

---

[19]Arellano, M., O. Bover: Another Look at the Instrumental Variable Estimation of the Error-components Models, *Journal of Econometrics*, 2003 (68) (1), pp. 29–51.
[20]Lu Xiaodong, Lian Yujun: Estimation of the Total Factor Productivity of Industrial Enterprises in China: 1999–2007, *China Economic Quarterly*, 2012 (11) (2), pp. 179–196.

public education expenditure and the scale and efficiency of financial development.

(i) Degree of openness

With reference to the practices in the previous literature, the degree of openness is measured by the ratio of the FDI and the total volume of exports–imports to GDP. The degree of openness may affect the transfer of agricultural labor through multiple channels. On the one hand, the higher the degree of openness of a region is, the more conducive to the introduction of advanced technology, the absorption of advanced management experience and the improvement of total factor productivity, thus further affecting the transfer of agricultural labor; on the other hand, China is now still at the peak of the transfer of labor, and the higher degree of openness leads to more active economic activities and a greater deepening of capital, thus promoting the transfer of labor from the agricultural sector to the non-agricultural sector. In addition, the degree of openness may also affect the transfer of agricultural labor from the perspective of factor allocation. Bentolila and Saint-Paul point out that any factor affecting the degree of imperfect market competition may affect factor allocation.[21] As for the specific situation of the Chinese market, the FDI and the total volume of imports–exports can be used to measure the degree of competition in the product market. The strengthening of market competition will reduce the cost of the transfer of agricultural labor.

(ii) Proportion of state-owned enterprises

The restriction of the system of household registration makes it difficult for the agricultural labor to become the staff of state-owned enterprises. A large proportion of state-owned enterprises indicates high monopoly power of state-owned enterprises, which tends to reduce the transfer of agricultural labor. In this chapter, the ratio of the total output of state-owned and state-owned holding industrial enterprises above the designated scale to the total output of all industrial enterprises above the scale has been adopted as a measurement of the proportion of state-owned enterprises.

---

[21]Bentolila, S., G. Saint-Paul: Explaining Movements in the Labor Share, *Contribution to Macroeconomics*, 2003 (3) (1), Article 9, pp. 9.

(iii) The level of public education expenditure

The per capita public education expenditure is used to measure the level of public education expenditure. In fact, public education expenditure is a resource allocation. Generally speaking, the urban residents have a higher level of education than rural residents, thus leading to a higher marginal output of investment in rural residents by public education expenditure. In case of an even urban–rural distribution of public education expenditure, the increase in the level of per capita education expenditure is conducive to promoting the transfer of agricultural labor. However, the unevenly distributed public education expenditure between urban and rural areas may hinder the transfer of agricultural labor.

(iv) Scale and efficiency of financial development

This chapter introduces the ratio of the total amount of loans to the GDP as an indicator of the scale of financial development and the ratio of the total amount of loans to total deposits as a proxy variable for financial efficiency. The two indicators may affect the urban–rural income gap and the transfer of agricultural labor to varying degrees in the specific environment of China's economic development. In terms of the distribution of financial resources, China's financial system shows a clear tendency toward urbanization, which is inclined to the state sector in credit allocation. Such an unbalanced development may hinder the transfer of agricultural labor.[22] According to the analysis of Zhang Qi *et al.* and Ye Zhiqiang *et al.*, financial development has significantly expanded the urban–rural income gap.[23] They also note that the improvement in financial efficiency with the development of financial scale may alleviate the tendency of urbanization and state-owned enterprises, and financial development may

---

[22]Wei, S., T. Wang: The Siamese Twins: Do State-owned Banks Favor State-owned Enterprises in China?, *China Economic Review*, 1997 (8) (1), pp. 19–29; Park, A., K. Sehrt, Tests of Financial Intermediation and Banking Reform in China, *Journal of Comparative Economics*, 2001 (29) (4): 608–644.

[23]Zhang Qi, Liu Mingxing, and Tao Ran: China's Financial Development and the Difference between Urban and Rural Income, *China Finance*, 2004 (1); Ye Zhiqiang, Chen Xiding, and Zhang Shunming: Can Financial Development Reduce the Urban–Rural Income Gap? — Evidence from China, *Journal of Financial Research*, 2011 (2), pp. 42–56.

bring about the narrowing of the urban–rural income gap. Yao Yaojun's analysis shows that the efficiency of financial development is negatively correlated with the income gap between the urban and rural areas, despite the positive correlation between the scale of financial development and the urban–rural income gap.[24]

(3) *Other factors*

In addition to the foregoing variables, the variable of the rate of urban unemployment and the variable of return on capital are also taken into account because they may affect the rate of the transfer of labor by affecting the demand for labor in the urban sector. In the regression analysis, the former is measured by the changes in the rate of urban unemployment and the latter is measured by the ratio of the total profit of industrial enterprises to the net value of fixed assets of industrial enterprises. In the benchmark regression, the rate of urban unemployment is measured by the rate of registered urban unemployment. Because of statistical problems, the indicator of the rate of registered urban unemployment cannot reflect the unemployment rate of China's urban sectors well. The more ideal measurement indicator is the rate of surveyed urban unemployment. However, the National Bureau of Statistics does not fully disclose the data regarding the rate of surveyed urban unemployment, and only microdata from the urban household surveys in some provinces are made available. Through the calculation of the microdata from the survey on urban households, it is possible to obtain the estimated data regarding the surveyed urban unemployment rate in the nine provinces from 1992 to 2009. Therefore, the surveyed urban unemployment rate is used to facilitate the regression analysis (the results show no significant difference, as reported in Exhibit B of Appendix B).

    To eliminate the possible impacts caused by price changes, the data for the nominal variable have been adjusted based on the CPI of various provinces and regions in 2000, such as per capita public education

---

[24]Yao Yaojun: Financial Development, Urbanization and Urban-Rural Income Gap in China — Co-integration Analysis and Granger Causality Test, *China Rural Survey*, 2005 (2), pp. 2–8+80.

Table 2.1. Statistics of Regression Variables of the Driving Factors of the Transfer of Agricultural Labor.

Variables	Number of observations	Mean	Standard deviation	Minimum	Maximum
The transfer of agricultural labor (logarithm)	530	2.694	1.454	−1.609	5.205
Urban–rural income gap (logarithm)	589	8.285	0.518	6.975	9.570
GDP growth rate	589	0.108	0.045	−0.043	0.345
Highway density (logarithm)	584	7.825	0.932	5.092	9.839
Loans/GDP	589	0.996	0.286	0.533	2.260
Loans/deposits	589	0.870	0.251	0.233	1.890
Total factor productivity (logarithmic)	587	−1.001	0.344	−1.805	−0.070
Agricultural labor productivity (logarithm)	583	2.882	0.698	0.846	4.364
FDI/GDP	576	0.035	0.036	0.000	0.243
Total volume of imports–exports/ GDP	589	0.299	0.397	0.032	2.173
Proportion of state-owned enterprises	584	0.511	0.202	0.094	0.899
Level of public education expenditure	483	3.280	3.099	0.374	20.15
Rate of registered urban unemployment (%)	565	3.370	0.966	0.400	7.400
Rate of surveyed urban unemployment (%)	162	6.367	3.184	1.338	14.49
Return on capital	589	0.096	0.083	−0.055	0.461
CPI (%)	589	5.178	7.021	−3.900	29.70

Source: *China Statistical Yearbook*, statistical yearbooks of various provinces and regions, traffic yearbooks of various provinces and regions, official website of the provincial department of transportation, *Compilation of Statistical Data of 60 Years in New China*, *Compilation of Agricultural Statistics Data of 60 Years in New China* and CEIC Database; the rate of surveyed urban unemployment has been estimated using the microdata from urban household surveys. The sample interval of each variable is from 1992 to 2010, and the sample interval of the communications infrastructure is from 1998 to 2010. Due to the missing data of some observations in individual provinces, municipalities and autonomous regions, the number of observations of each variable was not completely equal.

expenditure. In addition, the impact of inflation is controlled. The statistics of the above variables are reported in Table 2.1.

2. The results of the empirical analysis

With the use of the panel data of China's provinces and regions, the transfer of agricultural labor has been used as an explained variable to analyze the determinants of the transfer of agricultural labor. By reference to the practices in the previous literature, both SAR and SEM models are used for analysis in this section to overcome the influence of a potential spatial correlation and to carry out a maximum likelihood estimation. The same is true also for the setting of the spatial weight matrix. The weight coefficient of adjacent provinces is set as 1, and the weight coefficient of non-adjacent provinces is set as 0.[25] The weight matrix is standardized in the estimation of the specific measurement. For comparison purposes, the regression results under the two models are reported symmetrically in the regression table.

Table 2.2 shows the results of the baseline regression, indicating that the variable of the urban–rural income gap is significantly positive. This means that a larger urban–rural income gap leads to a stronger motivation for the transfer of agricultural labor and the greater transfer volume of agricultural labor, which is in line with the expectations. The coefficient of the growth rate of the GDP is significantly positive, indicating that economic growth increases the demand for non-agricultural labor, which is conducive to promoting the transfer of agricultural labor. The coefficient of the level of the scale of infrastructure is significantly positive, indicating that the improvement of the level of infrastructures is conducive to reducing labor transfer costs and promoting the transfer of agricultural labor, which is consistent with the expectations.

The estimated results of other influencing variables are also roughly in line with the expectations. The coefficient of the proportion of state-owned

---

[25]Luo Yongmin: An Analysis of the Economic Effects of the Urban–Rural Gaps of Infrastructures in China — Based on the Spatial Econometric Model with Panel Data, *Chinese Rural Economy*, 2010 (3), pp. 2–8+80. Guangdong and Hainan are considered as adjacent provinces in this section.

Table 2.2. Baseline Regression Results of the Driving Factors of the Transfer of Agricultural Labor.

Explanatory variables: Transfer of agricultural labor	SAR			SEM		
	(1)	(2)	(3)	(4)	(5)	(6)
Urban–rural income gap	0.399***	0.919***	0.853***	0.524***	0.943***	0.872***
	(0.133)	(0.168)	(0.166)	(0.149)	(0.177)	(0.175)
GDP growth rate	3.147***	3.469***	3.279***	3.301**	3.011***	2.861***
	(1.193)	(0.986)	(1.005)	(1.278)	(1.050)	(1.057)
Highway density (logarithm)	0.500***	0.549***	0.545***	0.518***	0.547***	0.534***
	(0.049)	(0.048)	(0.047)	(0.052)	(0.050)	(0.050)
Total factor productivity (logarithm)	−0.580***	−0.620***	−1.045***	−0.643***	−0.631***	−1.056***
	(0.202)	(0.176)	(0.193)	(0.206)	(0.176)	(0.194)
Agricultural labor productivity (logarithm)	−0.462***	−0.289***	−0.351***	−0.549***	−0.345***	−0.400***
	(0.075)	(0.068)	(0.068)	(0.084)	(0.071)	(0.071)
FDI/GDP	—	−9.683***	−8.770***	—	−10.23***	−9.306***
	—	(1.480)	(1.480)	—	(1.517)	(1.509)
Total volume of imports–exports/GDP	—	−0.018	−0.209	—	0.060	−0.127
	—	(0.155)	(0.156)	—	(0.154)	(0.156)
Proportion of state-owned enterprises	—	−1.511***	−1.446***	—	−1.852***	−1.790***
	—	(0.256)	(0.252)	—	(0.281)	(0.283)
Loans/GDP	—	−1.116***	−0.839***	—	−1.023***	−0.794***
	—	(0.185)	(0.188)	—	(0.189)	(0.189)
Loans/deposits	—	0.453*	0.164	—	0.321	0.134
	—	(0.257)	(0.259)	—	(0.261)	(0.259)
Level of public education expenditure	—	−0.118***	−0.135***	—	−0.133***	−0.143***
	—	(0.024)	(0.024)	—	(0.026)	(0.025)

(Continued)

Table 2.2.   (*Continued*)

Explanatory variables: Transfer of agricultural labor	SAR			SEM		
	(1)	(2)	(3)	(4)	(5)	(6)
Changes in the rate of registered urban unemployment (%)	—	—	0.040	—	—	0.012
	—	—	(0.077)	—	—	(0.079)
Return on capital	—	—	3.503^{***}	—	—	3.500^{***}
	—	—	(0.730)	—	—	(0.724)
CPI (%)	—	—	0.006	—	—	0.002
	—	—	(0.007)	—	—	(0.008)
P	0.230^{***}	0.114^{***}	0.096^{**}	/	/	/
	(0.045)	(0.041)	(0.041)	/	/	/
Λ	/	/	/	0.257^{***}	0.217^{***}	0.196^{***}
	/	/	/	(0.051)	(0.049)	(0.052)
Moran's I	0.248^{***}	0.217^{***}	0.173^{***}	0.253^{***}	0.229^{***}	0.195^{***}
R^2	0.891	0.885	0.892	0.890	0.883	0.889
Adjusted R^2	0.884	0.877	0.883	0.883	0.874	0.880
Log-likelihood	−721.7	−616.9	−603.6	−722.3	−611.7	−599.8
Number of observations	589	589	589	589	589	589

Note: *, **, and *** indicate statistical significance at 10%, 5%, and 1% levels, respectively. Moran's I is the result of the spatial correlation test. The coefficients ρ and λ are the spatial correlation coefficients of the SAR and the SEM, respectively. R^2, adjusted R^2 and log-likelihood reflect the goodness of the fit of the model.

enterprises is significantly negative, indicating that the larger the proportion of state-owned enterprises is the smaller the volume of labor transfer will be. The possible explanation is that the restriction of the household registration system may make it difficult for the agricultural labor to become the staff of state-owned enterprises, and thus, the agricultural labor mainly flows to the non-state-owned enterprises, leading to an increase in the proportion of state-owned enterprises. This indicates that the increased power of monopoly of state-owned enterprises may weaken the transfer of labor. The coefficient of the level of public education expenditure is significantly negative, indicating that the increase in the level of public education expenditure is not conducive to the rapid transfer and employment of agricultural labor. As a result, the biased expenditure of public education further reduces the employment opportunities for agricultural labor to cities in reality. Similarly, the current biased financial development is also not favorable for promoting the transfer of agricultural labor, and the improvement of financial efficiency plays a positive role to some extent. The improvement of agricultural labor productivity represented by the level of agricultural mechanization has a significant negative impact on the transfer of agricultural labor. This is possibly because of the fact that the opportunity costs of the transfer of agricultural labor increase with the increase in the output of agricultural products and agricultural labor income. In addition, the coefficient of capital return is significantly positive, indicating that the higher rate of capital return leads to greater investment incentives and a higher demand for non-agricultural labor, which is more favorable for promoting the transfer of agricultural labor.

The regression coefficient of the total factor productivity variable is significantly negative, indicating that the transfer of labor is weakened with the improvement of the level of technology. It is possibly because of the fact that the influence of total factor productivity on promoting the transfer of labor by output increase has been controlled by the variable of the growth rate of the GDP, the remaining influence shows that the technological progress is biased. The increase in the proportion of technology-intensive enterprises and capital-intensive enterprises reduces the demand for the transfer of agricultural labor, which is not conducive to promoting the transfer of agricultural labor. In addition, the FDI/GDP ratio also has a significant negative impact on the transfer of agricultural labor. This is possibly because of the fact that it is difficult for foreign enterprises to promote the transfer of agricultural labor due to higher requirements on human capital. However, the specific reasons still need to be further studied. Other variables such as CPI and the coefficient of the rate of registered urban unemployment are not significant, indicating that there may be no significant impact on the transfer of labor. However, the insignificant coefficient of the rate of registered urban unemployment may also be caused by the defects in the existing indicator of the rate of unemployment. However, the data from urban household surveys have been used to estimate the rate of surveyed urban unemployment in the nine provinces, and the results of the regression analysis are not significantly different (for the specific results, refer to Exhibit 1 of Appendix B).

3. Brief conclusions

The main driving factors of the transfer of agricultural labor have been analyzed by using the panel data of China's provinces and regions. The results of the analysis suggest that the urban–rural income gap, the improvement in the level of infrastructures, the increase in economic growth and return on capital and the decline in the proportion of state-owned enterprises or the development of the private sector are the main driving factors for the transfer of agricultural labor in China, and the current biased factors such as financial development and public education expenditure are not conducive to the transfer of agricultural labor.

In the event of a large number of surplus agricultural labor force to be transferred in the real economy, China has shown the signs of widening the urban–rural income gap and slowing down the momentum of the transfer of labor, arousing concern about the sustainability of the "transition dividend" in the academic and industrial circles. In view of the large number of agricultural labor force to be transferred, the potential "transition dividend" will continue to play its huge growth effect for a long time, and it is not pessimistic about whether China can successfully get out of the middle-income trap. According to the results of the test in this section, the transfer of agricultural labor can be greatly promoted by improving the construction of infrastructure and promoting the development of the private sector.

It should be especially noted that the improvement of the level of infrastructure not only effectively promotes the transfer of agricultural labor to the non-agricultural sector but also provides an important material basis for industrialization and urbanization. From an international comparison, the level of infrastructure has still a great deal of room for further improvement, despite the rapid growth in the scale of infrastructure in China in recent years.[26] The government should take the opportunity to strengthen the construction of infrastructure. Especially in a macroeconomic downturn, it is important to increase the economic efficiency and effectively raise the investments in infrastructures for the transfer of agricultural labor. In the short term, infrastructure investments, as a means of the government's expansionary fiscal policy, can boost domestic demand and prevent excessive economic decline in the context of the current economic slowdown. In the medium to long term, the expansion of infrastructure can improve the efficiency of economic operations, facilitate the transfer of agricultural labor, narrow the urban–rural income gap and create favorable conditions for a smooth economic transformation, thus laying a solid foundation for China's urbanization and modernization. Undoubtedly, it is necessary to pay attention to optimizing the direction and structure of government-led investments in infrastructure and appropriately encourage the introduction of some private capital in the course of practice to further utilize the functions of infrastructure in improving production efficiency and income distribution.

III. Technical Support for the Transfer of Agricultural Labor: The Revolution in Labor Productivity

One of the indispensable basic conditions for China's amazing achievements in economic development over the past 30 years is the constant improvement in the transformation and efficiency of China's structure of agricultural production. As China is a populous country, agriculture is of a particularly important significance as the foundation of the entire national economy. Since the reform and opening-up, China's agricultural labor force has kept shifting to the non-agricultural sector, which makes the proportion of the agricultural labor force in the total labor force decrease at an annual rate of more than 1 percentage point. The smooth transformation of China's economy can be achieved only when the level of the productivity of the agricultural labor force is high and more agricultural products are obtained with less labor consumption. Only in this way can

---

[26]Xu Jianguo, Zhang Xun: China's Sovereign Debt: Situation, Investments and Risk Analysis, *South China Journal of Economics*, 2013 (1), pp. 14–34.

more of the agricultural labor force be transferred to the non-agricultural sector in the society to effectively back up the development of non-agricultural sectors, as well as economic and social transformation.

It is very simple to explain why the development of a large country needs basic agricultural conditions. Improving the efficiency of traditional agricultural production is essential to the growth and transformation of a large economy with a population of more than one billion like China, especially the corresponding growth of agricultural labor productivity. Otherwise, the derivative law of the primary demand for food will fundamentally restrain the process of economic growth or indirectly restrict the process through the increase in agricultural prices beyond the acceptable range (especially for economies in the process of the transfer of agricultural labor). Marx once pointed out that the productivity of agricultural labor exceeding the individual needs of laborers is the foundation of all societies.[27] Modern developmental economics even views the growth of the productivity of agricultural labor as the premise for economic development because the food and raw materials produced by the agricultural sector constitute the conditions for the security of the basic materials that meet human existence and developmental needs. With the increase in the quantity of output per unit of labor, it is possible for the social economy to improve its efficiency by deepening the division of labor and to promote the development of material civilization. The practices of economic development in many countries, especially large countries in modern times, have provided extensive international experience to support and verify the above basic laws.

The observation of the trajectory of the changes in the productivity of agricultural labor is not only an important subject in agricultural economics but also an indispensable aspect for an understanding of the basic prerequisites for the overall transformation of China, a huge economy. Specifically, how has the productivity of agricultural labor changed in China in the 60-year history of the development of new China, especially since the reform and opening-up? What are the characteristics of the trend of the changes in labor productivity at different times and for different categories? Is labor productivity measured by different indicators that are comparable or different? What is the changing situation of the productivity of the marginal agricultural labor against the background of the

---

[27] *Capital*, Vol. 3, People's Publishing House, 1974, p. 885.

cross-sectoral transfer of the labor force and the interactive development of the two sectors in China? Besides, the systematic measurement of the productivity of agricultural labor is of great significance for a quantitative description of the improvement in the efficiency of agricultural production and for an understanding of the stage success of China's economic transformation and growth. Many studies have focused on the analysis of the productivity of agricultural labor in the domestic academic community, but some problems also exist, such as difference in purposes and lack of full and accurate understandings of China's agricultural labor productivity. According to a rough review of the literature, the situation of agricultural production in China has been studied from different perspectives, but there is still a lack of basic and systematic measurement of the productivity of agricultural labor over a long period of time.

Therefore, this section attempts to systematically estimate the changes in the productivity of agricultural labor through different methods based on the results of the existing research. The systematic estimation and analysis of the trend of change in the system of productivity of agricultural labor in more than 60 years since the founding of the PRC provide the realistic basis for the sustainable and stable transfer of agricultural labor in China. The productivity of agricultural labor is generally defined as the agricultural output brought by agricultural labor input per unit, which can be directly calculated based on the quantity of output and input of labor. It is one of the basic indicators for measuring the level of the efficiency of agricultural production. Besides, different specific indicators can also be used for measurement, depending on the units of measurement of input and output. Agricultural output can be measured either by the value of the market transaction or by the physical unit such as weight and volume. Agricultural labor input can be measured by time units such as hours and man-days. In the absence of support from microscopic investigation data, the number of agricultural laborers may also be used as an approximate measure, but it needs to be assumed that the length of labor and the intensity of the input of agricultural labor per year are roughly comparable in a chronological sense.

After the reform and opening-up, China changed to a different track to implement and gradually improve the national system of economic accounting and related statistical systems, providing agricultural added value and time series of agricultural labor as well as provincial data.

The overall trend of changes in the value-added agricultural average and marginal labor productivity is estimated according to the academic community's estimation of agricultural capital stocks and the update of this book. Moreover, the data regarding the long-term time series such as labor-day input and capital investment per unit area of land with generally stable and comparable data indicators, as well as the panel data of the provinces of origin of the major agricultural products in successive years, are provided according to the data from the national agricultural product cost-benefit survey conducted by the relevant departments of the Chinese government. Thus, it is possible to estimate the average and marginal labor productivity of the measurement of the physical quantity of major agricultural products. As a powerful supplement to the estimation of value, the data for the agricultural product cost-benefit survey have three advantages. First, the input from agricultural labor is measured with the number of working days, which helps to eliminate the uncertainty and error of the annual per capita investment of agricultural labor due to the length of the busy season of farming and leisure. Second, the use of physical quantity for statistics helps to eliminate the problems of intertemporal comparability which usually existed in the measurement of value, and even if the price indicator is adjusted to obtain comparable intertemporal data, it is still possible to meet problems involving the quality of the price data and possible uncertain statistical results. Third, the sample survey data based on the area of farmland can automatically control the impact of changes in the land area, facilitating the measurement and estimation of labor productivity.

Therefore, the average productivity of agricultural labor is systematically measured with the two groups of data from the value of the agricultural sector and the national agricultural product cost-benefit survey under the national system of economic accounting in China. The systematic estimation and analysis of the trend of change in the system of productivity of agricultural labor in more than 60 years since the founding of the PRC provide a realistic basis for the sustainable and stable transfer of agricultural labor in China. In addition, different data and methodologies have been adopted to estimate the marginal labor productivity of China's agriculture. Due to the limited length of the text, the specific process and results of the estimation can be found in the "Appendix C: Estimation of the Productivity of China's Agricultural Labor".

1. The productivity of agricultural labor measured by added value

Figure 2.4 shows the changes in the added value and labor force of the agricultural sector calculated at constant prices over the past 60 years since the founding of the PRC. The absolute value of agricultural added value has been on the rise, despite a decline in the proportion of agricultural added value in the GDP from 51% in 1952 to 28.2% in 1978 and then to 10.1% in 2011. The real added value measured at constant prices in 1978 increased from RMB 60.55 billion in 1952 to RMB 449.10 billion in 2011, an increase of 6.42 times. It rose to RMB 102.75 billion by 1978, an increase of 0.7 times. Since the reform and opening-up, it has continued to grow by 3.37 times. The number of members of the agricultural labor force increased from 173 million in 1952 to 391 million at its peak in 1991, with two great and slight decreases in 1958 and 1978, and then a rise to 266 million in 2011 (with a slight increase from 1998 to 2002).

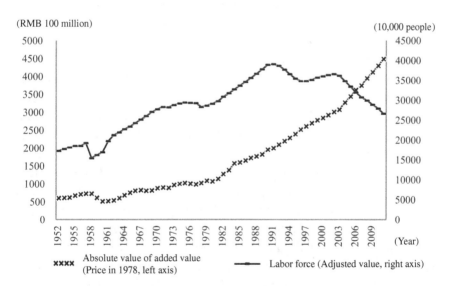

Figure 2.4. Agricultural added value and the number of the members of the labor force in China (1952–2011).

Source: *Agricultural Statistics Data of 60 Years in New China* and *China Statistical Yearbook* over the years.

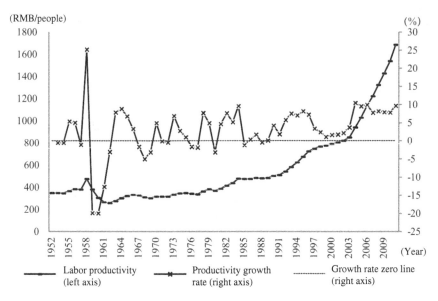

Figure 2.5.   The productivity of China's agricultural labor and its growth rate (1952–2011, at the price in 1978).

Source: Agricultural Statistics Data of 60 Years in New China and *China Statistical Yearbook* over the years.

Figure 2.5 shows the changes in the productivity of agricultural labor over the past 60 years since the founding of the PRC. The productivity of agricultural labor measured at constant prices in 1978 fell from RMB 350/ person in 1953 to RMB 343/person at the end of the Cultural Revolution in 1976, presenting a downward trend for more than 20 years. Under the planned economic system, it only increased by 3.7% over the 25 years even in comparison with the value of RMB 363/person in 1978 in the first year of reform and opening-up. After the reform and opening-up, labor productivity achieved rapid growth and rose to RMB 1,688/person in 2011, an increase of 4.7 times that of 1978, at an average annual growth rate of 4.8%. The growth rate of labor productivity during the period of the planned economic system fluctuated drastically in terms of stability of growth. For example, labor productivity experienced a 25% increase and a 20% decline in 1958 and 1959, respectively. In contrast, since the reform and opening-up, in addition to the increased growth rate and the reduced fluctuation in the growth rate, labor productivity has achieved rapid and stable growth, and especially since 2003, the growth rate has kept stable at 8%–10%.

2. The productivity of agricultural labor measured by physical quantity

The average labor productivity of major agricultural products is estimated using the national agricultural product cost-benefit survey data (the agricultural cost-benefit data).[28] The agricultural cost-benefit data survey is based on the basic statistical unit of mu. The raw data are generally the national and provincial data of the output per mu (kg/mu), labor (day/mu) and material costs (CNY/mu).[29] Average labor productivity can be calculated by the labor man-day and the quantity of physical output data produced per mu of land.

Grain is of special importance in agriculture. The realistic importance of the goal of food security makes agricultural policies revolve largely around food production and supply. The agricultural cost-benefit data especially provide the data for the average costs and benefits of "three kinds of grain (rice, wheat and corn)". Figure 2.6 shows the grain output per mu, labor consumption and capital input in China from 1953 to

---

[28]The national agricultural product cost survey began in 1953 (interrupted by the Cultural Revolution during the period 1966–1974). In 1984, the team of the agricultural cost survey was established for the national price system of all levels to be responsible for investigating the production cost and benefit of major agricultural products nationwide. The coverage of the survey gradually expanded to form a large-scale network of agricultural product cost survey consisting of 31 provinces (autonomous regions and municipalities directly under the Central Government), 312 prefecture-level (municipal) cities, 1,553 survey counties and more than 60,000 peasant households. The nationally surveyed varieties included 68 major agricultural products such as grain, oilseeds, cotton, flue-cured tobacco, silkworm cocoons, sugar, fruit, pigs, eggs and milk. The survey focused on the consumption of various materials including seeds, fertilizers, pesticides, agricultural machinery, irrigation, fuel power, tool materials, depreciation and repair and the expenditure of funds, including taxes, insurance, management fees, financial expenses, labor costs and land costs. The Price Division of the National Development and Reform Commission is currently taking charge of the survey.

[29]For live pigs, the statistical indicators are production per pig (kg/pig), labor man-days (days/pig) and material cost (CNY/pig).

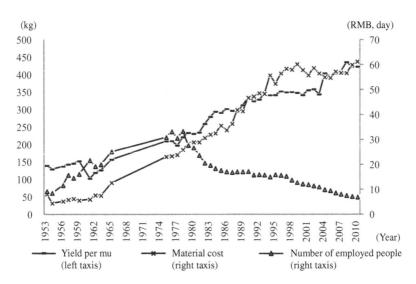

Figure 2.6.   China's grain output per mu, labor input and capital investments (1953–2010, at the price in 1978).

Source: The *Compilation of the Cost and Benefit Statistics of Major National Agricultural Products since the Founding of the PRC: 1953–1997* and the *Compilation of the Cost and Benefit Statistics of National Agricultural Products* over the years.

2010.[30] The capital input uses the "material cost"[31] in the survey as the proxy indicator and is adjusted by the price indicator of agricultural production materials based on 1978. As shown in the figure, the grain output per mu increased from 139 kg in 1953 to 221 kg in 1978 during the period of the planned economic system, with an increase of 59% in 25 years and an average annual growth of 1.87%. During the period of reform and opening-up, the grain output per mu continued to increase, reaching up to 424 kg in 2010, an increase of 92% from 1978 and an average annual growth of 1.99%. Since the establishment of the PRC, China's grain output per mu has shown a linear trend of growth in general as a whole.

---

[30]The data from 1966 to 1974 were missing and are represented by a straight line in Figure 2.6.

[31]After 1998, the "material cost" changed to "material and service cost". A comparison of the results shows a slight difference between them, and the ratio is generally stable. Therefore, they have not been adjusted here and will be processed accordingly in the analysis of following the measurement.

In contrast, the number of working days per mu presented the trend of rising first and then falling. Before the reform and opening-up, the labor input increased from 9.19 working days in 1953 to 33.3 working days in 1978, over a two-fold increase. The material cost calculated at constant prices in the same period increased from RMB 8.05 to RMB 25.92, similar to the growth rate of labor use. However, after the reform and opening-up, the labor input per mu kept decreasing. In 2010, it decreased to 6.9 working days, and the material cost continued to rise to RMB 61.3. During the period of the planned economy, both labor and capital increased and promoted the growth of the low yield per mu. On the contrary, after the reform and opening-up, the change in factor input, namely, the replacement of labor with capital, resulted in the rapid improvement of labor productivity.

Figure 2.7 shows the growth of the average labor productivity of grain. Before the reform and opening-up, the labor productivity of grain basically stagnated or even declined, with the minimum of 4.76 kg/d in 1961

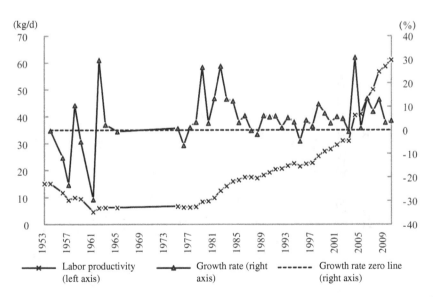

Figure 2.7. China's grain labor productivity and its growth rate (1953–2010).

Source: The *Compilation of the Cost and Benefit Statistics of Major National Agricultural Products since the Founding of the PRC: 1953–1997* and the *Compilation of the Cost and Benefit Statistics of National Agricultural Products* over the years.

and 6.65 kg/d in 1978, down by half from 15.15 kg/d in 1953. The signifi-cant decline in grain labor productivity and the stagnation of labor produc-tivity measured by the added value of agriculture show the low efficiency of the model of economic development in the period of the planned eco-nomic system from different angles. Since the reform and opening-up, the labor productivity has increased rapidly, reaching up to 31 kg/d in 2003, with an average annual growth rate of 6.35%. Subsequently, labor produc-tivity further increased at a fast rate, reaching up to 61.1 kg/day in 2010, with an average annual growth rate of 10.18% in that period. During the period of reform and opening-up (1978–2010), the annual growth rate was about 7.18%, a relatively high growth rate.

Figure 2.8 shows the average annual growth rate of contemporary labor productivity of 13 major agricultural products. Considering that the dead-line of some product data is different, the period from 1980 to 2010, when most products have data, roughly corresponds to the growth of the produc-tivity of agricultural labor in China during the period of reform and

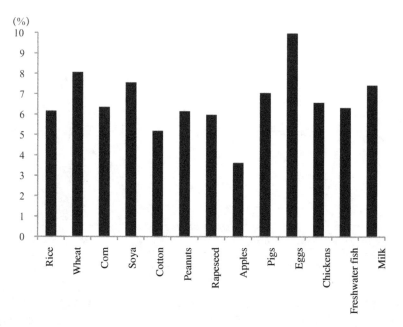

Figure 2.8.   Average annual growth rate of the labor productivity of major agricultural products (1980–2010).

opening-up. In terms of the 30-year average, the highest growth rate of labor productivity is eggs with an average annual growth rate of about 10%, while the lowest growth rate is apples with an annual growth rate of about 3.5%. Among them, the labor productivity of bulk agricultural products has achieved rapid and steady growth. The average growth rate of the four grain varieties is 7%. The fastest is wheat, at 8.1%, while the lowest is rice, at 6.3%.

Figure 2.9 shows the average annual growth rate of labor productivity of 13 major agricultural products in different periods since the reform and opening-up. Different agricultural products have different growth rates of labor productivity in different periods. For chickens, eggs, freshwater fish, milk and other animal products, productivity presents a trend of first rising and then falling. The eggs, chickens and freshwater fish achieved a growth

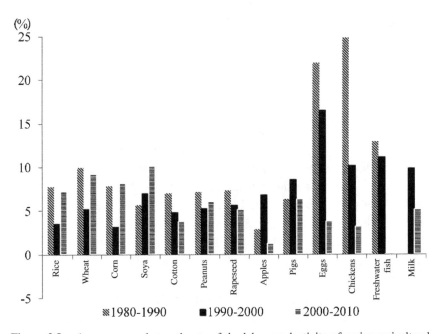

Figure 2.9. Average annual growth rate of the labor productivity of major agricultural products (1980–2010).

Source: The *Compilation of the Cost and Benefit Statistics of Major National Agricultural Products since the Founding of the PRC: 1953–1997* and the *Compilation of the Cost and Benefit Statistics of National Agricultural Products* over the years.

rate of labor productivity of 24.6%, 21.9% and 12.8%, respectively, in the 1980s and maintained the average annual growth rate of double digits in the 1990s. Moreover, the growth rate of productivity of milk as shown in the agricultural cost-benefit data has also maintained the high level of 9.8% since the 1990s. However, in the first decade of the 21st century, the growth rate of the four animal products dropped to 3.1%, 3.8%, −0.2% and 5.1%, respectively. Cotton, peanuts and rapeseed showed a trend of a slight downward decline in growth of productivity. Soybean productivity continued to rise, with an average annual growth rate of 5.6%, 7.0% and 10.2%, respectively, over the three decades. Pig productivity was high in the 1990s, about 8.3%, but slightly lower in the decade before and after the 1990s, about 6.3%. Apple productivity also showed a trend of high in the middle. In contrast to apples and pigs, the labor productivity of the three main grain products presented a trend of a higher level at both ends and a lower level in the middle. Rice, wheat and corn realized a productivity growth rate of 7.7%, 9.9% and 7.8% in the 1980s; 3.5%, 5.2% and 3.2% in the 1990s; and 7.3%, 9.2% and 8.1% in the first decade of the new century, respectively.

3. *Brief comments*

The economic development since the founding of the PRC has provided an empirical case of a very large country in both positive and negative aspects to illustrate the relationship between the improvement in the efficiency of agricultural production and the promotion of economic development. China's development failed to really embark on the track for many reasons in the period of a planned economy, which was consistent with the grim reality of stagnant productivity of agricultural labor at that time. This may be proved by the comparison of average agricultural added value and average grain output of labor before and after the reform and opening-up. The failure of the planned economic system to support the sustainable advancement of economic modernization has an important causal relationship with the restraint on the improvement in the productivity of agricultural labor by the agricultural economic system in violation of the economic laws at that time. On the eve of reform and opening-up, more than 70% of China's labor force still engaged in agriculture, and the average grain output per worker in 1976 was even lower than what it was in 1953. Over the past two decades and more, the Chinese people have not been able to address the problem of low levels of food and clothing, despite the adoption of agriculture-based policies and the continuous implementation of the grain goal through various means. This situation did not change historically until the late 1970s when China entered the period of reform and opening-up.

With the promotion of the transformation of the system of reform and opening-up, China's economy has grown at an average annual rate of about 10% over the past 30 years. As China's economic structure rapidly shifts toward industrialization and urbanization, China has initially entered the ranks of middle-income countries from the poorest international countries in terms of per capita income. All this has been achieved based on the rapid evolution of the function of agricultural production and the improvement in the capacity for agricultural production. Compared with the average values from 2009 to 2011 and the average values from 1975 to 1977 before the reform, the actual added value of agriculture in China increased by 3.3 times in the past 30 years, with an average annual growth rate of about 4.4%. Compared with the data in the first year of the reform in 1978, the total output of major agricultural products, such as grain, cotton and oilseeds, increased by 0.93 times, 2.15 times and 5.59 times, respectively, in 2012, with an average annual growth of about 2.0%, 3.4% and 5.7%; the total output of meat and milk increased by 3.35 times and 12.39 times from 1985, respectively, with an average annual growth of about 5.6% and 10.1%. In the same period, 260 million migrant workers shifted to the non-agricultural sector, and thus, the proportion of agricultural labor in the total labor force dropped from over 70% to less than 35%, with an average annual decline of more than 1 percentage point.

According to the overall developmental prospect on agriculture and the national economy, it is apparent that the productivity of China's agricultural labor is experiencing historic improvement and thus has completely gotten out of the Malthusian trap in the history of mankind. Consequently, China, as the country with the biggest population, is realizing a historic transformation while agriculture supports the law of economic development. The details of the estimated results of different methods of estimation may be varied, but together they form a basic conclusion, namely, compared with the long-term stagnation of or even a decline in the productivity of agricultural labor during the period of the planned economy, the revolution in labor productivity has been successfully realized in the agricultural sector during the period of reform and opening-up, which plays a fundamental role in supporting the rapid advancement of China's industrialization and urbanization, as well as the transformation of the contemporary economy.

IV. Summary

Since the reform and opening-up, China's agricultural labor force has continued to transfer to the non-agricultural sector on a large scale with the driving factors of the transfer of agricultural labor and the support of the productivity of agricultural labor, thus completely changing the labor market of China's non-agricultural sector and profoundly affecting China's investments, savings, technological progress and the fluctuation of its macroeconomic cycle. The agricultural labor force is the key to understanding the mechanism of China's economic development. Therefore, this book will combine the theory of the development of a dual economy and the theory of endogenous growth to analyze the three basic characteristics or riddles of China's economic development from the perspective of the transfer of agricultural labor in the next three chapters, that is, the riddle of China's rising return on capital, the riddle of China's rising savings rate and the riddle of "Okun's law" not being applicable to China.

Chapter 3

The Enigma of the Transfer of Agricultural Labor and the Rising Return on Capital

I. Introduction

Since the reform and opening-up, China has always maintained an extremely high rate of investment. Over a long period of time, however, China's return on capital has shown a sustained upward trend rather than a downward trend. According to the data published by the National Bureau of Statistics, China's rate of investment was never lower than 30% from 1980 to 2014, averaging 39.4%. In the 21st century, China's rate of investment has risen further, close to 50% recently, far higher than that of other countries in the world (as shown in Figure 1.2). Surprisingly, such a high rate of investment has not resulted in a falling return on capital in China. Massive empirical evidence provided by scholars in recent years shows that China's return on capital has been on the rise since the mid-to-late 1990s. Earlier, the World Bank and other organizations had reported an increase in China's return on capital over the previous period.[1] The results of the estimation of China's return on capital by Bai, Hsieh and

---

[1] The World Bank (WB) China Office: *China Quarterly Update*, May 2006.

Qian based on the data of the national income suggest that China's return on capital remained at the high level of more than 20% throughout the period of reform and opening-up, and it has also been on the rise in recent years.[2] In view of the results of the calculation of capital returns and the data regarding capital stock in financial accounting in industrial enterprises, the Research Group of the CCER China Economic Observer demonstrates that China's return on capital presents a feature of first falling then rising, and the nine series of indicators show a sustained trend of growth after the end of the last century.[3] By calculating the rate of return on industrial capital, Shu Yuan, Zhang Li and Xu Xianxiang also point out that the rate of return on capital in China has increased significantly over the past decade.[4] From the perspective of the theory of vintage capital, Fang Wenquan re-estimated the return on capital in China, and adjusted the rate of return on capital downward by 3%–5% by virtue of the revised rate of depreciation, but the overall change remains upward.[5] The results of the calculation of Zhang Xun and Xu Jianguo suggest that the total return on capital has risen steadily from 1998, but has dropped from 2009. Despite this, the return on industrial capital still presents an upward trend; for instance, the return on industrial fixed assets was up to 27.8% in 2012.[6] The upward trend of China's return on capital is clearly shown in the data from the report in Figure 1.3.

According to the basic assumption of the neoclassical theory of growth, the marginal output of capital will decrease with an increase in capital stock under a given level of technology and input of labor factors, that is,

---

[2]Bai, C., C. Hsieh and Y. Qian: The Return to Capital in China, *Brookings Papers on Economic Activity*, 2006 (2), pp. 61–88.

[3]Research Group of the CCER China Economic Observer: Measurements of China's Capital Return (1978–2006) — Microeconomic Underpinnings for the Recent Economic Boom in China, *China Economic Quarterly*, 2007 (6) (3), pp. 723–758.

[4]Shu Yuan, Zhang Li and Xu Xianxiang: An Analysis of the Chinese Industrial Capital Return and Allocation Efficiency: Calculation and Decomposition, *Economic Review*, 2010 (1), pp. 28–36.

[5]Fang Wenquan: China's Capital Returns: A Re-estimation from the Perspective of the Vintage Capital Model, *China Economic Quarterly*, 2012 (11) (2), pp. 159–178.

[6]Zhang Xun and Xu Jianguo: Re-measurement of China's Return on Capital, *World Economics*, 2014 (8), pp. 5–25.

the law of diminishing marginal returns of capital. As a developing country, China has always been viewed as a typical example of a country lacking technological progress. So how can the rising return on capital under a high rate of investment in the long run be explained? Sufficient attention has not been paid to the analysis of the reasons behind the rising return on capital, and not much of the literature has studied the reasons for the rising return on capital in theory, despite systematic estimations on the rate of capital return and discussions of the meaning of the rate of capital return on the rationality judgment of China's high rate of investment. However, this issue is of paramount importance for correctly understanding China's model of economic development and for judging the current economic situation. In the existing theory of economic development, there are mainly two frameworks of models with a theoretical possibility, namely, the new theory of growth and the theory of dual economic development. The former, through progress in endogenous biotechnology, and the latter, through the introduction of factors of the transfer of agricultural labor, may deduce the result of a constant and even rising return on capital theoretically. So can they provide an ideal explanation for China's rising return on capital?

For instance, the "model of knowledge spillover", as a typical representative of the new theory of growth proposed by Romer, Barro and Sala-I-Martin *et al.*, focuses on the "learning effect" and the "spillover effect" to overcome the law of diminishing marginal returns (collectively referred to as "technology spillover effect").[7] However, the AK property of this model actually implies a strong theoretical hypothesis not accomplished by China. To illustrate it, suppose that an enterprise *i* has an A_{it} level of technology of labor enhancement in the *t* year, and the total social capital stock is K_t, there is a positive relationship between the level of enterprise technology A_{it} and social capital stock K_t, thanks to the technology spillover effect. In the model of Romer *et al.*, it is assumed that $A_{it} = K_t$; more generally, it is set that $A_{it} = K_t^\sigma$, $\sigma \geq 0$ shows the elasticity of the technology spillover effect of investment.[8] The derivation shows that the marginal

[7] Romer, Paul M.: Increasing Returns and Long-Run Growth, *Journal of Political Economy*, 1986 (94) (5), pp. 1002–1037.

[8] *Ibid.*; Barro, Robert J. and X. Sala-I-Martin: *Economic Growth*, Cambridge: Massachusetts Institute of Technology, 2nd edition, 2004.

return on capital does not decrease progressively only when σ is greater than or equal to 1. It is Romer's assumption of $\sigma = 1$ (unit elasticity) which comes to the conclusion of a constant return on capital.[9] According to the results of the calculation of σ value by Li et al. based on the data and the latest method in the Penn World Table 6.3, the technology spillover effect does exist, but the estimation value σ of the corresponding caliber is only 0.552, far less than one.[10] In fact, the national estimation value σ is less than 1 for various income groups. In this chapter, the panel data and system GMM method of the industrial sector in 31 provinces, autonomous regions and municipalities in China from 1978 to 2010 are used to specifically calculate the σ value of the technology spillover effect in China, producing the result of 0.663. That is slightly higher than the world average, but still does not meet the requirement of not less than 1. This means that in the model of the knowledge spillover, China's return on capital is supposed to decline, not rise.

The Lewis model of a dual economy emphasizes the fact that the existence of a surplus labor in agriculture enables the non-agricultural sector to face an infinite supply of labor in the constant living wage, so that capital accumulation can also be achieved at the same rate of return on capital under the assumption of a constant wage.[11] However, the rising wages of migrant workers in China in recent years have made the theory lose its explanatory power. An analysis of the growth of wages by Zhang, Yang and Wang based on the data from surveys on Chinese agriculture reveals that China's real wages have had a significant upward trend since 2003, further inferring the arrival of the Lewis inflection point. This means that the assumption of the wage invariant has been disproved at least since then.[12] The results of the calculation obtained by Lu Feng on the wages of migrant workers in China indicates that the wages of migrant workers in

[9]Romer, Paul M.: Increasing Returns and Long-Run Growth, *Journal of Political Economy*, 1986 (94) (5), pp. 1002–1037.
[10]Li, J., K. Shen and R. Zhang: Measuring Knowledge Spillovers: A Non-Appropriable Returns Perspective, *Annals of Economics and Finance*, 2011 (12) (2), pp. 265–293.
[11]Lewis, W. A.: Economic Development with Unlimited Supplies of Labour, *Manchester School*, 1954 (22) (2), pp. 139–191.
[12]Zhang, X., J. Yang and S. Wang: China Has Reached the Lewis Turning Point, *China Economic Review*, 2011 (22) (4), pp. 542–554.

(RMB/month)

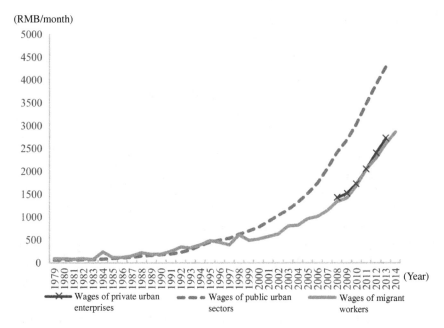

Figure 3.1.   Wages of urban sectors in China (1979–2014).

Source: CEIC and Lu Feng: Wage Trends among Chinese Migrant Workers: 1979–2010, *Social Sciences in China*, 2012 (7). Wages of migrant workers before 2007 came from Lu Feng (2012).

China have been on the rise over the past 30 years, especially regarding the nominal wage, which has increased by nearly 10% annually (Figure 3.1).[13] In reviewing the model of a dual economy, Lewis has pointed out that the hypothesis of constant wages has been proved to be invalid in many developing countries and is known as the biggest theoretical enigma of its time.[14] In any case, the hypothesis of non-diminishing return on capital in the Lewis model fails in China. Moreover, according to the model, an increase in wages means a decline in the return on capital.

Considering the specific situation of China, some scholars have studied the rising return on capital in combination with the characteristics of the

---

[13]Lu Feng: Wage Trends among Chinese Migrant Workers: 1979–2010, *Social Sciences in China*, 2012 (7), pp. 48–68+205.

[14]Lewis, W. A.: The Dual Economy Revisited, *Manchester School*, 1979 (47), pp. 211–229.

change in China's economic structure. Song, Storesletten and Zilibotti have constructed a model of a changing economy consisting of two types of enterprises to explain this phenomenon: In the process of privately owned enterprises with a relatively high amount of productivity gradually squeezing state-owned enterprises out of the market, the return on capital of the two types of enterprises remains unchanged, while the total return on capital increases due to the combination effect.[15] However, the basic assumption of such an explanation is not consistent with the actual situation in China. According to the calculations of the World Bank, the CCER China Economic Observer Research Group and this chapter (Figure 3.2), the capital return of China's private enterprises, state-owned enterprises and foreign-funded enterprises has been on the rise since 1998, showing basically the same growth trend. This indicates that the rising return on capital in China is attributable to the holistic factors covering the three types of enterprises.[16] Other scholars have also attempted to explain the main driving factors of China's rising return on capital by the decomposition method. Shu Yuan *et al.* have found through the decomposition of the industrial rate of capital return that the increase in the return on capital is mainly caused by its own growth effect, and the improvement in capital efficiency is mostly reflected in the total efficiency.[17] The decomposition of changes in China's return on capital by Huang Xianhai, Yang Jun and Xiao Mingyue shows that the main reason for the rising return on capital, instead of a decline with the growth of investments, is that technological progress increases the marginal output of capital.[18] These empirical

---

[15] Song Z., K. Storesletten and F. Zilibotti: "Growing Like China", *American Economic Review*, 2011 (101), pp. 196–233.

[16] The World Bank (WB) China Office: *China Quarterly Update*, May 2006; Research Group of the CCER China Economic Observer: Measurements of China's Capital Return (1978–2006) — Microeconomic Underpinnings for the Recent Economic Boom in China, *China Economic Quarterly*, 2007 (6) (3), pp. 723–758.

[17] Shu Yuan, Zhang Li and Xu Xianxiang: An Analysis of the Chinese Industrial Capital Return and Allocation Efficiency: Calculation and Decomposition, *Economic Review*, 2010 (1), pp. 28–36.

[18] Huang Xianhai, Yang Jun and Xiao Mingyue: An Analysis of the Transition of Capital Return in China — Based on the Perspective of Capital Deepening and Technical Progress, *Economic Theory and Business Management*, 2011 (11), pp. 49–56.

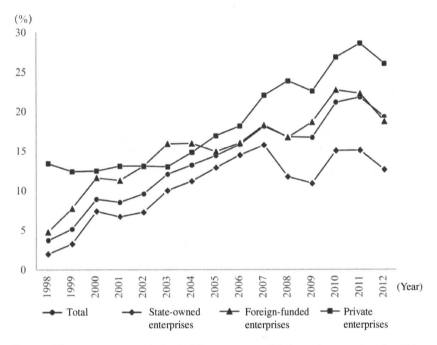

Figure 3.2. Return on capital of different types of industrial enterprises in China (1998–2012).

Note: The indicator of return on capital is a pre-tax profit rate of net assets, which is obtained by dividing the total amount of profits by the net assets (equity). The data of foreign-funded enterprises are obtained from the sum of the data of foreign investments, Hong Kong and Macao capital investments.

Source: *China Statistical Yearbook* over the years.

studies suggest that the fundamental factors promoting China's rising return on capital are supposed to boost China's technological progress and the efficiency of its capital aggregate, but further work is needed to make a clear explanation in theory.

The rising return on capital in China seems to be a developmental enigma. This chapter attempts to re-examine the transformation of the Chinese dual economic structure from the perspective of the transfer of the endogenous labor force and technological progress, and to solve the riddle by means of an analysis of the dynamic general equilibrium and an empirical analysis with the establishment of an expanded dual economic model. This chapter holds that China's economic development in recent years is a change in the dual economic structure with an endogenous growth mechanism, rather than the pure endogenous growth of the dual economy and a simple "Lewis" type of development of the dual economy. It is therefore necessary to combine the two theories organically to understand the coexistence of China's high investment rate and rising return on capital from the structural conditions of China as a developing country.

The expansion model established in this chapter not only relaxes the unit elasticity hypothesis of the model of knowledge spillover on the technology spillover effect but also presents a "strong condition" ($\sigma \geq 1$) and a "weak condition" ($\sigma \geq 1/2$) required for economies at different stages of development to maintain a constant or a rising return on capital. In view of China's background of change, the analysis in this chapter reveals that the transfer of the labor force and capital formation interact with each other to dynamically improve the level of technology. As a result, the requirement of the technology spillover effect for the realization of rising capital return is degraded from a "strong condition" to a "weak condition". Therefore, the theoretical analysis comes to the conclusion that the organic combination of the transfer of the labor force and the technology spillover effect promotes a rising return on capital in China. Evidence from an empirical analysis also reflects that China does have a technology spillover effect and fulfills the aforesaid "weak condition", thus leading to a tendency of a rising return on capital against the background of the continued migration of the labor force.

This chapter is organized as follows: The second part shows a review and discussion of the literature. The third part describes the theoretical model to explain the rising return on capital in China through a dynamic analysis of the general equilibrium. The fourth part describes the empirical analysis to examine the mechanism of the theoretical model in this chapter by means of a quantitative estimation of the level of China's technology spillover effect. The fifth part gives a summary.

II. Review and Discussion of the Literature

This chapter analyzes the transformation of China's dual economic structure from an endogenous perspective, and explains the rising return on capital in China with the help of the combination of endogenous labor transfer and technology spillover effect. Specifically, a model that is suitable for explaining China's economic development and even can be generalized to the economic structural transformation of developing countries will be built on the basis of the theory of dual economic development and the new growth theory and with the combination of the transfer of the labor force and the technology spillover effect. Therefore, it is necessary to make a brief review of the literature regarding the dual economic and new growth theories in relation to the theoretical analysis of this chapter.

The concept of dual economy was first proposed by Boeck in the study of Indonesia, who divided the country's social economy into a traditional sector and a modern capitalist sector run by Dutch colonizers. Higgins used different functions of production to reflect the differences between the traditional sector and the advanced sector from the dualism of production technology, and further described the characteristics of the dual economic structure of developing countries.[19] Lewis creatively raised the dual economic developmental model to link the dynamics of the development of the two sectors by means of an analysis of the transfer of the surplus labor, thus providing a basic analytical framework for explaining the economic development of developing countries.[20] Fei and Ranis put forward improvements to the Lewis model to emphasize the status and role of agricultural development in the development of a dual economy, and analyzed the balanced growth of the two sectors.[21] Jorgenson compared and analyzed the differences and similarities of the dual economic theory under the classical method and the neoclassical method, which broadened the research horizon of the dual economic theory.[22] Since then, the studies have focused on the analysis of labor transfer across departments. Harris and Todaro put forward the famous "Todaro model", and argued that the decision of the transfer of agricultural labor depended on the expected

---

[19]Zhang Peigang (Editor in chief): *New Development Economics*, Henan People's Publishing House, 2nd edition, 1999.

[20]Lewis, W. A.: Economic Development with Unlimited Supplies of Labour, *Manchester School*, 1954 (22) (2), pp. 139–191.

[21]Fei, J. and G. Ranis: A Theory of Economic Development, *American Economic Review*, 1961 (57), pp. 65–70.

[22]Jorgenson, D. W.: Surplus Agricultural Labour and the Development of a Dual Economy, *Oxford Economic Papers*, 1967 (19) (3), pp. 288–312.

income after transfer to the city rather than the actual income.[23] Based on the Todaro model, Neary analyzed the labor transfer on the condition of free flow of capital between the two sectors.[24] Some scholars divided urban sectors into formal and informal sectors, and established a more sophisticated model of labor transfer.[25]

China's economy is a typical dual economy. The large-scale transfer of agricultural labor constitutes one of the most important structural features of China's economic transformation. During the period of the planned economy, the division of urban and rural systems not only enabled China's agricultural sector to reserve a large number of surplus labor but also caused a huge transfer cost of the flow of labor. Since the reform and opening-up, the demand for labor has increased rapidly with the rapid development of the non-agricultural sector, and agricultural labor has kept transferring to the non-agricultural sector at an annual rate of about 8 million. In 2014, the number of migrant workers in China exceeded 270 million, and the proportion of agricultural labor decreased from over 70% in the early stage of the reform to about 30%. Besides, the transfer of agricultural labor has also been constantly strengthened and it has experienced a gradual process from rural non-agricultural sectors to small towns and township enterprises, and finally trans-provincial areas.[26] Therefore, both at the industrial level and at the spatial level, the allocation efficiency of China's labor resources is continuing to improve. Research shows that the transfer of agricultural labor is closely associated with the improvement in China's total factor productivity,[27] the rapid

---

[23]Harris, J. R. and M. P. Todar: Migration, Unemployment and Development: A Two-Sector Analysis, *American Economic Review*, 1970 (60) (1), pp. 126–142.

[24]Neary, J. P.: On the Harris-Todaro Model with Intersectoral Capital Mobility, *Economica*, New Series, 1981 (48) (191), pp. 219–234.

[25]Chandra, V. and M. Khan: Foreign Investment in the Presence of an Informal Sector, *Economica*, 1993 (60), pp. 79–103. ; Gupta, M. R.: Foreign Capital and the Informal Sector: Comments on Chandra and Khan, *Economica*, 1997 64 (254), pp. 353–363.

[26]Cai Fang: Growth and Structural Changes in Employment in Transitional China, *Economic Research Journal*, 2007 (7), pp. 5–15+23.

[27]Hu Yongtai: China's Total Factor Productivity: First Role of the Re-allocation of Agricultural labor, *Economic Research Journal*, 1998 (3), pp. 33–41.

development and exportation of the manufacturing industry,[28] the high savings rate and the high investment rate,[29] the change in the pattern of income distribution[30] and other important macroeconomic characteristic phenomena. Du Yang *et al.* discovered, through their latest research, that the flow of the labor force from rural areas to urban areas was conducive to expanding the size of the labor market and improving the total factor productivity of an urban economy, and the net benefits brought by the flow of labor were considerable, despite the negative impacts on the capital–output ratio and on the working hours.[31]

Furthermore, the agricultural labor in the real economy often faces various obstacles and transfer costs instead of free movement between the two sectors. The phenomenon of "semi-urbanization", once prevalent in Latin America and other regions, is evident in the process of the transfer of China's agricultural labor force, and even more prominent in some aspects.[32] The semi-urbanization of the rural migrant population is reflected in social life, actions, recognition, and system level, with a long-term trend.[33] This means that in reality, the transfer of China's agricultural labor force encounters a variety of obstacles, including moving out, moving in and flow barriers, as well as the impact of transfer costs. With the awareness of the importance of transfer costs, Gupta *et al.* built a labor transfer model considering transfer costs.[34] Therefore, the existence of transfer costs should also be taken into account in the specific analysis of

---

[28]Young, A.: Gold into Base Metals: Productivity Growth in the People's Republic of China during the Reform Period, *Journal of Political Economy*, 2003 (111), pp. 1220–1261.

[29]Li Yang and Yin Jianfeng: High Savings, High Investment, and China's Economic Growth in the Process of Labor Transfer, *Economic Research Journal*, 2005 (2), pp. 4–15+25.

[30]Li Daokui, Liu Linlin and Wang Hongling: The U Curve of Labor Share in GDP during Economic Development, *Economic Research Journal*, 2009 (1), pp. 71–83.

[31]Du Yang, Cai Fang, Qu Xiaobo and Cheng Jie: Sustain the China Miracle: Reaping the Dividends from Hukou Reforms, *Economic Research Journal*, 2014 (8), pp. 4–13+78.

[32]Jacoby, Erich H.: The Coming Backlash of Semi-Urbanization, *Ceres (FAO Review)*, 1970 (3) (6), pp. 48–51.

[33]Wang Chunguang: A Study of the Floating Rural People's "Semi-Urbanization", *Sociological Studies*, 2006 (5), pp. 111–126+248.

[34]Gupta, M. R.: Foreign Capital and the Informal Sector: Comments on Chandra and Khan, *Economica*, 1997 (64) (254), pp. 353–363.

the flow of China's agricultural labor force, so as to successfully explain the transfer mode with an increase in the total number of migrant workers in China and the growth of wages. For this reason, this chapter will introduce heterogeneous agricultural labor transfer costs and a micro-transfer decision-making mechanism.

The introduction and development of the dual economic theory provide a basic analytical framework for understanding the Chinese economy. However, to analyze China's specific economic problems, an important issue remains to be solved. The standard theory of a dual economy does not explain the technological progress, so it is hard to make an ideal explanation for the rising return on capital in China. In the Lewis model, the rate of return on capital remains constant and does not rise under the assumption of constant wages. In view of the rising wages for migrant workers in China, the return on capital is supposed to fall. This is because the Lewis model ignores the endogenous technological progress in the process of China's economic transformation. So far, studies have introduced the concept of endogenous growth into the dual economic model, and especially, they have endogenized the technological progress of the agricultural sector or the non-agricultural sector through the "learning by doing" model.[35] This chapter will focus on the analysis of the technology spillover effect with the endogenous growth theory to address the endogenous problems of technological progress.

The emergence and development of an endogenous theory are aimed at eliminating the reliance of sustained economic growth on the exogenous assumption of technological progress under the framework of neoclassical growth. Its basic idea is to determine the sustained economic growth within a system by means of endogenous technological progress. Depending on different generational mechanisms of technological progress, the endogenous growth model can be roughly divided into two categories. The former is the external model or the knowledge spillover

---

[35]Chen Zongsheng and Li Defu: A Growth Model of Dual Economy with Endogenous Agricultural Technology Progress — The Re-analysis of "East Asian Miracle" and the Chinese Economy, *Economic Research Journal*, 2004 (11), pp. 16–27; Guo Tao and Song Deyong: An Endogenous Growth Model of Dual Economy about Rural Labor Transfer, *South China Journal of Economics*, 2006 (8), pp. 77–84.

model, which assumes that knowledge accumulation or technological progress is the "by-product" of economic activities such as investment or production.[36] The latter is the R&D model or the innovation model, which regards technological progress as the result of original research and development consciously conducted by enterprises.[37]

Lin Yifu and Zhang Pengfei pointed out that the source of technological progress has been varied at different stages of development. The most developed countries are standing at the forefront of industrial technology. Original technological innovation can only derive from new technological inventions, so that more capital and manpower are needed to develop new technologies. Developing countries may achieve technological innovation by introducing new technologies from more developed countries. Such non-original research and development is characterized by low costs, low risks and high benefits, which are in line with the comparative advantages of developing countries.[38] Xu Jianguo believed that, for developing countries, investment was the most important way of obtaining technological progress, because the backward countries' new investment contained the advanced technologies at that time, conducive to promoting the accumulation of human capital and technological progress in the use of new capital goods.[39] Thus, different characteristics of technological progress exist between developing countries and developed countries. In contrast, the R&D model is more suitable to explaining the technological progress of developed countries, while the spillover model is more suitable to explaining the technological progress of developing countries.

---

[36] Arrow, Kenneth J.: The Economic Implications of Learning by Doing, *The Review of Economic Studies*, 1962 (29) (3), pp. 155–173; Romer, Paul M.: Increasing Returns and Long-Run Growth, *Journal of Political Economy*, 1986 (94) (5), pp. 1002–1037; Barro, Robert J. and X. Sala-I-Martin: *Economic Growth*, Cambridge: Massachusetts Institute of Technology, 2nd edition, 2004.

[37] Romer, Paul M.: Endogenous Technological Change, *Journal of Political Economy*, 1990 (98) (5), pp. 71–102; Aghion, P. and P. Howitt: A Model of Growth through Creative Destruction, *Econometrica*, 1992 (60), pp. 323–351.

[38] Lin Yifu and Zhang Pengfei: The Advantage of Later Comers, Technology Imports and Economic Growth of Developing Countries, *China Economic Quarterly*, 2005 (5) (1), pp. 53–74.

[39] Xu Jianguo: Capital Accumulation and Technological Progress, Working Paper of the China Center for Economic Research, No. C2013001, 2013.

Among spillover models, the knowledge spillover model of Romer, Barro and Sala-I-Martin[40] is most closely related to the characteristics of the technological progress of enterprises since China's reform and opening-up. Based on Arrow's idea of "learning by doing", the model concludes that enterprises should learn knowledge and accumulate experience in the process of investment and production, so as to achieve technological progress, and moreover, the spillover effect of knowledge should be considered, so that the technological progress of an enterprise will quickly spread to the whole society. This idea can be traced back to Smith's discussion of machine improvement in *The Wealth of Nations*.[41] The reason why the knowledge spillover model is more consistent with the characteristics of China's technological progress is that the model emphasizes the relationship among investment, production and technological progress. China has maintained a high investment rate for a long time, while the return on capital has continued to rise rather than fall. It is the result of the interaction between investment and technological progress. The Research Group for China's Economic Growth and Macroeconomic Stability points out that China's technological progress and productive investment maintain a stable proportional relationship.[42] Many scholars find that the endogenous growth of "learning by doing" or "learning by investment" exists in China's economic development, and "learning by doing" makes an important contribution to China's total factor productivity and economic growth.[43]

---

[40]Romer, Paul M.: Increasing Returns and Long-Run Growth, *Journal of Political Economy*, 1986 (94) (5), pp. 1002–1037. Barro, Robert J. and X. Sala-I-Martin: *Economic Growth*, Cambridge: Massachusetts Institute of Technology, 2nd edition, 2004.

[41]Arrow, Kenneth J.: The Economic Implications of Learning by Doing, *The Review of Economic Studies*, 1962 (29) (3), pp. 155–173.

[42]Research Group for China's Economic Growth and Macroeconomic Stability, Learning by Doing, Low Cost Competition and Conversion of Economic Growth Patterns, *Economic Research Journal*, 2006 (4), pp. 5–15.

[43]Li Yang, Yin Jianfeng: High Savings, High Investment, and China's Economic Growth in the Process of Labor Transfer, *Economic Research Journal*, 2005 (2), pp. 4–15+25; Blanchard, O. and F. Giavazzi: Rebalancing Growth in China: A Three-Handed Approach, *China & World Economy*, 2006 (14) (4), pp. 1–20; Zhang Yan: Empirical Test on China's Economic Growth Path through the Learning by Doing Model, *Public Finance Research*, 2009 (6), pp. 35–40.

The foregoing discussions reveal that China's economic development can be regarded as a dual economic development with an endogenous growth mechanism. To explain the rising rate of return on capital and sustained economic growth in China, it is necessary to make an organic combination of the theory of a dual economy and the theory of endogenous growth to construct an extended dual economic model.

III. Theoretical Model

Under the basic framework of a dual economy, this section introduces the frictional heterogeneous transfer of agricultural labor and endogenous technological progress to establish an extended dual economic model applicable to the characteristics of China's economic development, thus providing a theoretical framework for an explanation for the continuous rise of China's rate of return on capital. This section will show that the combination effect of the transfer of labor and technology spillover can guarantee a sustained rising return on capital in China, though China does not fulfill the assumptions of constant wages and unit elasticity of the technology spillover effect implied by the Lewis model and the new growth theory in the explanation of the unchanged (or rising) rate of return on capital.

1. Model specification

It is assumed that an economy consists of two sectors, namely, the agricultural sector (expressed by subscripted a) and the non-agricultural sector (expressed by subscripted b). The two sectors have an initial labor population of N_a and N_b, respectively, and a total labor population $N = N_a + N_b$. For the sake of a simplified analysis, population growth is not considered for the time being.

The production function of a representative enterprise i in the non-agricultural sector is assumed to be: $Y_{it} = K_{it}^{\alpha}(A_{it}L_{it})^{1-\alpha}$; where, K_{it} and L_{it} represent the capital and labor used by enterprise i, respectively; A_{it} represents the technical level of enterprise i; α represents the elasticity of capital output; subscripted t represents the period. The enterprise achieves technological progress in the process of investment, so the technical level

A_{it} of the enterprise is positively correlated with capital stock K_{it}. Besides, the technical level A_{it} of an enterprise is positively correlated with K_t, because of the spillover effect.[44] This chapter uses more general assumptions than Romer *et al.* It is assumed that $A_{it} = K_t^\sigma$, and $\sigma \geq 0$ is the technology spillover elasticity of investment.[45] Therefore, the production function of an enterprise in the non-agricultural sector is formalized as

$$Y_{it} = K_{it}^\alpha (K_t^\sigma L_{it})^{1-\alpha}. \tag{1}$$

Under such assumptions, the enterprise retains the characteristic of constant returns to scale (CRTS), but the entire society has increasing returns to scale (IRTS) due to the existence of the learning effect and the spillover effect. The aforesaid production function is also consistent with that used by Yao Yang.[46]

Total employment in the non-agricultural sector is $L_{bt} = \sum_i L_{it}$, and total capital stock is $K_t = \sum_i K_{it}$.

Given the rate of return on capital r_t, wage rate w_t and total social capital stock K_t, the enterprise chooses the optimal amount of capital K_{it} and labor input L_{it} to maximize its profit:

$$\max \pi_{it} = K_{it}^\alpha (K_t^\sigma L_{it})^{1-\alpha} - r_t K_{it} - w_t L_{it}.$$

First-order conditions:

$$r_t = \alpha K_t^{\sigma(1-\alpha)} K_{it}^{\alpha-1} L_{it}^{1-\alpha}, \tag{2}$$

$$w_t = (1-\alpha) K_t^{\sigma(1-\alpha)} K_{it}^\alpha L_{it}^{-\alpha}. \tag{3}$$

[44]Arrow, Kenneth J.: The Economic Implications of Learning by Doing, *The Review of Economic Studies*, 1962 (29) (3), pp. 155–173; Romer, Paul M.: Increasing Returns and Long-Run Growth, *Journal of Political Economy*, 1986 (94) (5), pp. 1002–1037; Barro, Robert J. and X. Sala-I-Martin, *Economic Growth*, Cambridge: Massachusetts Institute of Technology, 2nd edition, 2004; Xu Jianguo: Capital Accumulation and Technological Progress, Working Paper of the China Center for Economic Research, No. C2013001, 2013.
[45]Romer, Paul M.: Increasing Returns and Long-Run Growth, *Journal of Political Economy*, 1986 (94) (5), pp. 1002–1037.
[46]Yao Yang: The High Equilibrium Trap — The Needham Paradox Revisited, *Economic Research Journal*, 2003 (1), pp. 71–79+94.

In case of equilibrium, all manufacturers make the same optimal decision, that is, they choose the same amount of capital K_{it} and labor L_{it}. Therefore,

$$r_t = \alpha K_t^{\sigma(1-\alpha)} \left(\frac{L_{it}}{K_{it}} \right)^{1-\alpha} = \alpha K_t^{\sigma(1-\alpha)} \left(\frac{L_{bt}}{K_t} \right)^{1-\alpha}, \qquad (4)$$

$$w_t = (1-\alpha) K_t^{\sigma(1-\alpha)} \left(\frac{K_{it}}{L_{it}} \right)^{\alpha} = (1-\alpha) K_t^{\sigma(1-\alpha)} \left(\frac{K_t}{L_{bt}} \right)^{\alpha}. \qquad (5)$$

The production function of the agricultural sector is set as $Y_{at} = R_{at}^{\gamma} (A_{at} L_{at})^{1-\gamma}$, where A_{at} is the agricultural technology level, R_{at} is the agricultural land, L_{at} is the agricultural labor and $1 - \gamma$ is the elasticity of labor output. Similarly, it is assumed that the level of agricultural technology is also positively correlated with the total capital stock of the society, that is, $A_{at} = A_a K_t^{\sigma}$, where $A_a > 0$ represents the degree of technology assimilation and the transformation of the agricultural sector to the non-agricultural sector. Since agricultural land is basically constant, the unit is 1, and then the agricultural production function can be expressed as

$$Y_{at} = (A_a K_t^{\sigma} L_{at})^{1-\gamma}. \qquad (6)$$

Further, let us turn to the cross-sectoral transfer of labor. In the case that the labor force moves freely between the two sectors without transfer costs, the equilibrium condition of the labor market is the equal marginal labor productivity of the two sectors, namely, $\text{MPL}_{at} = \text{MPL}_{bt}$. However, as described earlier, farmers face various obstacles and hidden costs in reality when they move to cities to work. Therefore, even if the level of wages of the non-agricultural sector is higher than that of the agricultural sector, the transfer of labor will still be insufficient. In this chapter, the various obstacles that lead to the insufficient transfer of agricultural labor are summarized as the existence of transfer costs. According to the empirical analysis, the marginal labor productivity of the agricultural sector is always far lower than that of the non-agricultural sector in China, that is,

$MPL_{at} < MPL_{bt}$, indicating that the transfer of labor has reached an equilibrium when the existence of transfer costs makes the marginal output of the two sectors not equal.[47] At the same time, it is noted that there is heterogeneity in the transfer of labor, and the transfer costs vary with the characteristics of the labor force.[48]

Suppose that the transfer cost of a farmer $i\theta$ is θ. After all farmers are arranged in accordance with the size of transfer costs, a certain distribution will be formed. Let us set the distribution function as $\theta \sim G(\theta) = P(x \mid x \leqslant \theta)$. The condition for a farmer $i\theta$ to move to the non-agricultural sector for employment is that the wage w_t in the non-agricultural sector is higher than the transfer costs θ, that is, $w_t \geq \theta$. Given the wage w_t in the non-agricultural sector, the farmers whose transfer costs are less than the wage w_t in the non-agricultural sector will transfer, and the farmers whose transfer costs are greater than the wage w_t in the non-agricultural sector will not transfer, unless a higher level of wages is available. So, the transfer ratio of farmers is $m_t = P(\theta \mid \theta \leqslant w_t) = G(w_t)$. As a matter of fact, the macroscopic equilibrium, $MPL_{at} = MPL_{bt}$, has no restrictive effect due to the existence of transfer costs and the fact that $MPL_{at} < MPL_{bt}$ in China.

To simplify the analysis, let us suppose θ obeys the uniform distribution over $[u_1, u_2]$. Given the non-agricultural sector wage w_t, the ratio of agricultural labor transfer is as follows:

$$m_t = \frac{w_t - u_1}{u_2 - u_1}. \tag{7}$$

[47]Zhang Ping and Guo Xibao: Structural Change Effect in the Economic Growth of China — Measurement Method Based on Marginal Labor Productivity, *Journal of Shanxi University of Finance and Economics University*, 2011 (4), pp. 6–13.

[48]Xiong Jie and Teng Yangyang: The Impact Mechanism and Testing of the Transfer of Rural Heterogeneous Labor on the Income Difference of Urban and Rural Areas — Based on the Reasoning and Empirical Analysis of the Lewis Dual Economic Theory, *Chinese Journal of Population Science*, 2010 (1), pp. 31–40. Gennaioli, N., La Porta, R., Lopez-de-Silanes, F. and Shleifer, A.: Human Capital and Regional Development, *The Quarterly Journal of Economics*, 2013 (128) (1), pp. 105–164.

Non-agricultural sector employment supply:

$$L_{bt} = N_b + m_t N_a. \tag{8}$$

Through the combination of Eq. (7) and Eq. (8),

$$L_{bt} = N_b + \frac{w_t - u_1}{u_2 - u_1} N_a. \tag{9}$$

This proves that the labor supply of the non-agricultural sector is positively correlated with the level of labor capital due to the heterogeneous transfer costs, and does not enjoy an infinite labor supply as a result of the surplus labor in the agricultural sector.

2. Equilibrium analysis

(1) Labor market equilibrium

Taking into account the curve regarding the demand and supply of the labor market of the non-agricultural sector, namely, that represented by Eqs. (5) and (9), when the labor demand is equal to the labor supply, the labor market reaches an equilibrium, to figure out the following equilibrium condition:

$$L_{bt} = N_b - \frac{N_a u_1}{u_2 - u_1} + \frac{N_a}{u_2 - u_1}(1 - \alpha)K_t^{\sigma(1-\alpha)}\left(\frac{K_t}{L_{bt}}\right)^{\alpha}. \tag{10}$$

After solving Eq. (10), we can obtain the non-agricultural employment amount L_{bt} at equilibrium and then the wage w_t. Both of them are functions of capital stock K_t, that is, $L_{bt} = L_b(K_t)$ and $w_t = w(K_t)$.

(2) Mode of an increase in both the total number of migrant workers and their wages

In this section, let us analyze the transfer mode of an increase in both the total number of migrant workers and their wages through specific solutions. To simplify the analysis, it is assumed that the initial state of the

transfer is also equalizing, that is, $\frac{N_b}{N_a} = \frac{u_1}{u_2 - u_1}$, and then $N_b - \frac{N_a u_1}{u_2 - u_1} = 0$.
Thus, Eq. (10) can be converted into the following:

$$L_{bt} = \frac{N_a}{u_2 - u_1}(1-\alpha)K_t^{\sigma(1-\alpha)}\left(\frac{K_t}{L_{bt}}\right)^{\alpha}. \tag{11}$$

By solving the process, the solution of L_{bt} is $L_{bt} = [\frac{N_a}{u_2-u_1}(1-\alpha)]^{\frac{1}{1+\alpha}}K_t^{\frac{\sigma(1-\alpha)+\alpha}{1+\alpha}}$.
Suppose the constant $B = [\frac{N_a}{u_2-u_1}(1-\alpha)]^{\frac{1}{1+\alpha}}$, thus

$$L_b t = BK_t^{\frac{\sigma(1-\alpha)+\alpha}{1+\alpha}}. \tag{12}$$

Furthermore, the wage w_t of the non-agricultural sector is obtained by the following:

$$w_t = \frac{u_2 - u_1}{N_a}L_b(K_t) = (1-\alpha)B^{-\alpha}K_t^{\frac{\sigma(1-\alpha)+\alpha}{1+\alpha}}. \tag{13}$$

According to Eqs. (12) and (13), both the equilibrium of non-agricultural employment L_{bt} and wage w_t are the increasing functions of capital stock K_t under this model. With the accumulation of capital, the wages of the non-agricultural sector continue to rise, so that agricultural labor is constantly shifting, and non-agricultural employment is constantly growing. The existence of heterogeneous transfer costs does not result in an infinite labor supply to the non-agricultural sector from the large number of surplus labor in the agricultural sector, thus further making the Lewis constant wage hypothesis invalid in China.[49] Therefore, the transfer of agricultural labor in China is manifested as a pattern of an increasing number of migrant workers and wages. After a review of the dual economic model, Lewis points out that the failure of the constant wage hypothesis in most developing countries is the biggest theoretical puzzle of its time, and the analysis in this chapter may help to solve this puzzle.[50]

---

[49]Lewis, W. A.: Economic Development with Unlimited Supplies of Labour, *Manchester School*, 1954 (22) (2), pp. 139–191.
[50]Lewis, W. A.: The Dual Economy Revisited, *Manchester School*, 1979 (47), pp. 211–229.

(3) Analysis of the trend of change in the rate of return on capital

The phenomenon of rising return on capital in China in recent years is theoretically explained in this section. In this model, the change in the return on capital r_t is affected by three factors: (1) With the accumulation of capital K_t, the law of diminishing marginal output makes the rate of return on capital have a decreasing trend; (2) with the accumulation of capital K_t, the marginal output of labor increases, which attracts agricultural labor to move to the non-agricultural sector, so that the marginal output of capital increases, and the rate of return on capital tends to rise; (3) with the accumulation of capital K_t, new investments promote technological progress and improve the marginal output of capital through the technology spillover effect, further leading to an upward trend in the rate of return on capital. Therefore, the ultimate change in the rate of return on capital depends on three factors, which may be illustrated by a mathematical derivation.

Substituting Eq. (12) into Eq. (4), we can obtain the following:

$$r_t = \alpha B^{1-\alpha} K_t^{\frac{2(1-\alpha)\left(\sigma - \frac{1}{2}\right)}{1+\alpha}}. \tag{14}$$

According to Eq. (14), when $\sigma < 1/2$, the return on capital r_t is the decreasing function of the capital stock K_t. When $\sigma = 1/2$, the return on capital r_t is constant. When $\sigma > 1/2$, the return on capital r_t is the increasing function of the capital stock K_t. Thus, it is apparent that, with the accumulation of capital, the trend of return on capital in China depends on whether the technology spillover parameter σ reaches the critical value 1/2. The return on capital can stay the same or even rise only if $\sigma \geq 1/2$.

For the purpose of comparison, the condition required to keep the marginal output of capital from declining is $\sigma \geq 1$[51] in the model of Romer, Barro and Sala-I-Martin. This is because of the fact that in the absence of

[51]Romer, Paul M.: Increasing Returns and Long-Run Growth, *Journal of Political Economy*, 1986 (94) (5), pp. 1002–1037; Barro, Robert J. and X. Sala-I-Martin: *Economic Growth*, Cambridge: Massachusetts Institute of Technology, 2nd edition, 2004.

the transfer of the labor force, the expression of return on capital is changed to $r_t = \alpha K_t^{\sigma(1-\alpha)} \left(\frac{N_b}{K}\right)^{1-\alpha} = \alpha N_b^{1-\alpha} K_t^{(\sigma-1)(1-\alpha)}$. Thus, only if $\sigma \geq 1$, can the return on capital keep increasing with the accumulation of capital. This chapter calls it a "strong condition" for the increasing rate of return on capital. In the extended dual economic model in this chapter, the rate of return on capital can remain stable or increase with the accumulation of capital only if there is a transfer of agricultural labor and σ is not less than 1/2. This means that the factors of the transfer of agricultural labor lower the threshold of increasing return on capital. This chapter calls it a "weak condition" for the increasing rate of return on capital. In particular, in case of $1/2 < \sigma < 1$, that is, the technology spillover intensity meets the weak condition instead of the strong condition, the return on capital will increase with capital accumulation in an economy with a continuous transfer of labor, while the return on capital will decrease with capital accumulation in an economy without any transfer of labor.

According to the aforementioned model discussions, the continuous rising return on capital in China depends on whether the technology spillover parameter (σ) meets the weak condition, that is, $\sigma \geq 1/2$, in the context of a continuous large-scale transfer of agricultural labor. The theoretical derivation result provides the basic test proposition of the empirical analysis: if the parameter of China's technology spillover meets the condition of $\sigma \geq 1/2$, the interpretation of China's rising return on capital in this chapter is acceptable. Otherwise, the theoretical interpretation in this chapter lacks the explanatory power of reality. In the next section, we will focus on it by the practical estimates of the parameter (σ) of China's technology spillover.

IV. Empirical Analysis

The theoretical derivation of the previous section shows that, with the accumulation of capital, the increase in the return on capital in China depends on whether the intensity of the technology spillover meets the weak condition, that is, $\sigma \geq 1/2$. In this section, the panel data of the industrial sectors in 31 provinces, autonomous regions and municipalities on the Chinese mainland from 1978 to 2010 are used to estimate the parameter (σ) of China's technology spillover, thus testing the mechanism of the theoretical model of this chapter.

1. General measure of the technology spillover effect

Following the theoretical discussions on the learning effect and the spill-over effect by Arrow and Romer *et al.*, some scholars started to empiri-cally measure the size of the technology spillover effect.[52] Li *et al.* used the data of the Penn World Table 6.3 and the latest methods to measure the extent of the knowledge spillover. In this chapter, the parameter (σ) of the technology spillover is equivalent to the v value[53] of knowledge enhanced elasticity defined in their model. According to their calculations, a tech-nology spillover does exist. The σ value of the whole sample based on the total capital stock and per capita capital stock method is 0.552 and 0.778, respectively. Although the intensity of the spillover is less than 1 and does not fulfill the strong condition, it fulfills the weak condition of $\sigma > 1/2$. Therefore, under the model framework in this chapter, the rate of return on capital in China is an increasing function of the capital stock, and keeps rising with the accumulation of capital.

2. China's technology spillover effect and its rising return on capital

The estimation of the parameter of the technology spillover by Li *et al.* reflects the world average. To estimate the intensity of China's technology spillover, this section uses the panel data of industrial sectors in 31 prov-inces, autonomous regions and municipalities on the Chinese mainland from 1978 to 2010, and estimates China's spillover parameter σ by the total capital stock method of Li *et al.*

---

[52]Arrow, Kenneth J.: The Economic Implications of Learning by Doing, *The Review of Economic Studies*, 1962 (29) (3), pp. 155–173; Romer, Paul M.: Increasing Returns and Long-Run Growth, *Journal of Political Economy*, 1986 (94) (5), pp. 1002–1037.
[53]Li, J., K. Shen and R. Zhang: Measuring Knowledge Spillovers: A Non-Appropriable Returns Perspective, *Annals of Economics and Finance*, 2011 (12) (2), pp. 265–293.

The regression equation is as follows:

$$\ln y_{it} = \pi_{0i} + \pi_1 \ln k_{it} + \pi_2 \ln K_t + \varepsilon_{it}, \qquad (15)$$

where y_{it} is the average labor output of province i in the year t, which is obtained by Y_{it}/L_{it} (dividing the industrial GDP of each province by the labor force of industrial enterprises). K_{it} is the average labor capital of province i in the year t, which is obtained by K_{it}/L_{it} (dividing the net value of fixed assets of the industrial enterprises above the designated size of each province by the labor force of industrial enterprises). K_t is the total capital of the industrial enterprises in China in the year t, which is obtained by adding the net value of fixed assets of industrial enterprises above the designated size of all of the provinces. The data come from the *Statistical Yearbook* of provinces and regions, the *China Statistical Yearbook* and the *Statistical Data Compilation of China's Industrial Transportation and Energy for 50 Years*.

Where Eq. (15) can be derived from Eq. (1), that is, according to $Y_{it} = K_{it}^\alpha (K_t^\sigma L_{it})^{1-\alpha}$, the following can be derived:

$$\ln\left(\frac{Y_{it}}{L_{it}}\right) = \alpha \ln\left(\frac{K_{it}}{L_{it}}\right) + \sigma(1-\alpha)\ln K_t. \qquad (16)$$

It can be seen that the corresponding relation between the model parameter and the regression equation coefficient is, $\alpha = \pi_1, \sigma(1-\alpha) = \pi_2$. After estimation of the parameters π_1 and π_2, the formula $\sigma = \pi_2/1 - \pi_1$ is used to construct Wald statistics to statistically infer the parameter σ.

To ensure the robustness of the estimation results, Table 3.1 shows the estimation results of the simple least squares regression (1), the least squares regression of the control time effect (2), the fixed effect panel regression (3) and the dynamic panel regression (system GMM, (4)). According to the results of the estimation set forth in Table 3.1, China's economic growth has a technology spillover effect and fulfills the weak condition. The four estimation methods share the same regression results basically, indicating the appropriateness of model specification and the robustness of the regression results. The estimated coefficient $\ln k_{it}$, namely, α estimate, in the four regression methods are 0.503, 0.475, 0.510

and 0.464, respectively, all of which are around 0.5 and are consistent with the estimates of Young, Bai Chong'en and Qian Zhenjie[54] on the capital share of China's industrial sectors. The coefficient $\ln k_{it}$ is estimated to be 0.458, 0.451, 0.430 and 0.355 in the four regression methods, all of which are around 0.4. The statistically inferred value σ is 0.922, 0.860, 0.877 and 0.633 in the four regression methods, all of which are ranged from 0.5 to 1 in line with the weak condition which supports the rise of China's return on capital. The value of the estimate of the least squares method is 0.922 max, higher than the estimate of the parameter of the world's average spillover of Li *et al.*[55] However, macrovariate regression is prone to suffer non-stationary and endogenous problems, and the estimate obtained by the least squares method is likely to be biased, as indicated by Li *et al.* In contrast, the systematic GMM method can overcome the endogenous problems of macro variables and weak instrumental variables by introducing endogenous variables' horizontal and differential lag terms as instrumental variables, so the results of the estimation are more reliable.[56] In Table 3.1, the systematic GMM regression passes the Arellano–Bond test and the Hansen over-identification test, indicating the appropriateness of model specification. The inferred value σ is 0.663, close to the estimate of the world average of Li *et al.* (within the range of 0.552 and 0.778 estimated).[57] Therefore, a reasonable estimate of the parameter (σ) of China's technology spillover for the transfer of agricultural labor and China's economic development should be 0.663.

---

[54]Young, A.: Gold into Base Metals: Productivity Growth in the People's Republic of China during the Reform Period, *Journal of Political Economy*, 2003 (111), pp. 1220–1261; Bai Chong'en and Qian Zhenjie: The Factor Income Distribution in China: The Story behind the Statistics, *Economic Research Journal*, 2009 (3), pp. 27–41.

[55]Li, J., K. Shen and R. Zhang: Measuring Knowledge Spillovers: A Non-Appropriable Returns Perspective, *Annals of Economics and Finance*, 2011 (12) (2), pp. 265–293. Blundell, R. W. and S. R. Bond: Initial Conditions and Moment Restrictions in Dynamanel Data Models, *Journal of Econometrics*, 1998 (87), pp. 115–143.

[56]Blundell, R. and S. R. Bond: GMM Estimation with Persistent Panel Data: An Application to Product Functions, *Econometric Reviews*, 2000 (19) (3), pp. 321–340.

[57]Li, J., K. Shen and R. Zhang: Measuring Knowledge Spillovers: A Non-Appropriable Returns Perspective, *Annals of Economics and Finance*, 2011 (12) (2), pp. 265–293.

Table 3.1.   Estimates of the Parameters of China's Technology Spillover.[58]

Explained variable	Least squares method (1)	Least squares method (2)	Fixed effects (3)	Systematic GMM (4)
	0.503***	0.475***	0.510***	0.464***
	(0.023)	(0.023)	(0.085)	(0.091)
	0.458***	0.451***	0.430***	0.355***
	(0.020)	(0.028)	(0.054)	(0.096)
σ inferred value	0.922***	0.860***	0.877***	0.663***
	(0.017)	(0.043)	(0.051)	(0.099)
Individual effect	No	No	Yes	Yes
Vintage effect	No	Yes	Yes	Yes
R^2	0.938	0.943	0.985	0.271
				0.183
				1.000
Observed value	974	974	974	974

Note: The statistical inference for σ is based on the Wald test, and the null hypothesis is H0: $\sigma = 0$. The content in parentheses shows robust standard errors. *** represents significance at the 1% significance level. In the systematic GMM estimation, the p values of the A-Bond first order, the second-order test and the Hansen test are shown in the column of R^2.

It can be concluded that China's economic growth meets the weak condition of $\sigma > 1/2$ for the rise in return on capital with the accumulation of capital, which explains why the return on capital keeps rising in the case of high investment in China. However, China does not meet the strong condition of $\sigma > 1$ for the rise in return on capital. So, the rise in return on capital cannot be separated from the combination of the transfer of agricultural labor. At present, China is able to guarantee a rise in return on capital, which is attributable to the existence of the effect of technology

---

[58]Considering the economic particularities of Tibet, some literature excludes the panel data of provinces and regions for regression analysis. Similarly, this section makes a robustness test with the exclusion of the Tibet sample. Considering the great economic particularities of Beijing and Shanghai, this section also makes a robustness test with the exclusion of Tibet, Beijing and Shanghai at the same time. The estimated results of both kinds of exclusions show that the exclusion of specific provincial samples has no significant impact on the estimated results of Table 3.1 (due to limited space, no specific results are indicated here).

spillover on the one hand, and the reduction in the threshold condition for guaranteeing the increase in return on capital due to the transfer of labor on the other hand. Therefore, the combined effect of the transfer of labor and the technology spillover factor is a key condition for explaining the coexistence of a high investment rate and a rising return on capital in a specific period of time in China.

V. Recent Performance of China's Return on Capital

Since the global financial crisis in 2008, China's capital return volatility has expanded and even presented a downward trend in the short term (see Figure 1.3). According to the result of the calculation of Zhang Xun and Xu Jianguo, the overall return on capital has continued to rise since 1998 and fell in 2009. However, the return on industrial capital has still increased, and in 2012, the return on industrial fixed assets reached up to 27.8%.[59] How can the recent performance of China's return on capital be understood? How should we consider the role of the theoretical mechanism proposed by this book in this process?

The book argues that the recent performance of China's return on capital mostly reflects the cyclical factors, as well as the subsequent effects of over-stimulated investment policies. Subject to the global financial crisis at the end of 2008, the profitability of Chinese enterprises, especially exporting enterprises, was affected to some extent in the short term, and the rate of return on capital was confronted with the pressure of decline. The in-depth cause was that, to cope with the global financial crisis, China launched a package of a plan for investment stimulus from the end of 2008 to the end of 2010, namely, the "Four Trillion Plan". It is the main reason for the overall downward trend of China's return on capital in recent years. On the one hand, large-scale plans for stimulus investments reduce the efficiency of investments, and many investments flow into the industries with excess capacity without the formation of productive capital, thus directly leading to a decline in the rate of return on capital. On the other

---

[59] Zhang Xun and Xu Jianguo: Re-measurement of China's Return on Capital, *The Journal of World Economics*, 2014 (8), pp. 5–25.

hand, stimulus investment also lowers the effect of the technology spill-over and further reduces the return on capital, so that it is hard to expect the "learning by doing" effect or embedded technology progress in large stimulus investments. As a matter of fact, the recent decline in China's return on capital reflects the general law of investment and return on capital, which does not prove the failure of the mechanism of the model in this book, but instead, it reversely verifies the effectiveness of the mechanism in this book. The recent performance of China's return on capital also fully demonstrates that the plan for investment stimulus is only a short-term measure. In the medium and long term, the measures that rely on the investment plan to forcibly stimulate economic growth will not only fail to work but will also result in a decline in the return on capital subsequently and will affect the incentive to invest.

Though the recent decline in China's return on capital reflects the short-term factors to a large extent, it does not necessarily indicate the involvement of China's economy in the process of declining return on capital. However, in the long run, China's economy will be doomed to reach this stage. The rising rate of return on capital and the sustained rapid economic growth in China in the past two decades are partially attribut-able to the effect of the technology spillover in the investment and produc-tion process, and partially attributable to the supporting role of the transfer of agricultural labor. In the future, the transfer of agricultural labor will end eventually and the effect of the technology spillover will gradually lose its late development advantages as China gets closer to the techno-logical frontier. At that time, the rate of return on capital in China will gradually decline, and the same is true for the investment rate and eco-nomic growth. In this regard, the example of Japan may offer a possible prospect for China. The pre-tax profit margin of the manufacturing industry in Japan from 1955 to 2009, as shown in Figure 3.3, can reflect the long-term trend of Japan's return on capital, indicating that Japan also experienced a period of rising return on capital of about 20 years from the 1950s to the 1970s, very similar to the situation of rising return on capital in China (but Japan had a more volatile return on capital). This is the period during which Japan accelerated the transfer of surplus agricultural labor. From 1955 to 1975, the proportion of agricultural labor decreased

Figure 3.3. Japan's manufacturing pre-tax profit margin (1955–2009).

Note: The pre-tax profit margin of Japan's manufacturing industry is calculated from current profits/ equity. Current profits, Equity come from the Ministry of Finance-Financial Statements Statistics of Corporations by Industries, Quarterly; the original data are quarterly data, and the annual profit margin is calculated from the sum of current profits of four quarters of each year/equity in the fourth quarter.

from 40.2% to 13.9% in Japan, with an average annual decline of 1.3 percentage points, very similar to China's current situation. In the 1980s, Japan saw that the proportion of agricultural labor gradually stabilized, the transfer of agricultural labor nearly ceased, and the rate of return on capital began to decline continuously, returning to the neoclassical economic growth framework of diminishing marginal returns. Given Japan's similarities with China's economy in all respects, the long-term trend in Japan's return on capital gives a very possible prospect for China's economy. Undoubtedly, China should make every effort to delay the arrival of this stage through a series of measures, for instance, Du Yang *et al.* called for the reform of the household registration system to reap dividends, so as to further promote the transfer of agricultural labor, and avoid the situation in which China "ages before getting rich" or it falls into the "middle-income trap".[60]

---

[60]Du Yang, Cai Fang, Qu Xiaobo and Cheng Jie: Sustain the China Miracle: Reaping the Dividends from Hukou Reforms, *Economic Research Journal*, 2014 (8), pp. 4–13+78.

VI. Conclusions

In recent years, the rate of return on capital shows a rising trend while China maintains a high investment rate. This phenomenon is inconsistent with the law of diminishing marginal return on capital, and it is difficult to explain it well under the existing theoretical framework. This chapter reexamines the structural transformation of China's economy from the perspective of endogenous factors, and establishes an expanded dual economic model on the basis of highlighting the effects of the transfer of agricultural labor and technology spillover, so as to explain the coexistence of a high investment rate and a rising rate of return on capital in China in recent years. The study shows that the combination of the transfer of labor and technology spillover is a key condition to explain the above special phenomenon.

The extended model in this chapter not only relaxes the effect of the technology spillover united with the elasticity assumption of the model of knowledge spillover in the analysis of the condition for the rising capital return but also distinguishes the "strong condition" ($\sigma \geq 1$) and "weak condition" ($\sigma \geq 1/2$) required for an economy in different stages of development to keep the return on capital constant or rising. By promoting investment and production, the transfer of labor has a dynamic promoting effect on the level of technology, which reduces the requirement of maintaining the rising return on capital from strong condition to weak condition. According to the empirical analysis of the panel data of different provinces and regions in China from 1978 to 2010, China's economic growth does have a technology spillover effect that meets the weak condition, and combines with the continuous transfer of large-scale agricultural labor to support the improvement of the return on capital.

The results of the study in this chapter can provide a reference for understanding the characteristics of China's economic developmental stage and its future trend of evolution. In recent years, China's rate of return on capital has kept rising and its economy has grown at a fast rate, which is partially attributable to the spillover effect of technology in the process of investment and production, and partially attributable to the supporting role of the transfer of agricultural labor. Now, the proportion of agricultural labor in China is still above 30%. Compared with the steady-state level usually below 10% in developed countries, nearly a quarter of the agricultural labor will continue to gradually transfer to the non-agricultural sector in the next 20 years or so. However, the report on the monitoring survey on migrant workers in recent years shows that the transfer of agricultural labor in China has slowed down. According to the study in this chapter, China's technology spillover effect only meets the weak condition, which is insufficient to support the rise or mainte-nance of the return on capital. As the boom of the transfer of labor fades, it is recommended that China should create new growth mechanisms to ensure that the overall rate of return on capital is kept at a high level. A great deal of room is available for policy adjustment. At present, we should actively implement the policies conducive to the transfer of agri-cultural labor, bring into full play the combined effect of the transfer of labor and technology spillover in the improvement of the rate of return on capital and maintain rapid economic growth. Meanwhile, we should formulate and implement the policies favorable to technological innova-tion, and improve the level of the effect of technology spillover, thereby making preparations for fulfillment of the strong condition of capital return rate in the future.

Chapter 4

Riddle of the Transfer of Agricultural Labor and the Rise of the Rate of Household Saving in China

I. Introduction

China's national rate of saving has been on the rise steadily since the reform and opening-up. In recent years, the rate of saving has grown faster, from 37.6% in 2000 to 52.6% in 2010, and then to 49.5% in 2014 (see Figure 1.4). On the one hand, the internal structure between low consumption and high savings is prone to imbalance; on the other hand, the savings–investment gap is also expanding, causing external imbalances.[1] Greenspan considered that the high rate of saving in developing countries resulted in a long-term low interest rate, which was the root cause of the housing bubble and the global financial crisis over the past 20 years.[2] Therefore, it is of paramount importance to explain the reasons for

---

[1]Fan Gang and Lv Yan: Economic Developing Stage and National Saving Expansion: Extend by the Lewis'Dual Economy Model, *Economic Research Journal*, 2013 (3).
[2]Greenspan, A.: The Fed Didn't Cause the Housing Bubble, *The Wall Street Journal*, 2009 (11), A15, pp. 1–4.

China's high national rate of saving and thus make clear how to alleviate structural imbalances.

To understand the root cause of the rise in the national savings, it is necessary to decompose the structure of national savings first. According to departments, national savings can be divided into resident savings, enterprise savings and government savings. Figure 4.1 shows the proportion of those three types of savings in the national savings since 2000. In 2009, the three types of savings accounted for 48.3%, 41.9% and 9.8% of national savings, respectively, clearly showing the dominant position of residents and enterprises in the national savings. In recent years, the rate of saving of residents (household rate of saving) and the rate of saving of enterprises have both showed an upward trend to jointly raise the overall national rate of saving. Therefore, the discussion of resident savings and enterprise savings is conducive to understanding the national rate of saving. Fan Gang and Lu Yan explain why the rate of enterprise savings has been rising in recent years.[3] It is believed that China is still in the dual economy state before the Lewis turning point, and the existence of a surplus labor force puts the labor force in a weak position in the game of labor and capital, further leading to a slow increase in wages; with the reform of the system and the market opening, the production efficiency of enterprises has been greatly improved, but this part of value is more occupied by capital. With the expansion of the scale of capital, profits will accumulate at a higher rate and eventually form large-scale enterprise savings.

China's household savings rate also kept rising from 31.1% in 2000 to 40.4% in 2009 (Figure 4.2). In spite of a slight decrease in recent years, the proportion of resident savings is still large and will further increase under the guidance of the policy of "increasing the disposable income of residents", which will play a significant role in determining the trend of the national savings rate in the future. In addition, according to the international comparative study of Blanchard and Giavazzi, the rate of saving of Chinese enterprises and the government's rate of saving are not

---

[3]Fan Gang and Lu Yan: Economic Developing Stage and the Expansion of National Savings: Extend by the Lewis Dual Economy Model, *Economic Research Journal*, 2013 (3), pp. 19–29.

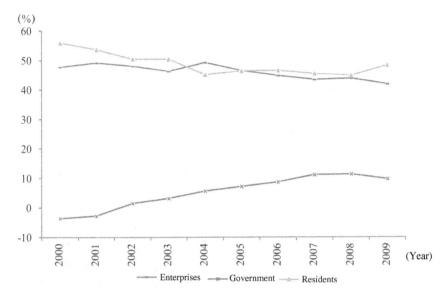

Figure 4.1. Proportion of three-sector savings in the national savings (2000–2009).

Source: 2001–2010 Fund Flow Statement in the *China Statistical Yearbook*.

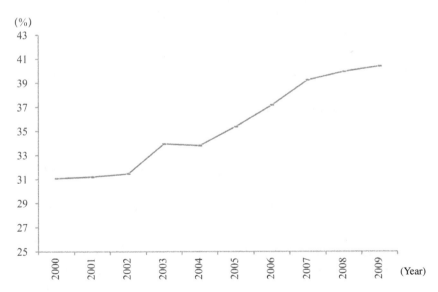

Figure 4.2. The rate of China's household saving (2000–2009).

Source: 2001–2010 Fund Flow Statement in the *China Statistical Yearbook*.

exceptional in transnational comparisons, and the high rate of saving in China is still closely associated with high rate of household saving.[4] Thus, this chapter focuses on studying the reasons for the rise in the rate of household saving in China in recent years, and further explores the trend of the national rate of saving.

In essence, the rate of household saving is an equilibrium decision made by households to maximize utility under a given budget constraint. However, the current discussions of household decision-making in China cannot be separated from the typical urban–rural dual structure. As a matter of fact, the constraints faced by urban and rural residents vary greatly, and the same is also true for the decision-making of consumption and savings. Specifically, urban enterprises tend to underwrite a certain level of social medical insurance[5] for urban households. Thus, urban residents have a significantly higher level of social medical security than rural residents,[6] which makes rural residents need more savings to address their pension, medical and other problems,[7] thus leading to the higher rate of saving of rural residents. Meanwhile, most rural residents in China are in the "subsistence" level and have little income to save, thus limiting their high rate of saving. Figure 4.3 shows the difference in the rate of saving between urban and rural households in China. Before 2004, the rural residents had a higher rate of saving than urban residents, while after 2004, the contrary was the case.

It should be noted that the urban and rural residents in Figure 4.3 are divided according to permanent residence. Under the current dual economic framework, the members of the agricultural labor force are constantly shifting to the non-agricultural sector with the capital deepening of the non-agricultural sector. Due to the restrictions of the household registration system, the process of transfer divides households into three types naturally, namely, urban residents, migrant workers working in

---

[4] Blanchard, O. and F. Giavazzi: Rebalancing Growth in China: A Three-Handed Approach, *China & World Economy*, 2006 (14) (4), pp. 1–20.

[5] *Ibid.*

[6] Kanbur, R. and X. Zhang: Fifty Years of Regional Inequality in China: A Journey through Central Planning, Reform, and Openness, *Review of Development Economics*, 2005 (9) (1), pp. 87–106.

[7] Kuijs, L.: How Will China's Saving-investment Balance Evolve? World Bank Policy Research Working Paper, No. 3958, 2006.

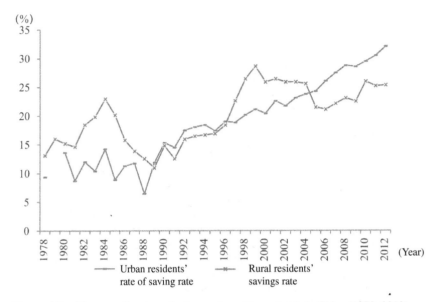

Figure 4.3.   The rate of saving of urban and rural households in China (1978–2012).

Note: The rate of saving of urban residents is calculated from their average disposable income minus their annual average consumption expenditure, and then divided by their average disposable income. The rate of saving of rural residents is calculated from their per capita net income minus their average annual consumption expenditure, and then divided by their per capita net income.

Source: *China Statistical Yearbook*.

cities and rural residents. Urban residents include a large number of migrant workers who are of rural registered permanent residence actually. Migrant workers have a much lower level of income and of social security than urban residents, significantly constraining household consumption–savings decision-making, and affecting the rate of saving.

To further investigate the composition of the rate of household saving and analyze the reasons for its rise, it is absolutely necessary to separate the rates of saving of the three groups. With different data sources, Table 4.1 summarizes the rates of saving of urban registered residents, migrant workers and rural registered residents employed in rural areas. As shown in the table, the year 2002 and 2007 (data available) witnessed the highest rate of saving of migrant workers. In 2002, urban registered residents had a lower rate of saving than rural registered residents employed in rural areas, while in 2007, the contrary was the case.

Table 4.1.   The Rates of Saving of Urban Registered Residents, Migrant Workers and Rural Registered Residents Employed in Rural Areas.

Group	2002 (%)	2007 (%)
Rural registered residents employed in rural areas	25.90	22.14
Migrant workers	25.98	33.29
Urban registered residents	22.60	31.76

Note: (1) For the sake of the calculation of the rate of saving of rural registered residents employed in rural areas, this chapter assumes that only a small number of urban residents move to rural areas for production and living, so the rate of saving of rural residents in Figure 4.3 can be directly applied. (2) The data regarding the rate of saving of migrant workers in 2002 and 2007 and that regarding the rate of saving of urban registered residents in 2007 were extracted from the CHIPS database. (3) The data regarding the rate of saving of urban residents in 2002 were directly extracted from the data regarding the rate of saving of urban residents in 2001 in Figure 4.3. Because the respondents to the urban household survey under the statistical caliber were national non-farm residents before 2001 and changed to national urban and township residents in 2002 and later, the migrant workers were excluded from the data regarding the rate of saving of 2001, and it was reliable to use the rate of saving of 2002 for approximation.

Under the current dual economic framework, the agricultural labor is continuously shifting to the non-agricultural sector to become migrant workers. According to Table 4.1, the migrant workers have the highest level of rates of saving among the three groups. Therefore, in the process of the transfer of labor, the growth of migrant workers has led to the rise of the rate of household saving and the overall national rate of saving. This chapter attempts to use the general equilibrium model to explore the difference in rates of saving among urban residents, migrant workers working in cities and rural residents, the relationship of the rates of saving among the three groups and the reasons for the changes in that relationship, and to further explain the continuous rise in the rate of China's household savings and that of national savings in recent years. This chapter holds that the difference in level of social security enjoyed by rural registered residents has a great deal of room for further improvement. Under the motivation of preventive savings, the rate of saving has been increased, but the savings are subject to the constraint of the minimum level of consumption. The income of migrant workers rises greatly,[8] leading to an increase in the savings rate of migrant workers. The consumption and savings behaviors of the three groups determine the trend of the rate of household saving in China, and the growth of migrant workers with a high rate of saving is an important reason for the increase in the rate of household saving in recent years.

Therefore, this chapter discusses the reasons for the rise in the rate of household saving and in that of national saving in China from the perspective of the transfer of agricultural labor under the dual economic framework. For this end, a general equilibrium model is established to analyze the households' consumption–savings decisions, and divide the total rate of saving into three groups, namely, the rate of saving of urban residents, that of migrant workers and that of farmers. The migrant workers have a higher marginal propensity to save (MPS) than farmers and urban residents due to the difference in the level of social security and of income. With the continuous transfer of agricultural labor to the non-agricultural sector, the group of migrant workers keeps expanding with the accumulation of capital in the non-agricultural sector, and their behavior regarding a high rate of saving also promote the rise of the rate of household saving and the national rate of saving.

This chapter is organized as follows: The second part shows a review of the literature, the third part explains the reasons for the rise in the rate of household saving and in the rate of national saving in China with a theoretical model, the fourth part gives a description of an analysis of the economic significance and the fifth part is a conclusion and gives some policy suggestions.

II. Review of the literature

Quite a lot of the literature has discussed household savings from the classical theory. Previous studies have explained China's high rate of saving from different perspectives.[9] However, a high rate of saving is not a

---

[8]Lu Feng: Wage Trends among Chinese Migrant Workers: 1979–2010, *Social Sciences in China*, 2012 (7), pp. 48–68+205.

[9]Specifically, the existing literature mainly studies China's savings rate from the perspective of equilibrium and disequilibrium. In terms of disequilibrium, China's high savings

necessary condition for the continuous rise in the rate of saving. The studies on the rise in the rate of household saving in China have proceeded in recent years. First, according to the life-cycle hypothesis, economic agents make consumption–savings decisions based on the income of their entire expected lifetime.[10] Thus, the increase in the proportion of the working group in the total population can lead to an increase in the rate of saving under the assumption of homogeneity of economic subjects[11]; however, the conclusion is far from being consistent with the actual situation in China.[12] However, if the actual invisible unemployment of Chinese farmers is taken into consideration, the proportion of the actual working group caused by the transfer of agricultural labor to the non-agricultural sector with higher productivity can better explain why the Chinese rate of saving continues to rise. Second, the low degree of financial development may cause economic entities to suffer strong credit constraints at the initial stage, thus leading to a higher rate of saving, which is the reverse support for the life-cycle hypothesis in essence.[13] However, the efficiency of China's financial system has kept improving and the rate of saving has

---

rate is explained by the shortage of a commodity market and a credit market and the rationing system (Feltenstein *et al.*, 1990; Ma, 1993; Wang and Chern, 1992; Fleisher *et al.*, 1994; Wang and Kinsey, 1994). In terms of equilibrium, the explanations mainly include three categories: (1) Keynesian savings function, indicating the savings rate is highly correlated with income (Wong, 1993; Qian, 1988; World Bank, 1988); (2) Permanent income hypothesis, indicating only unexpected income can bring about an increase in the rate of saving (Chow, 1985; Qian, 1988; Wong, 1993; Wang, 1995); (3) Life-cycle hypothesis, indicating an economic entity makes saving decisions based on its expected lifetime income (Jefferson, 1990; Pudney, 1993; Dessi, 1991), see Kraay (2000). In addition, Banerjee *et al.* (2010) supported the life-cycle hypothesis from the perspective of the family planning policy.

[10]Modigliani, F.: The Life Cycle Hypothesis of Saving and Intercountry Differences in the Saving Ratio, *Induction, Growth and Trade*, 1970, pp. 197–225.

[11]Modigliani, F. and S. L. Cao: The Chinese Saving Puzzle and the Life-cycle Hypothesis, *Journal of Economic Literature*, 2004 (42) (1), pp. 145–170; Horioka, C. Y. and J. Wan: The Determinants of Household Saving in China: A Dynamic Panel Analysis of Provincial Data, *Journal of Money, Credit and Banking*, 2007 (39) (8), pp. 2077–2096.

[12]Chamon, M. D. and E. S. Prasad: Why are the Rates of Saving of Urban Households in China Rising, *American Economic Journal: Macroeconomics*, 2010, pp. 93–130.

[13]Kuijs, L.: How Will China's Savings–Investment Balance Evolve? World Bank Policy Research Working Paper, No. 3958, 2006.

also risen in recent years, thus challenging the effectiveness of this explanation. Cultural difference is one of the reasons for the high rate of saving of the Eastern Asian countries, but due to the time invariance of culture, it is hard to explain the rise of the rate of saving in recent years, and it is necessary to combine it with a constant factor of change to achieve an ideal explanation.[14] Du and Wei, together with Wei and Zhang, propose the competitive savings theory and hold that China's gender imbalance makes Chinese families save wealth in order to gain a high degree of competition on the marriage market, which leads to a rising rate of saving.[15] In fact, this kind of pursuit of wealth and even social position is the "spirit of capitalism"[16] raised by Max Weber, with its existence widely recognized. However, the study of Chamon and Prasad shows that the rates of saving across all age groups are rising in China, which cannot simply be explained by the preparation for high competition on the marriage market. Therefore, there may be a more fundamental factor pushing up the rates of saving across all age groups in China.[17]

Another classic explanation for the rising rate of saving is income uncertainty and precautionary saving. Supporters believe that residents' income is subject to great uncertainty because of the shortcomings in China's social security system and medical system, and residents' excessive savings for self-insurance and future pensions have pushed up the rate of saving in China. In fact, this is a generalization of the life-cycle hypothesis.[18] However, according to some studies, the precautionary

---

[14]Wei, S. J. and X. Zhang: The Competitive Saving Motive: Evidence from Rising Sex Ratios and Savings Rates in China, *Journal of Political Economy*, 2011 (119) (3), pp. 511–564.

[15]Du, Q. and S. J. Wei: A Sexually Unbalanced Model of Current Account Imbalances, NBER Working Paper, No. 16000, 2010; Wei, S. J. and X. Zhang: The Competitive Saving Motive: Evidence from the Rising Sex Ratios and Savings Rates in China, *Journal of Political Economy*, 2011 (119) (3), pp. 511–564.

[16]Bakshi, G. S. and Z. Chen: The Spirit of Capitalism and Stock-Market Prices, *American Economic Review*, 1996, pp. 133–157.

[17]Chamon, M. D. and E. S. Prasad: Why are the Rates of Saving of Urban Households in China Rising, *American Economic Journal: Macroeconomics*, 2010, pp. 93–130.

[18]Blanchard, O. and F. Giavazzi: Rebalancing Growth in China: A Three-Handed Approach, *China & World Economy*, 2006 (14) (4), pp. 1–20. Chamon, M. D. and E. S. Prasad: Why are the Rates of Saving of Urban Households in China Rising, *American*

saving theory may explain why China has a high rate of saving, rather than why China's rate of saving keeps rising. With the improvement in China's social and health care systems and the decrease in the income uncertainty, the rate of saving should decline, which is obviously inconsistent with the reality.[19] This chapter argues that most precautionary savings studies overlook one important fact, that is, against the background of China's dual economic structure, the urban and rural social and medical security systems also have a duality: urban residents enjoy a much higher level of social and medical security than rural residents, leading to a tendency of a higher rate of saving on the part of rural residents than of urban residents.[20] However, the level of the rate of saving is also limited by the lowest level of consumption, which becomes more significant in the event of a lower level of income. Therefore, rural residents are not doomed to have a higher rate of saving than urban residents. The limitation of the minimum level of consumption forces rural residents to take the suboptimal saving decision and consume in advance, thus reducing their rate of saving. More and more people will no longer be limited by minimum consumption only with the general improvement of the level of income, so as to achieve the individual intertemporal optimization of the rate of consumption and the rising rate of saving as a whole.

The foregoing analysis of the mechanism takes into account the duality of the rate of household saving in China and the difference in the rate of saving between urban and rural residents. However, the analysis is not complete, and the rate of saving of urban and rural residents is not certain according to the above inference. In fact, a special group with a growing scale and proportion emerges in the process of China's economic

---

Economic Journal: Macroeconomics, 2010, pp. 93–130. Chamon, M., K. Liu and E. Prasad: Income Uncertainty and Household Savings in China, IMF Working Paper, 2010, pp. 1–34.

[19] Wei, S. J. and X. Zhang: The Competitive Saving Motive: Evidence from Rising Sex Ratios and Savings Rates in China, *Journal of Political Economy*, 2011 (119) (3), No. 511–564.

[20] Kanbur, R. and X. Zhang: Fifty Years of Regional Inequality in China: A Journey through Central Planning, Reform, and Openness, *Review of Development Economics*, 2005 (9) (1), pp. 87–106; Blanchard, O. and F. Giavazzi, Rebalancing Growth in China: A Three-Handed Approach, *China & World Economy*, 2006 (14) (4), pp. 120.

transformation, that is, migrant workers who are rural residents transferred to the urban non-agricultural sector for employment. Migrant workers have two important characteristics. First, migrant workers still have their registered permanent residence in the countryside, so that they are rural residents and can only enjoy a lower level of medical and social security, thus leading to a higher tendency of saving than urban residents. Second, the income of migrant workers in the urban sector is close to or even higher than that of some urban household residents, which is several times the income they can earn in the employment of agricultural sector. Therefore, they have gradually gotten rid of the restrictions of the minimum level of consumption. With these two characteristics, migrant workers have the highest rate of saving among the three groups. The statistics show that since the reform and opening-up, agricultural labor has been transferring to the urban sector with an annual average of 8 million. The total number of migrant workers reached up to 270 million in 2014, accounting for more than 50% of the people employed in the non-agricultural sector in China. The model described later analyzes in detail that, due to the limitation of the minimum level of consumption and the urban–rural gap in the level of social and medical security, the number of migrant workers is growing in the context of the transformation of China's dual economic structure and the continuous transfer of agricultural labor, which has been and will continue to push up China's overall rate of household saving.

In fact, according to the studies of Lewis and Jorgenson, the dual economic model either based on the classical hypothesis or on the neoclassical hypothesis reveals that the national rate of saving of a developing country will rise with the further development of the non-agricultural sector relative to the agricultural sector.[21] Previous studies have recognized the importance of the characteristics of a dual economic structure for China's economy, and regarded it as a breakthrough point to explain the soaring rate of saving in China in recent years. For example, Li Yang, Yin Jianfeng *et al.* believe that the continuous transfer of the surplus labor

---

[21] Lewis, W. A.: Economic Development with Unlimited Supplies of Labour, *Manchester School*, 1954 (22) (2), pp. 139–191; Jorgenson, D. W.: Surplus Agricultural Labour and the Development of a Dual Economy, *Oxford Economic Papers*, 1967 (19) (3), pp. 288–312.

force from agriculture to industry (industrialization), from rural villages to cities (urbanization), and from state-owned enterprises to non-state-owned enterprises (marketization) leads to the inevitable result of a high degree of savings of enterprises.[22] Fan Gang *et al.* point out that the reason for the substantial increase in enterprise savings is the improvement in enterprise productivity and the continuous transfer of surplus rural labor brought by the reform and opening-up.[23] Ba Shusong holds that the reasons for the increase in enterprise savings in China in the previous stage are that the increase in labor costs caused by demographic changes is not reflected in the real costs of enterprises, and enterprises fail to transfer the super-high profits generated by cost distortion into the expenses of workers such as pensions, medical care and insurance, resulting in a significant increase in enterprise savings.[24] Fan Gang and Lu Yan also explore the reasons for the rise in China's rate of saving under the dual economic structure.[25] However, in spite of the consideration of the transformation of China's dual economic structure, the foregoing studies on China's rate of saving proceed from the perspective of enterprise profits and capital accumulation, rather than from household savings. Therefore, this chapter will merge with the minimum consumption theory, the life-cycle theory and the precautionary saving theory based on the framework of analysis of the theory of the development of the dual economy to study the consumption–savings decisions of the three different groups under various constraint conditions, and further to establish a dynamic economic model that reflects the characteristics of the dual economy transition of a developing country to explain why China maintains a rising rate of household saving and even a rising national rate of saving under rapid economic growth.

---

[22]Li Yang, Yin Jianfeng: Anatomy of China's High Rate of Saving, *Economic Research Journal*, 2007 (6), pp. 15–27.

[23]Fan Gang, Wei Qiang and Liu Peng: Internal and External Imbalance and the Reform of China's Fiscal and Tax Policy, *Economic Research Journal*, 2009 (8), pp. 19–27.

[24]Ba Shusong: External Rebalancing: Rate of Saving and Capital Flow, *New Finance*, 2011 (1), pp. 6–12.

[25]Fan Gang and Lu Yan: Economic Developing Stage and National Saving Expansion: Extension by the Lewis Dual Economy Model, *Economic Research Journal*, 2013 (3), pp. 19–29.

III. Theoretical Model

In this chapter, the subjects under the dual economic structure are divided into three categories, namely, u, people who have urban household registration and work in cities; a, people who have rural household registration and work in rural areas; m, people who have rural household registration and work in cities. Suppose that in the t stage, the population with urban household registration is $N_{ut} = L_{ut}$; the number of people with rural household registration is N_{at}, of whom, the number of migrant workers working in cities is L_{mt}, and the number of people staying in rural areas to engage in agricultural production is $L_{at} = N_{at} - L_{mt}$. In this chapter, the number of urban registered population and rural registered population is temporarily given, thus the total population is also given.

1. Production

Agricultural sector production function:

$$Y_{at} = L_{at}^{\gamma} = (N_{at} - L_{mt})^{\gamma},\tag{1}$$

where $0 < \gamma \le 1$.

Non-agricultural sector production function:

$$Y_{ut} = K_t^{\alpha}(A_{ut}L_{ut} + A_{mt}L_{mt})^{1-\alpha},\tag{2}$$

where A_{ut} and A_{mt} represent the difference in efficiency between urban workers and migrant workers. Such an efficiency difference is caused either by a difference in human capital or by specialization (migrant workers were originally employed in agriculture).

The three groups share the same preference, but face different budget constraints. For one reason, they enjoy different levels of social insurance. Rural residents with household registration have a lower level of social insurance than urban residents. Thus, the following assumptions are made:

Hypothesis 1: Suppose that the proportion of the insurance purchasing amount of urban workers, migrant workers and farmers to their incomes is θ_u, θ_m and θ_a, respectively, which are in line with $\bar{\theta} = \theta_u > \theta_m = \theta_a = \underline{\theta}$.

Enterprises are obliged to purchase endowment insurance equal to $\varphi(\theta)$ of the income of workers' salaries, which means that workers will enjoy the endowment insurance benefits in the proportion $\theta + \varphi(\theta)$ in the second phase, where θ and $\varphi(\theta)$ are exogenous constants, and $\varphi(\theta)$ are continuously and monotonously increasing. That is, $\varphi'(\theta) > 0$, and suppose $\varphi(0) = 0$. It is known that

$$\varphi(\overline{\theta}) > \varphi(\underline{\theta}). \tag{3}$$

The profit maximization decision of the agricultural sector complies with the following requirements:

$$\max L_{at}^{\gamma} - (1 + \varphi(\underline{\theta}))W_{at}L_{at}.$$

F.O.C.

$$W_{at} = \frac{\gamma L_{at}^{\gamma-1}}{1 + \varphi(\underline{\theta})} = \frac{\gamma(N_{at} - L_{mt})^{\gamma-1}}{1 + \varphi(\underline{\theta})}. \tag{4}$$

Now, it should be noted that the non-agricultural sector has surplus profits. For simplicity, let us just assume that profits dissipate and do not accumulate.

With the given interest rate r_t, urban worker wage W_{ut} and migrant worker wage W_{mt}, a non-agricultural sector enterprise uses the optimal amount of capital K_t, the number of urban workers L_{ut} and the number of migrant workers L_{mt} to maximize the following profit function πt:

$$\max \pi t = K_t^{\alpha}(A_{ut}L_{ut} + A_{mt}L_{mt})^{1-\alpha} - (1 + \varphi(\overline{\theta}))W_{ut}L_{ut}$$
$$- (1 + \varphi(\underline{\theta}))W_{mt}L_{mt} - r_t K_t.$$

To solve this maximization problem, we get

$$W_{ut} = (1-\alpha)K_t^{\alpha}(A_{ut}L_{ut} + A_{mt}L_{mt})^{-\alpha}A_{ut} / (1 + \varphi(\overline{\theta})). \tag{5}$$

$$W_{mt} = (1-\alpha)K_t^{\alpha}(A_{ut}L_{ut} + A_{mt}L_{mt})^{-\alpha}A_{mt} / (1 + \varphi(\underline{\theta})). \tag{6}$$

$$r_t = \alpha K_t^{\alpha-1}(A_{ut}L_{ut} + A_{mt}L_{mt})^{1-\alpha}. \tag{7}$$

Thus,

$$\frac{W_{ut}}{W_{mt}} = \frac{A_{ut}}{A_{mt}} \frac{(1+\varphi(\underline{\theta}))}{(1+\varphi(\overline{\theta}))}. \tag{8}$$

It is apparent that the wage ratio of the two types of workers depends on the difference in relative productivity and the level of social insurance that enterprises need to provide, and is directly proportional to the difference in relative productivity and inversely proportional to the level of relative social insurance.

2. *Preference*

The lifetime utility maximum V of a typical household meets the generational overlap model, namely,

$$\max V = \ln(C_t - \overline{C}) + \beta\ln(C_{t+1} - \overline{C}) - D,$$

$$\mathrm{st} : C_t = W_t - S_t - \theta W_t,$$

$$C_{t+1} = \left[S_t + (\theta + \varphi(\theta))W_t \right](1 + r_{t+1}),$$

where C_t and C_{t+1} are the ordinary consumption of the first phase and the second phase, respectively, $\overline{C}$ is the minimum level of consumption needed by households to maintain the survival of each phase[26]; D is the cost of the transfer of cross-sectoral labor. For urban residents and farmers, D is equal to 0; migrant workers face certain transfer costs.[27] In this

---

[26]Gollin, Douglas, Stephen L. Parente and Richard Rogerson: The Food Problem and the Evolution of International Income Levels, *Journal of Monetary Economics*, 2007 (54) (4), pp. 230–1255.

[27]In reality, the agricultural labor transfers between the two sectors with a cost and often encounters many flow barriers and transfer costs. The phenomenon of "semi-urbanization" (Jacoby, Erich H.: The Coming Backlash of Semi-Urbanization, Ceres (FAO Review), 1970 (3) (6), pp. 48–51) is common in Latin America and other regions, and also evident in the process of the transfer of China's agricultural labor. The term, "migrant worker", reflects the identity of most transferred workers, their lifestyles and industrialization input contradictions of labor factors. The semi-urbanization of China's rural floating population is not only reflected in the level of social life, action and identity but also more obviously reflected in the level of the system. The mutual strengthening of the three levels results in

chapter, for the convenience of analysis, the cost arising from hindering the transfer of agricultural labor is collectively referred to as the transfer cost, and the direct decline in the transfer of agricultural labor is the utility level of migrant workers, that is, $D > 0$. β is the subjective discount rate; W_t is the income of the family in the first phase. The combined budget constraint formula:

$$C_t + \frac{C_{t+1}}{1+r_{t+1}} = W_t(1+\varphi(\theta)). \tag{9}$$

To solve the maximization problem, the first-order condition meets

$$C_t = \frac{1+\varphi(\theta)}{1+\beta}W_t + \frac{\bar{C}}{1+\beta}\left(\beta - \frac{1}{1+r_{t+1}}\right). \tag{10}$$

Thus, it is possible to obtain the rate of household consumption as follows:

$$c_t = \frac{C_t}{W_t} = \frac{1+\varphi(\theta)}{1+\beta} + \frac{\bar{C}}{(1+\beta)W_t}\left(\beta - \frac{1}{1+r_{t+1}}\right). \tag{11}$$

In a broad sense, savings should include household savings and an insurance purchase, then the generalized rate of saving is as follows:

$$s_t = \frac{S_t + \theta W_t}{W_t} = \frac{\beta - \varphi(\theta)}{1+\beta} - \frac{\bar{C}}{(1+\beta)W_t}\left(\beta - \frac{1}{1+r_{t+1}}\right). \tag{12}$$

---

a sustained trend of change in the semi-urbanization of the rural floating population (Wang Chunguang: A Study of Floating Rural People's "Semi-Urbanization", *Sociological Studies*, 2006 (5), pp. 111–126+248). This means that the transfer of labor will encounter various obstacles in reality, including the obstacles to move out, move in and flow, and the impact of transfer costs. Gupta (Gupta, M. R.: Foreign Capital and the Informal Sector: Comments on Chandra and Khan, *Economica*, 1997 (64) (254), pp. 353–363) has long recognized the importance of transfer costs and constructed a model of the transfer of labor with the introduction of a transfer cost.

According to Eq. (12), Lemma 1 can be derived in this chapter:

Lemma 1: The generalized rate of household saving defined in Eq. (12) satisfies the following properties:

(1) The higher the social security level, the lower the rate of household saving, namely,

$$\frac{\partial s_t}{\partial \theta} = -\frac{\varphi'(\theta)}{1+\beta} < 0. \tag{13}$$

(2) Suppose $\beta(1 + r_{t+1}) > 1$, the higher the level of household income, the higher the rate of saving, namely,

$$\frac{\partial s_t}{\partial W_t} = \frac{\bar{C}}{(1+\beta)W_t^2}\left(\beta - \frac{1}{1+r_{t+1}}\right) > 0. \tag{14}$$

(3) Under the hypothesis of (2), it is further assumed that

$$\bar{C}\left(\beta - \frac{1}{1+r_{t+1}}\right)\left(\frac{1}{W_m} - \frac{1}{W_u}\right) < \varphi(\bar{\theta}) - \varphi(\underline{\theta}) < \bar{C}\left(\beta - \frac{1}{1+r_{t+1}}\right)\left(\frac{1}{W_a} - \frac{1}{W_u}\right). \tag{15}$$

It is known $s_{at} < s_{ut} < s_{mt}$, that is, the migrant workers have a higher rate of saving than urban residents, and the urban residents have a higher rate of saving than rural residents.

The conclusion derived from Lemma 1 (3) is consistent with the 2007 patterns of the rate of saving of the three groups. This chapter further discusses the rationality of the hypothesis in Lemma 1. With regard to the hypothesis in (2) that the level of income induced by the lowest level of consumption is positively correlated with the rate of saving, namely, $\beta(1 + r_{t+1}) > 1$, it has been discussed abundantly in literature. Dynan *et al.* have shown that in the event of a sufficiently high rate of return on investment, the restriction of the minimum level of consumption makes the level of income positively correlated with the rate of saving.[28] Now, China's capital output ratio remains to be improved, and China's return on capital

---

[28]Dynan, Karen E., Jonathan Skinner and Stephen P. Zeldes: Do the Rich Save More? *Journal of Political Economy*, 2004 (112) (2), pp. 397–444.

104   *China's Rural Labor Migration and Its Economic Development*

remains high. Considering the exogenous discount factor, the hypothesis is reasonable and does not affect the conclusions of the model.[29] This also explains the phenomenon that migrant workers have a higher rate of saving than rural residents. In the event of a low income level, the intertemporal optimal level of consumption will be lower than the minimum level of consumption. In this case, the limitation of the minimum level of consumption forces rural residents to take the suboptimal saving decision and consume in advance, thus reducing the rate of saving and capital accumulation. More and more people will no longer be limited by the minimum consumption only with the general improvement in the level of their income, so as to achieve an individual intertemporal optimization of the rate of consumption and a rising rate of saving as a whole. The intuitive meaning of the hypothesis in (3) is that the difference in social security between urban and rural areas is still large enough to fall within the range of Eq. (15). To sum up, although migrant workers receive a slight increase in the level of their income after transfer into cities, they have a higher rate of saving than urban residents due to their low level of social security. In spite of a high level of social security for urban residents, the farmers remain at subsistence level, resulting in a lower rate of saving of farmers than that of urban residents, which is in agreement with the overall rate of saving of the three groups in this chapter in 2007.

The model in this chapter can also be used to explain the pattern of the rate of saving of 2002. As can be seen from Table 4.1, the migrant workers have a higher rate of saving than rural residents, and yet a higher on than urban residents in 2002. The rate of saving of farmers in 2007 was also lower than that in 2002. In fact, since 2004, the level of social security of China's rural residents has been significantly improved, leading to a change in the pattern of savings in 2007, that is, the rate of saving of urban and rural residents was reversed, meaning that the urban residents had a

[29]Lee, Houng, Syed Murtaza and Xueyan Liu: Is China Over-Investing and Does It Matter? IMF Working Paper, 12/277, 2012; Bai, C., C. Hsieh and Y. Qian: The Return to Capital in China, Brookings Papers on Economic Activity, 2006 (2), pp. 61–88; Research Group of CCER China Economic Observer: Measurements of China's Capital Return (1978–2006) — Microeconomic Underpinnings for the Recent Economic Boom in China, *China Economic Quarterly*, 2007 (6) (3), pp. 723–758; Xu Jianguo and Zhang Xun: China's Sovereign Debt: Situation, Investment and Risk Analysis, *South China Journal of Economics*, 2013 (1), pp. 14–34.

higher rate of saving. In Eq. (15), the urban–rural social security gap was larger than the upper limit defined in Eq. (14) in 2002, namely,

$$\varphi(\bar{\theta}) - \varphi(\underline{\theta}) > \bar{C}\left(\beta - \frac{1}{1+r_{t+1}}\right)\left(\frac{1}{W_a} - \frac{1}{W_u}\right) > \bar{C}\left(\beta - \frac{1}{1+r_{t+1}}\right)\left(\frac{1}{W_m} - \frac{1}{W_u}\right).$$

(16)

Now, the rate of saving is $s_{ut} < s_{at} < s_{mt}$, that is, the pattern of the rate of saving described in the data in 2002. As stated later in this chapter, the transfer of agricultural labor can constantly push up the rate of saving no matter whether Eq. (15) or Eq. (16) is established, namely, both in 2002 and 2007.

3. Equilibrium

Next, let us discuss the model equilibrium. Rural residents may choose whether to move to the city. In fact, with the capital accumulation of the non-agricultural sector, the labor demand increases and the population with rural household registration earns more money after transfer to cities, but that transfer of labor causes the migrant workers to have to bear transfer costs. Therefore, the transfer of labor will reach an equilibrium, under which the population with rural household registration has no difference before and after transfer:

$$\ln(C_{mt} - \bar{C}) + \beta \ln(C_{m,t+1} - \bar{C}) - D = \ln(C_a - \bar{C}) + \beta \ln(C_{a,t+1} - \bar{C}),$$

namely,

$$\ln\left[\frac{1+\varphi(\underline{\theta})}{1+\beta}W_{mt} - \frac{\bar{C}}{1+\beta}\left(1+\frac{1}{1+r_{t+1}}\right)\right]$$

$$+ \beta \ln\left[\frac{1+\varphi(\underline{\theta})}{1+\beta}\beta(1+r_{t+1})W_{mt} - \frac{\bar{C}}{1+\beta}(\beta r_{t+1} - 2)\right] - D$$

$$= \ln\left[\frac{1+\varphi(\underline{\theta})}{1+\beta}W_{at} - \frac{\bar{C}}{1+\beta}\left(1+\frac{1}{1+r_{t+1}}\right)\right]$$

$$+ \beta \ln\left[\frac{1+\varphi(\underline{\theta})}{1+\beta}\beta(1+r_{t+1})W_{at} - \frac{\bar{C}}{1+\beta}(\beta r_{t+1} - 2)\right].$$

Suppose

$$W_{mt} = \tau W_{at}. \tag{17}$$

It is known that τ relies heavily on the transfer cost D and it is easy to prove $\frac{\partial \tau}{\partial D} > 0$ and $\tau > 1$. Thus, the larger the transfer cost, the greater the wage gap between migrant workers and farmers. In this regard, the general equilibrium definition of the economy can be obtained.

Definition 1: The general equilibrium condition of an economy consists of the first-order condition of maximizing profits in two sectors, the equilibrium of the transfer of labor and the consumption–savings decisions of the three main groups.

Given the registered population of urban and rural areas, the level of wages of the three types of people can be solved, and the number of those involved in the transfer of labor is the number of migrant workers. The number of migrant workers meets the following formula:

$$\frac{(1-\alpha)K_t^{\alpha} \left(A_{ut}L_{ut} + A_{mt}L_{mt}\right)^{-\alpha} A_{mt}}{\gamma(N_{at} - L_{mt})^{\gamma-1}} = \tau. \tag{18}$$

With the implicit function $L_{mt} = L_{mt}(K_t)$ obtained, it is less difficult to know $L'_{mt}(K_t) > 0$. Besides, the wages of the three types of people can be written as a function of the capital stock, and comply with $W'_{at}(K_t) > 0$, $W'_{mt}(K_t) > 0$, $W'_{ut}(K_t) > 0$. Thus, Lemma 2 is deduced:

Lemma 2: With the continuous accumulation of capital in the non-agricultural sector, there are transfers of labor from the agricultural sector to the non-agricultural sector, during which the rise in wages takes place for farmers, migrant workers and urban workers.

It should be pointed out that, in the absence of a transfer of labor, capital accumulation in the non-agricultural sector just increases the wages of urban workers, without any impact on the income of farmers.[30] In this sense, free migration makes income more equal.

---

[30]It is true when the changes in the relative price of industrial products and agricultural products are not considered, or when the price of the two kinds of commodities is determined by the world price; otherwise, agricultural income will go upward with an increase in the price of agricultural products.

In addition, an economy does not encounter a transfer of labor from the beginning. According to Eq. (18), assume $L_{mt} = 0$, it can solve $K_{0t} = K_t = A_{ut}L_{ut}\left[\frac{\tau\gamma N_{at}^{\gamma-1}}{(1-\alpha)A_{mt}}\right]^{1/\alpha}$. This is the initial capital stock necessary for labor to start transferring, which depends on the relative proportion of urban and rural registered population in the early stage of the economy. In addition, the higher the transfer costs, the higher the initial capital demand for transfer of labor. Therefore, in an economic sense

$$L_{mt}(K_t)\begin{cases} = 0, \text{ if } K_t \leqslant A_{ut}L_{ut}\left[\dfrac{\tau\gamma N_{at}^{\gamma-1}}{(1-\alpha)A_{mt}}\right]^{\frac{1}{\alpha}} \\[3em] > 0 \text{ and meets Eq. (15), } K_t > A_{ut}L_{ut}\left[\dfrac{\tau\gamma N_{at}^{\gamma-1}}{(1-\alpha)A_{mt}}\right]^{\frac{1}{\alpha}} \end{cases} \quad (19)$$

(1) *Capital accumulation and economic growth*

Next, let us discuss the capital accumulation and economic growth in the process of a transfer of labor. The capital accumulation equation is as follows:

$$K_{t+1} = S_t = \frac{\beta - \varphi(\bar{\theta})}{1+\beta}W_{ut}(K_t)L_{ut} + \frac{\beta - \varphi(\theta)}{1+\beta}W_{mt}(K_t)L_{mt}(K_t)$$
$$+ \frac{\beta - \varphi(\theta)}{1+\beta}W_{at}(K_t)L_{at}(K_t), \quad (20)$$

where $L_{mt}(K_t), W_{ut}(K_t), W_{mt}(K_t), W_{at}(K_t)$ meet Eqs. (4), (8), (17) and (18). Under $K_{t+1} = F(K_t)$ in Eq. (20), Lemma 3 can be obtained:

Lemma 3: Assume $\beta > \varphi(\theta)$, the function $F(K)$ satisfies

(1) $\lim\limits_{K \to 0} F(K) \geqslant 0$;

(2) $\forall K \in (0, K_0) \cup (K_0, \infty)$, thus, $F'(K) \geqslant 0$, where K_0 is the initial capital stock required for the transfer, i.e. $F(K)$ monotone increasing.

(3) $\lim\limits_{K \to 0} F'(K) = \infty$, $\lim\limits_{K \to \infty} F'(K) = 0$.

With Lemma 2, the following Theorem 1 can be deduced.

Theorem 1: Under the equilibrium by Definition 1, an economy must have at least one stable equilibrium.

The proofs of Lemma 3 and Theorem 1 are provided in the appendix attached to this chapter. Intuitively, the stable equilibrium obtained from Theorem 1 is a long-term process, while Lemma 3 shows that the capital of the economy keeps accumulating before the stable equilibrium is reached, so as to realize economic growth. In addition, the free transfer of the labor force can enable the economy to reach a higher balance between capital and output, as described in Theorem 2:

Theorem 2: The transfer of labor helps raise the steady-state capital stock and economic developmental level.

The proof of Theorem 2 is also provided in the appendix attached to this chapter.

(2) *Rate of saving*

Next, the rate of saving under the dual economic framework is discussed. According to the foregoing model of generational overlap, the demographic structure of a country in the period t is made up of the three categories of young people born in the period t and the three categories of old people born in the period $t - 1$. Therefore, the total national rate of saving depends on the respective rates of saving of these six categories of people and their proportion in the population structure. It should be pointed out that the three categories of old people born in the period $t - 1$ consume all the capital income in the period t, leading to a rate of saving of 0.

Theorem 3: The total national rate of saving of a country depends on the total rate of saving of the young people, the rate of saving (0) of the old people and the aging structure of the population; the rate of saving of the young people depends on the rates of saving of the three categories of young people, as well as the structure of the labor force.

Due to the differences in the level of social security and in income, and the existence of the transfer costs, with the constant transfer of agricultural labor to the non-agricultural sector, namely, with the increasing number of migrant workers L_{mt}, both the total rate of saving of young people and the overall rate of saving will keep rising as long as the differences in the levels of social security meet Eq. (15) or (16).

It is proved that

(1) In this chapter, the total rate of saving s_{1t} of savers (that is, young people or workers) is taken into account first, then

$$s_{1t} = \frac{s_{ut}W_{ut}L_{ut} + s_{mt}W_{mt}L_{mt} + s_{at}W_{at}L_{at}}{W_{ut}L_{ut} + W_{mt}L_{mt} + W_{at}L_{at}}.$$

By substituting the relationship of the income from wages of the three groups, the income from wages can be eliminated and the following equation can be obtained:

$$s_{1t} = s_{mt}\frac{\frac{s_{ut}}{s_{mt}}\frac{A_{ut}}{A_{mt}}\frac{1+\varphi(\theta)}{1+\varphi(\bar{\theta})}L_{ut} + \frac{1}{\tau}\frac{s_{at}}{s_{mt}}N_{at} + \left(1 - \frac{1}{\tau}\frac{s_{at}}{s_{mt}}\right)L_{mt}}{\frac{A_{ut}}{A_{mt}}\frac{1+\varphi(\theta)}{1+\varphi(\bar{\theta})}L_{ut} + \frac{N_{at}}{\tau} + \left(1 - \frac{1}{\tau}\right)L_{mt}}. \tag{21}$$

Thus,

$$\frac{ds_{1t}}{dL_{mt}} = s_{mt}\frac{\left(1 - \frac{s_{ut}}{s_{mt}} + \frac{1}{\tau}\frac{s_{ut}}{s_{mt}} - \frac{1}{\tau}\frac{s_{at}}{s_{mt}}\right)\frac{A_{ut}}{A_{mt}}\frac{1+\varphi(\theta)}{1+\varphi(\bar{\theta})}L_{ut} + \frac{1}{\tau}(1 - s_{at})N_{at}}{\left[\frac{A_{ut}}{A_{mt}}\frac{1+\varphi(\theta)}{1+\varphi(\bar{\theta})}L_{ut} + \frac{N_{at}}{\tau} + \left(1 - \frac{1}{\tau}\right)L_{mt}\right]^2}. \tag{22}$$

In Eq. (15) or (16), $s_{mt} > s_{ut}$ and $s_{mt} > s_{at}$, and $\tau > 1$, it is known $\frac{ds_{1t}}{dL_{mt}} > 0$. Therefore, with the increasing number L_{mt} of migrant workers, i.e. with the advancing of the process of the transfer of labor, China's total rate of saving of laborers s_{1t} will keep increasing. It should be noted that, as long as a certain gap exists between the levels of urban and rural social security, the model in this chapter is able to simultaneously explain the rising pattern of the rate of saving in the two periods before and after the improvement of the level of social security in 2004, which is also the current reality of the difference between the levels of urban and rural social security in China.

The model also reveals that capital accumulation and wage increase can bring about an increase in the laborer's rate of saving, which is mainly because of the restrictions imposed by the minimum level of consumption on savings. In fact, in the early stage of a country's economic development, the rate of saving will increase due to the rise in the level of income. However, in view of the reality in China, the model suggests that the most important key reason for the rise in the laborer's rate of saving is the change in the structure of labor workers: in the absence of a transfer of labor, the average social rate of saving falls between that of farmers and that of urban residents. Due to the cost of transfer and the deepening of capital accumulation, a certain monetary compensation should be given to the farmers once the transfer of labor starts, so as to motivate them to engage in production in the non-agricultural sector as migrant workers, thus enabling the transfer of labor to proceed. The lack of social security causes the sustained high rate of saving of migrant workers, and the improvement of the level of income makes the rate of saving rise further, so that the laborers of the whole society have a faster growth rate in their total savings than the total labor remuneration, thus raising the average rate of saving of the group of laborers in the entire society.

(2) Next, a country's total national rate of saving s_{2t} is considered:

$$s_{2t} = \frac{s_{ut}W_{ut}L_{ut} + s_{mt}W_{mt}L_{mt} + s_{at}W_{at}L_{at}}{Y_{bt} + Y_{at}}.$$

It is simplified to get the following:

$$s_{2t} = \frac{\gamma s_{mt}}{1+\varphi(\theta)} \frac{\frac{s_{ut}}{s_{mt}}\frac{A_{ut}}{A_{mt}}\frac{1+\varphi(\theta)}{1+\varphi(\bar{\theta})}L_{ut} + \frac{1}{\tau}\frac{s_{at}}{s_{mt}}N_{at} + \left(1 - \frac{1}{\tau}\frac{s_{at}}{s_{mt}}\right)L_{mt}}{\frac{\gamma}{1-\alpha}\frac{A_{ut}}{A_{mt}}L_{ut} + \frac{N_{at}}{\tau} + \left(\frac{\gamma}{1-\alpha} - \frac{1}{\tau}\right)L_{mt}}. \tag{23}$$

Thus,

$$\frac{ds_{2t}}{dL_{mt}} = \frac{\gamma s_{mt}}{1+\varphi(\theta)}$$

$$\frac{\frac{A_{ut}}{A_{mt}}L_{ut}\left[\frac{\gamma}{1-\alpha} - \frac{\gamma}{\tau(1-\alpha)s_{mt}}\frac{s_{at}}{s_{mt}} - \frac{\gamma}{1-\alpha}\frac{s_{ut}}{s_{mt}}\frac{1+\varphi(\theta)}{1+\varphi(\bar{\theta})} + \frac{1}{\tau}\frac{s_{ut}}{s_{mt}}\frac{1+\varphi(\theta)}{1+\varphi(\bar{\theta})}\right] + \frac{N_{at}}{\tau}\left(1 - \frac{s_{at}}{s_{mt}}\frac{\gamma}{1-\alpha}\right)}{\left[\frac{\gamma}{1-\alpha}\frac{A_{ut}}{A_{mt}}L_{ut} + \frac{N_{at}}{\tau} + \left(\frac{\gamma}{1-\alpha} - \frac{1}{\tau}\right)L_{mt}\right]^2}. \tag{24}$$

Thus, when

$$\frac{A_{ut}}{A_{mt}}L_{ut}\left[\frac{\gamma}{1-\alpha} - \frac{\gamma}{\tau(1-\alpha)}\frac{s_{at}}{s_{mt}} - \frac{\gamma}{1-\alpha}\frac{s_{ut}}{s_{mt}}\frac{1+\varphi(\theta)}{1+\varphi(\bar{\theta})} + \frac{1}{\tau}\frac{s_{ut}}{s_{mt}}\frac{1+\varphi(\theta)}{1+\varphi(\bar{\theta})}\right]$$

$$> \frac{N_{at}}{\tau}\left(\frac{s_{at}}{s_{mt}}\frac{\gamma}{1-\alpha} - 1\right), \tag{25}$$

it is known that $\frac{ds_{2t}}{dL_{mt}} > 0$.

The fulfillment of the conditions in Eq. (25) is further discussed:

(1) In case of the same elasticity of labor output of the two sectors, i.e. $\gamma = 1 - \alpha$, $\frac{ds_{2t}}{dL_{mt}} > 0$ is permanently established;
(2) Generally speaking, the agricultural sector has a greater elasticity of labor output than the non-agricultural sector, i.e. $\gamma > 1 - \alpha$. When the cost of the transfer is large enough, the transfer of labor makes China's total rate of saving rise.

To prove it, it is assumed that the cost of transfer is infinite, i.e. $\tau \to \infty$, Eq. (25) is changed to

$$\frac{\gamma}{1-\alpha} \frac{A_{ut}}{A_{mt}} L_{ut} \left[1 - \frac{s_{ut}}{s_{mt}} \frac{1+\varphi(\theta)}{1+\varphi(\bar{\theta})} \right] > 0. \qquad (26)$$

It is also easily deduced that Eq. (26) is permanently established. However, when the cost of transfer is approaching 0, no difference exists regardless of transfer, that is, farmers and migrant workers have the same level of wages, leading to $\tau \to 1$. In this case, Eq. (25) is changed to

$$\frac{A_{ut}}{A_{mt}} L_{ut} \left[\left(\frac{\gamma}{1-\alpha} - 1 \right) \left(1 - \frac{s_{ut}}{s_{mt}} \frac{1+\varphi(\theta)}{1+\varphi(\bar{\theta})} \right) + \left(1 - \frac{\gamma}{1-\alpha} \frac{s_{at}}{s_{mt}} \right) \right]$$

$$> N_{at} \left(\frac{s_{at}}{s_{mt}} \frac{\gamma}{1-\alpha} - 1 \right). \qquad (27)$$

If $1 - \frac{\gamma}{1-\alpha} \frac{s_{at}}{s_{mt}} < 0$, the left side and right side of Eq. (27) are negative and positive, respectively, so Eq. (25) may not be true. Define

$$G(\tau) = \frac{A_{ut}}{A_{mt}} L_{ut} \left[\frac{\gamma}{1-\alpha} - \frac{\gamma}{\tau(1-\alpha)} \frac{s_{at}}{s_{mt}} - \frac{\gamma}{1-\alpha} \frac{s_{ut}}{s_{mt}} \frac{1+\varphi(\theta)}{1+\varphi(\bar{\theta})} + \frac{1}{\tau} \frac{s_{ut}}{s_{mt}} \frac{1+\varphi(\theta)}{1+\varphi(\bar{\theta})} \right]$$

$$- \frac{N_{at}}{\tau} \left(\frac{s_{at}}{s_{mt}} \frac{\gamma}{1-\alpha} - 1 \right). \qquad (28)$$

It is easy to prove that, $G(\tau)$ is a monotonous function of the cost of transfer, so there is a threshold value $\bar{\tau}$ of the cost of transfer.

When $\tau > \bar{\tau}$, the transfer of labor may also bring about an increase in the total rate of saving. Intuitively, the larger cost of the transfer of labor between urban and rural areas leads to a greater labor remuneration gap between migrant workers and farmers. In the process of the transfer of labor, the contribution of the total rate of the growth of savings of migrant workers is greater than that of the rate of the growth of total labor remuneration, which leads to a rise in the rate of total saving of the whole society.

(3) The gap in the level of social security can change the trend of the rate of saving: Under a shrinking gap in the level of social security, the rate of saving can maintain an upward trend only when the cost of transfer becomes higher; when the level of social security is completely equalized, the total rate of savings of the society declines constantly with a continuous transfer of labor.

The preceding conclusions can be directly inferred from Eq. (25). It should be noted that the narrowing of the gap in the level of social security will not necessarily lead to a decline in the rate of saving, but will slow down the rise of the rate of saving. The total rate of saving will drop only if the gap in levels of social security is small enough or even equal. Intuitively, given the gap in the levels of social security in the previous period, the narrowing of the gap in the current period means a relative increase in the level of social security of rural registered residents. Based on the decision of the maximization of utility, the rate of saving of rural residents will decrease relatively, leading to a reduction of or even to a decline in the total rate of saving of the entire society.

IV. Analysis of the Economic Significance

The model deduction in this chapter has demonstrated that the transfer of agricultural labor can push up the rate of household saving in China at the present stage. On such a basis, the marginal conditions for a decline in the rate of saving are also given in this chapter. Since this chapter only explains the reasons for the rise in the rate of household saving consistent with the conclusion of the model, the rate of household saving basically presents a monotonous rising trend in the sample interval, so the results of

Table 4.2. The Analysis of the Economic Significance on the Rise in the Rate of Household Saving (2000–2009).

Calculation caliber	Caliber description	Calculation results (%)
Real rates of household saving	Increase in the rate of real household saving	9.30
Caliber 1	Income share of farmers = per capita annual net income of rural households * number of rural population/labor remuneration Income share of migrant workers = total nominal wages of migrant workers/labor remuneration Income share of urban residents = 1 − (income share of farmers + income share of migrant workers)	5.69
Caliber 2	Income share of farmers = added value of the primary industry/ labor remuneration Income share of migrant workers = total nominal wages of migrant workers/ labor remuneration Income share of urban residents = 1 − (income share of farmers + income share of migrant workers)	5.96

Note: The caliber of the permanent population is applied in both the per capita annual net income of rural households and the number of the rural population, which can rule out migrant workers.

Source: The data of the total nominal wages of migrant workers are extracted from Lu Feng's study (2012), and the rest come from the *China Statistical Yearbook* over the years.

the calibration simulation of model parameters are estimated to roughly conform to the expected conclusion. Given the limited space available, a simple analysis of the economic significance is carried out on the rise in the rate of household saving with the idea of a deductive model, that is, how much the model can explain the rise in the rate of household saving in recent years. Specifically, this chapter uses the data regarding the rate of saving in Table 4.1 and the income shares of the three groups calculated based on the existing data to figure out the rise in the rate of saving from 2000 to 2009, when it keeps rising. Table 4.2 shows the results of the basic calculation.

Table 4.2 gives the calculated results of the two calibers. In this chapter, caliber 1 was used to calculate the income share of farmers and migrant workers, which is the ratio of the total income of rural residents and the total nominal wages of migrant workers to the labor remuneration, and further to figure out the income share of urban residents. The calculation results show that the model in this chapter can explain the increase in the rate of saving by 5.69 percentage points from 2000 to 2009, with the explanatory power of 61.2%. Caliber 2 was used to calculate the income share of farmers by the ratio of the added value of the primary industry to labor remuneration. To calculate the income share of migrant workers and that of urban residents, the same method is used. The results of the calculation show that the model can explain the increase in the rate of saving by 5.96 percentage points from 2000 to 2009, with the explanatory power of 64.1%. Both results show that the model in this chapter is of strong explanatory power for the rise of the rate of household saving. It should be noted that the calculation of the economic significance takes into account the overall effect of the level of income and the change in the structure of the population: after a farmer moves into the city to become a migrant worker, the increased level of income enables him/her to overcome the limitations of minimum consumption, and due to the effect of social security, the MPS improvement leads to a further increase in the rate of saving. The growing number of migrant workers and the increasing income share result in an increase in the rates of household saving. Due to data limitations, the calculation in this chapter does not separate the two types of effects, which is the direction for the research as a follow up to this book.

V. Conclusions

From the perspective of the transfer of agricultural labor, this chapter explores the reasons for the rise in the rate of household saving and the national rate of saving in China under the dual economic framework. In this chapter, a general equilibrium model is established to analyze the households' consumption–saving decisions, and the total rate of saving is divided into the rate of saving of urban residents, the rate of saving of migrant workers and the rate of saving of farmers. The migrant workers have a higher MPS than farmers and urban residents due to the difference in the level of social security and the level of income. With the continuous transfer of agricultural labor to the non-agricultural sector, the group of migrant workers keeps expanding with the accumulation of capital in the non-agricultural sector, and their high degree of saving also promotes the rise in the rate of household saving and that of national saving.

China's excessively high rate of saving has resulted in severe internal and external structural imbalances in the country, and even global structural imbalances to a certain extent, further resulting in a housing bubble and a financial crisis. This chapter explains the reasons for China's rising high rate of saving from the perspective of household savings, and thus makes clear how to alleviate the structural imbalances. The research in this chapter suggests that narrowing the urban–rural gap in the level of social medical security will be an effective measure for improving the level of consumption of residents and reduce the rate of saving. The reason why the transfer of the labor force pushes up the rate of household saving is that the level of social medical security enjoyed by the migrant workers still has a great deal of room for further improvement, despite a significant increase in income. Thus, the migrant workers always maintain a high precautionary tendency toward saving, and do not convert their increased amount of income into effective consumption. Therefore, establishing a unified system of social medical security and improving the level of social medical security available to rural residents can promote the consumption of farmers, especially migrant workers, reduce the rate of household saving and thus help reduce the national rate of saving. In addition, improving the level of social medical security of migrant workers can also increase the labor cost of enterprises, lower the huge surplus profits of enterprises and the enterprise rate of saving, and thus reduce the national rate of saving. From the perspective of sociology, a unified system of social medical security is essential to achieve social equity. As citizens with equal rights, they are supposed to enjoy equal rights and interests in social medical security. Closing the urban–rural gap in social medical security will also be conducive to reducing the real urban–rural income gap in the context of a widening urban–rural income gap.

Apart from the establishment of a unified system of social medical security, reducing the cost of the transfer of agricultural labor is also an effective measure for reducing the rate of saving. The study in this chapter reveals that the greater the cost of the transfer of labor in urban and rural areas, the greater the labor remuneration gap between migrant workers and farmers. In the process of the transfer of labor, the contribution of the growth rate of total savings of migrant workers is greater than that of the growth rate of total labor remuneration, which leads to the rise in the rate of the total saving of the whole society. Therefore, reducing the cost of the transfer of agricultural labor will boost the transfer of the labor force, support the development of non-agricultural sectors, narrow the labor remuneration gap between migrant workers and farmers, and reduce the effect of a rising rate of saving arising from the transfer of labor. In terms of the level of policy, the government can greatly reduce the cost of the transfer of agricultural labor by strengthening the construction of infrastructure that is conducive to the transfer of labor, safeguarding the rights and interests of migrant workers in cities, and other measures.

Chapter 5

The Transfer of Agricultural Labor and the Okun Relationship in China

I. Introduction

As a standard model in modern macroeconomics textbook, Okun's law, in essence, analyzes the correlation between a country's macroeconomic cycle and the changes in the labor market, and its specific form is to reveal the stable negative correlation between a country's unemployment rate and actual output. According to the analysis of the empirical relationship between unemployment and actual output based on the 1947–1960 quarterly data of the United States, Okun finds that the correlation coefficient between unemployment and actual output is −3.2, that is, every increase of 1% in the unemployment rate will correspond to a decrease of 3.2% in the output.[1] Okun's law suggests that, regardless of a decline or an increase, the unemployment rate will be favorable for the production of goods or services, making the unemployment rate inversely related to the change in the real GDP. Undoubtedly, the statistical links revealed by Okun's empirical model do not imply the one-way causation between unemployment and output change.

---

[1]Arthur M. Okun: Potential GNP, Its Measurement and Significance, in American Association, *Proceedings of the Business and Economics Statistics Section*, 1962, 98–103.

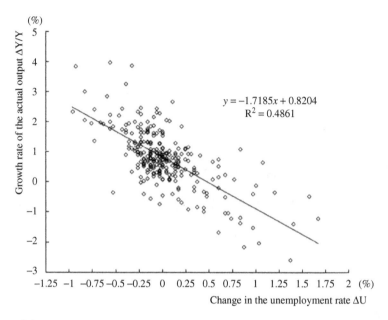

Figure 5.1. Okun's law in the United States (1948 Q2–2013 Q4).

Source: Bureau of Economic Analysis, BEA and Bureau of Labor Statistics, BLS.

In the opinions of Okun, the reason why the coefficient between the unemployment rate and the change in production is more than 1 is because production is also affected by other factors that change with the unemployment rate.[2] Figure 5.1 shows the quarterly data about the change in unemployment rate and the economic growth rate in the United States from 1948 to 2013, indicating that the Okun relationship can be significantly established.

Since the late 1970s, China has begun to implement the reform and opening-up policy and has gradually established a market economy structure, with an average annual growth rate of nearly 10% over the past 30 years. However, with the intensification of the market-oriented reform, the unemployment stress in China was further aggravated in the late 1990s, impelling the government to focus more on the objectives of its

---

[2]Okun points out that such factors include the rate of labor participation, labor time, labor productivity, etc. For instance, the labor time will increase by overtime in the context of a booming economy and a declining unemployment rate.

employment policy. Much literature has been published in the academic world to study the correlation between the model of Okun's law and Chinese data. Surprisingly, the data in Figure 1.8 show that the significant inverse correlation as described by Okun's law does not exist between China's GDP growth rate and the official unemployment rate.

Researchers have investigated the applicability of Okun's law in China from different perspectives. Some scholars have discovered that no significant correlation exists between the change in the registered urban unemployment rate and the economic growth rate in China, and that the changes in the real GDP growth rate and unemployment rate deviate greatly from the assumptions of Okun's law.[3] Some studies also indicate that the negative correlation between the growth rate of China's economy and the growth rate of employment proves the inapplicability of Okun's law in China.[4] Some scholars have set up five versions of the model for the empirical form of Okun's law, such as the difference model, the gap model and the asymmetry model, and have tested them, and the results show that none of them is applicable to the Chinese situation.[5] The studies on the classification of Okun equations in the expansion period and the recession period reveal that the coefficient of the unemployment rate to the growth rate is very small, every deviation of about 20 percentage points from the trend value in the growth rate corresponds to a change of about 1 percentage point in the unemployment rate, and the positive coefficient in the expansion stage is inconsistent with the theoretical hypothesis.[6] According to the estimation of Okun equations in the three industries based on the data of the three industries, a significant correlation as described by Okun exists between the primary and secondary industries,

---

[3]Jiang Wei and Liu Shicheng: Okun's Model and China's Empirical Study (1978–2004), *Statistics and Decision*, 2005 (24); Li Han and Pu Xiaohong: An Analysis of the Applicability of Okun's Law's in China, *Commercial Research*, 2009 (6), pp. 21–22.
[4]Yin Bibo and Zhou Jianjun: China's High Economic Growth and Low Employment: Empirical Study of Okun's Law in China, *Finance & Economics*, 2010 (1), pp. 56–61.
[5]Fang Fuqian and Sun Yongjun: Applicability of Okun's Law in China, *Economics Information*, 2010 (12), pp. 20–25.
[6]Lin Xiumei and Wang Lei: A Study of Non-linear Dynamic Correlation between Economic Growth and Unemployment Rate — Reconsideration of Okun's Law, *The Journal of Quantitative Economics*, 2006 (1), pp. 64–73.

and the Okun coefficient estimating symbol of the tertiary industry is positive, which deviates from the prediction meaning of Okun's law.[7]

The aforementioned basic empirical facts and research results on the correlation between unemployment rate and macroeconomic fluctuations all show that it is improper to directly apply the model of Okun's law from the existing textbooks to China. What is the root cause of this phenomenon? What is the real form of China's Okun relationship? In view of the empirical observation of the special correlation between China's labor market and macroeconomic cycle fluctuations, this chapter holds that for China as a transitional economy, the short-term change in the transfer of agricultural labor relative to its long-term trend is a key variable reflecting the correlation between the labor market and the macroeconomic cycle.

For instance, according to the data in Figure 1.9, the trend of agricultural labor decreases in the context of the transformation of China's employment, however, the decreasing number relative to its trend in a given year is significantly associated with the macro-cyclical changes measured by the GDP growth rate. To be specific, employment in the primary industry decreases at a slow rate in the years with a high macroeconomic growth, while the contrary is the case in the years with a low macroeconomic growth. As shown in Figure 5.2, there is a significant positive correlation between a change in non-agricultural employment and the macroeconomic cycle. Employment transformation means the growth trend of non-agricultural employment. However, non-agricultural employment has a significant positive correlation with changes in the macroeconomic cycle; this means that non-agricultural employment increases significantly in the years with a high macroeconomic growth, while the contrary is the case in the years with a low macroeconomic growth.

Thus, for the purpose of understanding the correlation between China's labor market and the changes in the macroeconomic cycle in the transition period, it is essential to break the limitation of the standard Okun model which only uses the unemployment rate to represent the changes in the labor market, and to construct a generalized model of Okun's law with the appropriate introduction of the variables of the transfer of agricultural

---

[7]Zou Wei and Hu Xuan: Research on the Deviation of China's Economy against Okun's Law and Unemployment, *The Journal of World Economy*, 2003 (6), pp. 40–47+80.

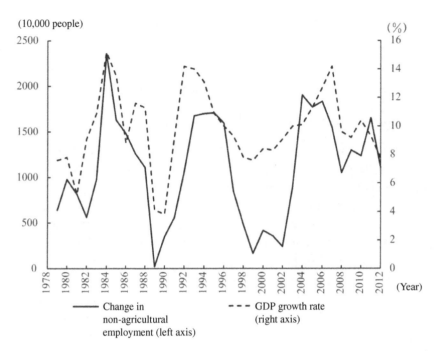

Figure 5.2.   Changes in employment and GDP growth rate of China's non-agricultural Industry (1979–2012).

Note: Non-agricultural employment refers to the employment in the secondary and tertiary industries. The data come from the *China Statistical Yearbook* over the years.

labor. Compared with the generalized Okun model, the standard Okun model is only applicable to the special case in developed countries. To explore the inapplicability of Okun's law in China, we go beyond the basic assumptions of the standard model in textbooks and find a more general connection between the labor market and the macroeconomic fluctuation in economies at different stages of development. Therefore, this chapter deduces the generalized Okun model to empirically analyze China's Okun relationship from the perspective of Okun's law, and tests the generalized Okun's law with transnational panel data.

This chapter is organized as follows: The second section describes the ideas of the analysis and derives the generalized Okun model, the third section empirically analyzes China's Okun relationship from the generalized Okun's law, the fourth section tests the generalized Okun's law with transnational panel data and the fifth section shows conclusions and policy recommendations.

II. Ideas of Analysis and Model Derivation

1. Analysis of the ideas of the research

We propose two issues for discussion on China's Okun relationship according to the empirical observation of the correlation between China's labor market and fluctuations in the macroeconomic cycle. First, as an economy with rapid transformation of economic and growth structure, China experiences a high degree of and continuous transfer of agricultural labor, so that the fluctuation in the macroeconomic cycle is closely associated with the speed of the transfer of agricultural labor. The agricultural labor shifts to the non-agricultural sector and further affects economic growth with the change in the employment in the non-agricultural sector; in turn, the fluctuations in the economic growth rate restrict the scale and rhythm of the transfer of agricultural labor through the change in the demand for non-agricultural labor. Second, in the period of the research that is the object of this chapter, the statistical object of a meaningful unemployment rate generally refers to the phenomenon of unemployment among the urban population.[8] The urban–rural divide in the system of household registration makes the employment of the urban population shield the macroeconomic fluctuations to a certain extent. Besides, independently of macroeconomic fluctuations, the institutional and policy changes, such as the return of educated young people to cities in the early stage of reform and the breakthrough in the reform of state-owned enterprises at the end of the last century, will cause greater difficulties in urban employment in a specific period. The definition of urban unemployment rate in China and its characteristics of change cause the Okun's law that only focuses on the correlation between the rate of economic growth and the unemployment rate to be "not applicable" to China.

---

[8]In the context of the rural family land contract system generally implemented, the vast majority of farmers own a certain area of contracted land, so it is hard to define the agricultural labor unemployment rate of operational significance. In fact, no data on time series of agricultural unemployment are available for use.

Scholars have found the inapplicability of the standard Okun's law in China and are seeking correction. Some scholars analyze the causes of the inapplicability of Okun's law from the perspective of unemployment data and attempt to use other surrogate variables of the unemployment rate.[9] Some scholars also investigate the correlation between economic growth and employment indicator or employment volume instead of the unemployment rate, that is, a deformed Okun's law.[10] Such studies are of positive significance for understanding unemployment phenomena and appropriate measurement methods in China. However, with the mature developed countries as the real prototype, the standard Okun model ignores the operational characteristics of the labor market reflected by the transfer of labor, a structural variable. Consequently, it is difficult to truly solve the riddle of the inapplicability of Okun's law in China. With the importance of the transfer of agricultural labor in the study of the Okun relationship in China in mind, Li Defu incorporated the transfer of agricultural labor into the framework of an analysis of the Okun relationship, constructed the model of the Okun relationship including the transfer of labor, and tested relevant data based on the estimated rate of the transfer of agricultural labor in China.[11] Li Defu's literature is an important bit of literature with unique insights into the Okun relationship in China. However, some issues still remain to be discussed and improved. For example, in terms of the model derivation, the appropriateness of assuming that agriculture does not contribute to economic growth can be explored; the surge of labor data in 1990 as a result of the fourth national population census still needs to be properly processed; it is improper to directly use the registered urban unemployment rate officially announced, which needs to be appropriately adjusted according to the actual situation of China's labor market.

---

[9]Cai Fang: Consistency of China's Statistics on Employment: Stylized Facts and Implications for Public Policies, *Chinese Journal of Population Science*, 2004 (3), pp. 4–12+81.

[10]Zou Wei and Hu Xuan: Research on the Deviation of China's Economy against Okun's Law and Unemployment, *The Journal of World Economy*, 2003 (6), pp. 40–47+80.

[11]Li Defu: Theory of Phillips Curve and Okun's Law of Dual-Economy, *The Journal of World Economy*, 2005 (8), pp. 53–61.

With reference to relevant research results, this chapter clearly proposes and tests the generalized Okun's law, and further studies the Okun relationship in China in detail from two aspects for expansion and deepening. First, based on the concept of a generalized Okun's law and the deduction of relevant models, the transnational panel data of more than 100 countries have been used to test whether the generalized Okun's law is consistent with the extensive international comparative experience. Second, an attempt is made to improve and perfect the expression and estimation of China's Okun relationship. For example, the model derivation takes into account the impacts of the transfer of labor on the output of both the non-agricultural and agricultural sectors, meaning the overall impacts of the transfer of labor on economic output are analyzed and tested. This improvement makes clear the economic benefits of the difference in productivity between the two sectors brought by the transfer of labor. In addition, in terms of empirical analysis, the unemployment rate in China is examined in more detail, and in addition to the officially released registered urban unemployment rate, multiple unemployment indicators are constructed for a regression analysis. Finally, in terms of data processing of the indicators of the transfer of labor, different measurement indicators, including the change in employment in the primary industry and the number of migrant workers, have been selected to deal with the surge of labor data in 1990, so as to improve the robustness of the results of the empirical test.

2. Theoretical model derivation

This section derives a more general Okun relationship that is applicable to countries with labor transition, i.e., a generalized Okun model that includes both the transfer of agricultural labor and the change in the unemployment rate.

It is assumed that an economy is composed of two sectors, i.e., an agricultural sector a and a non-agricultural sector b, and the economically active population of the two sectors is N_{at} and N_{bt}, respectively; the employed population is L_{at} and L_{bt}, respectively; the production function is: $Y_{at} = at \times L_{at}$; $Y_{bt} = bt \times L_{bt}$, respectively, where at and bt refer to the average labor productivity of the agricultural sector and non-agricultural sector, respectively. The total economic output is $Y_t = Y_{at} + Y_{bt}$, and the total employment is: $L_t = L_{at} + L_{bt}$, the overall average labor productivity is $c_t = \frac{Y_t}{L_t}$. To simplify the form, the time subscript t is omitted in the following analysis; adding "•" to the top of the variable indicates the derivative of the variable with respect to time.

Growth rate of total output:

$$g = \frac{\dot{Y}}{Y} = \frac{\dot{Y}_a + \dot{Y}_b}{Y} = \frac{Y_a}{Y} \frac{\dot{Y}_a}{Y_a} + \frac{Y_b}{Y} \frac{\dot{Y}_b}{Y_b} = \theta_a g_a + \theta_b g_b.$$

where $g_a = \frac{\dot{Y}_a}{Y_a}$ means the output growth rate of the agricultural sector; $g_b = \frac{\dot{Y}_b}{Y_b}$ means the output growth rate of the non-agricultural sector; $\theta_a = \frac{Y_a}{Y}$ means the share of agricultural output in the total output; $\theta_b = \frac{Y_b}{Y}$ means the share of non-agricultural output in the total output; $\theta_a + \theta_b = 1$, indicating that the sum of the output shares of the two sectors is equal to 1.

Suppose no "unemployment" exists in the agricultural sector, that is, $L_a = N_a$; but unemployment exists in the non-agricultural sector, $L_b = N_b - U_b = N_b - U$; the growth rate of economically active population is η for both sectors. Since an economy in transition undergoes a continuous transfer of large-scale agricultural labor to the non-agricultural sector (set the total transfer of labor as M), the employment growth of the non-agricultural sector consists of three parts, namely, the natural growth of the economically active population in the non-agricultural sector ηN_b, the change in the unemployment population $\dot{U}$, and the growth of the transfer of labor from the agricultural sector $\dot{M}$. Therefore, the employment growth in the agricultural sector $\dot{L}_a = \eta N_a - \dot{M}$, employment growth rate $\frac{\dot{L}_a}{L_a} = \frac{\eta N_a - \dot{M}}{L_a} = \eta - \frac{\dot{M}}{L_a}$; the employment growth in the non-agricultural sector $\dot{L}_b = \eta N_b + \dot{M} - \dot{U}$, employment growth rate $\frac{\dot{L}_b}{L_b} = \frac{\eta N_b + \dot{M} - \dot{U}}{L_b}$.

Therefore, the overall economic growth rate is

$$g = \theta_a g_a + \theta_b g_b$$

$$= \theta_a \left(\frac{\dot{a}}{a} + \frac{\dot{L}_a}{L_a} \right) + \theta_b \left(\frac{\dot{b}}{b} + \frac{\dot{L}_b}{L_b} \right)$$

$$= \theta_a \left(\varphi_a + \eta - \frac{\dot{M}}{L_a} \right) + \theta_b \left(\varphi_b + \frac{\eta N_b + \dot{M} - \dot{U}}{L_b} \right)$$

$$= \left[\theta_a (\varphi_a + \eta) + \theta_b \left(\varphi_b + \frac{\eta N_b}{L_b} \right) \right] + \left(\theta_b \frac{\dot{M}}{L_b} - \theta_a \frac{\dot{M}}{L_a} \right) - \theta_b \frac{\dot{U}}{L_b}$$

$$= \left[\theta_a (\varphi_a + \eta) + \theta_b \left(\varphi_b + \frac{\eta}{1-u} \right) \right] + \left(\frac{bL_b}{Y} \frac{L}{L_b} \frac{\dot{M}}{L} - \frac{aL_a}{Y} \frac{L}{L_a} \frac{\dot{M}}{L} \right) - \theta_b \frac{\dot{U}}{L_b}$$

$$= \left[(\theta_a \varphi_a + \theta_b \varphi_b) + \left(\theta_a \eta + \theta_b \eta \frac{1}{1-u} \right) \right] + \frac{(b-a)}{c} \frac{\dot{M}}{L} - \theta_b \frac{N_b}{L_b} \frac{\dot{U}}{N_b}$$

$$= \beta_0 + \beta_1 m + \beta_2 \dot{u},$$

where $\beta_0 = (\theta_a \varphi_a + \theta_b \varphi_b) + (\theta_a \eta + \theta_b \eta \frac{1}{1-u}) \approx (\theta_a \varphi_a + \theta_b \varphi_b) + (\theta_a + \theta_b)\eta = \varphi + \eta$; $\varphi_a = \frac{\dot{a}}{a}$ represents the growth rate of labor productivity in the agricultural sector, $\varphi_b = \frac{\dot{b}}{b}$ represents the growth rate of labor productivity in the non-agricultural sector, $\varphi = \theta_a \varphi_a + \theta_b \varphi_b$ is the weighted average growth rate of labor productivity, $\beta_1 = \frac{b-a}{c} \geqslant 0$, indicating that the movement of labor from the low-productivity agricultural sector to the high-productivity non-agricultural sector increases the total output; $m = \frac{\dot{M}}{L}$ is the proportion of the newly increased transfer of agricultural labor to the non-agricultural sector in the total employment; $\beta_2 = -\theta_b \frac{N_b}{L_b} = -\theta_b \frac{N_b}{N_b - U} = -\frac{\theta_b}{1-u} \approx -\theta_b$; $u = \frac{U}{N_b}$ is the ratio of the number of unemployed people in the non-agricultural sector to the number of the economically active population in the non-agricultural sector, indicating the unemployment rate. $\dot{u} = \frac{U}{N_b}$ indicates the change in unemployment.

In conclusion, a general form of Okun's law, that is, a generalized Okun's law model, is obtained:

$$g = \beta_0 + \beta_1 m + \beta_2 \dot{u}, \tag{1}$$

where β_0 can be interpreted as the economic growth rate without a transfer of labor and a change in the unemployment rate, which is also equal to the sum of the growth rate of labor productivity plus the growth rate of the population. Due to the continuous transfer of labor in the economies in transition, the potential economic growth rate should be $g_n = \beta_0 + \beta_1 m_n = \varphi + \eta + \beta_1 m_n$, where m_n is a stable rate of the transfer of labor. Thus, the gap model of the generalized Okun's law is obtained:

$$g - g_n = \beta_1 (m - m_n) + \beta_2 \dot{u}. \tag{2}$$

The generalized Okun's law has two basic meanings. First, the more general Okun relationship, which describes the correlation between macroeconomic cycle and the labor market of economies in different stages of development, should take into account the variable of the transfer of labor, that is, the ratio of the transfer of labor (m) and the change in the unemployment rate jointly affect the rate of economic growth. Second, the standard Okun's law model is applicable to the situation where the influence of the m variable declines in developed economies, which can be regarded as a special case of the generalized model. Compared with mature economies, the country in transition has $\beta_1 m_n$ additionally in the potential growth rate and $\beta_1 m$ additionally in the real growth rate.

China's economic transition has an even more special situation. The variable of the urban unemployment rate may affect China's Okun relationship less in view of the facts that China's unique institutional conditions block the impact of changes in the macroeconomic cycle on urban employment to a certain extent, and that the factors beyond the scope of the macroeconomic cycle, such as the return of China's educated youth to cities and the breakthrough in the reform of state-owned enterprises in the past few decades, have the greatest impact on the short-term changes in the urban unemployment rate. Therefore, it is speculated that the experience form of the Okun relationship that adapts to China's transition period is as follows:

$$g - g_n = \beta_1(m - m_n).\qquad(3)$$

With the continuous process of the transfer of labor, the proportion of agricultural labor in China will gradually decline to the level of developed countries. In addition, with the advancing of the reforms of the household registration system and related fields, the integration of China's urban and rural labor market will gradually improve. The disappearance of these structural factors is expected to make China's unemployment rate and macroeconomic fluctuations more closely linked. When China's economic transformation is basically completed, the Okun relationship in China is expected to be subject to the following textbook model:

$$g - g_n = \beta_2 \dot{u}.\qquad(4)$$

In the subsequent section, the application form of the generalized Okun's law in China is first tested by observing relevant empirical data in China, and then transnational panel data are used to investigate whether the generalized Okun's law is consistent with extensive international empirical evidence.

III. Analysis of the Generalized Okun Relationship in China

This section uses the generalized Okun model and the relevant data of China to analyze the Okun relationship applicable to China in the transition period. It consists of three parts. The first part introduces and discusses the measurement indicators and data of the variables of the transfer of labor and preliminarily observes the correlation between the transfer of labor and macroeconomic fluctuation. The second part discusses the indicator of the unemployment rate in China and constructs three kinds of adjusted indicators of the unemployment rate for econometric analysis. The third part shows the regression analysis of the generalized Okun model including the transfer of labor and the change in the unemployment rate.

1. Indicator and measurement of the variable of the transfer of agricultural labor in China

The proportion of agricultural labor in China has been decreasing since the reform and opening-up, which is consistent with extensive international experience. Over the past more than a century, the average proportion of agricultural labor in the Organisation for Economic Co-operation and Development (OECD) countries declined from 53% to about 10% at present; the proportion of agricultural labor in China decreased from more than 70% on the eve of reform to 33.6% in 2012, and will decrease to nearly 10% by 2030 as estimated.[12] The total number of employees in China increased from 463 million in 1978 to 767 million in 2012, of which the number of people employed in the primary industry increased from 327 million in 1978 to a peak of 391 million in 1991 and gradually decreased to 258 million in 2012.[13]

Consistent with the earlier theoretical model derivation logic, the following formula is used to estimate the newly increased transfer of agricultural labor $\dot{M}$ and its ratio m:

(1) $\dot{M}$ = Change in employment in the non-agricultural sector + change in the number of the unemployed — non-agricultural labor force in the previous period × growth rate of the economically active population.

(2) $m = \dot{M}$ ÷ total social employment in the previous year ×100.

Here, the method of calculation of the new labor transfer $\dot{M}$ and its ratio m is basically the same as that of Li Defu (2005). However, the total number of social employment rather than the sum of non-agricultural employment in the secondary and tertiary industries is used as the denominator indicator in the calculation of m.[14]

It is also necessary to discuss and make appropriate adjustments to the surge in the number of the economically active population and

---

[12]Lu Feng and Yang Yewei: Measurement of Factors behind the Decline of the Agricultural Labor Share in the Total Labor Force of China (1990–2030), *Chinese Journal of Population Science*, 2012 (4), pp. 15–26+113.

[13]Data from the *China Statistical Yearbook 2013*.

[14]The formula used by Li Defu (2005) for calculating the transfer rate m is: $m = \dot{M}$/total employment of the secondary and tertiary industries in the previous year ×100, that is, the denominator is the employment of the non-agricultural sector.

subcategories of employment before 1990. According to the data for the economically active population provided by the *China Statistical Yearbook*, the economically active population in 1990 increased by nearly 100 million from 1989, with a rate of increase of 17.3%. In view of the abnormal changes in the statistics of the economically active population in 1990 brought by the fourth national population census, the following method is used for adjustment: assume that the real growth rate of the economically active population in 1990 is equal to the average of the growth rate of the economically active population of 1989 and 1991, and the growth rate of the economically active population in each of the years before 1990 accords with that as indicated in the statistical yearbook, thus acquiring the time series data of the adjusted economically active population. Employment data at the end of the year are adjusted in a similar manner to the economically active population.

The estimated results of the transfer of labor in the primary industry and its proportion in the total employment as shown in Figure 5.3 show

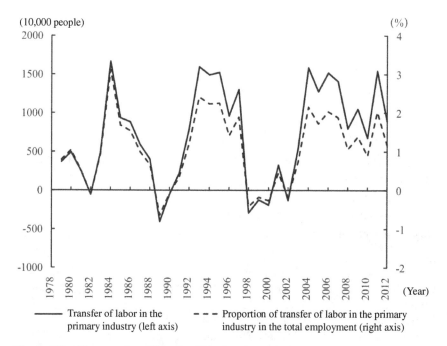

Figure 5.3.   The transfer of labor in China's primary industry and its proportion in the total employment (1979–2012).

Source: The China Statistical Yearbook over the years, estimated by the author.

Figure 5.4.   China's GDP growth rate and the rate of the transfer of labor in the primary industry (1979–2012).

Source: The China Statistical Yearbook over the years, estimated by the author.

that the average annual transfer of agricultural labor in China from 1979 to 2012 was 7.18 million, with an average rate of transfer of 1.08 percentage points. Figure 5.4 shows the correlation between the GDP growth rate and the rate of the transfer of agricultural labor, clearly indicating that there is a significant positive correlation between them.

Considering the prevalence of the form of "migrant workers" as the subject of the transfer of agricultural labor in China's specific institutional environment, the number of migrant workers provides another measurement indicator of the transfer of labor. Lu Feng introduced and discussed the transfer of migrant workers in China and its periodic characteristics.[15]

---

[15]Lu Feng: *Reflection on Economic Catch-up by a Large Country — An Understanding of China's Open Macro Economy (2003–2013) (Volume 1)*, Peking University Press, 2014, Edition 1.

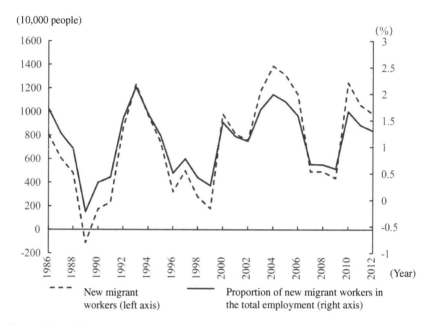

Figure 5.5. China's new migrant workers and their proportion in the total employment (1986–2012).

Source: The total employment is shown in the *China Statistical Yearbook* over the years. For the number of new migrant workers from 1985 to 2010, refer to Lu Feng's literature (2014, Vol. 1, p. 469, Figure 1). The data about the number of new migrant workers in 2011 and 2012 are sourced from the National Bureau of Statistics (2013).

Restricted by the availability of data, the data of migrant workers started in 1985. Figures 5.5 and 5.6 show the volume of transfer and the rate of migrant workers and compare them with the economic growth rate, indicating that the speed of the transfer of migrant workers has a generally positive correlation with the macroeconomic cycle.

2. Discussion on the indicator of China's urban unemployment rate

In the derivation of the theoretical model, the unemployment rate in this chapter is defined as the ratio of unemployment in the non-agricultural sector to the economically active population in the non-agricultural sector. However, it is necessary to find relatively reasonable alternative

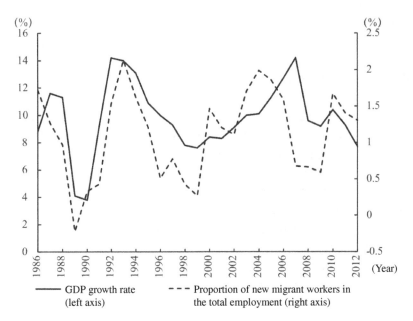

Figure 5.6. GDP growth rate and the rate of transfer of new migrant workers in China (1986–2012).

Source: For economic growth rate data, refer to *China Statistical Yearbook* over the years.

indicators for an empirical test due to limited data availability. The indicator of China's unemployment rate officially announced is the registered urban unemployment rate,[16] which is mainly questioned by the following two aspects. First, the indicator does not take into account the possible unemployment of the rural labor force, or it is assumed that no unemployment exists in agricultural labor. This issue must be approached rationally

---

[16]Registered urban unemployment rate is the ratio of urban registered unemployment to the sum of urban units' employment (excluding rural labor, employed retirees and employees from Hong Kong, Macao and Taiwan and foreign countries), off-duty workers in urban units, urban private owners, self-employed entrepreneurs, urban private enterprises employees and freelancers, and the registered unemployed people in cities and towns. Urban registered unemployed people refer to those who have non-agricultural household registration and the ability to work under a certain age (16 years old to retirement age), request for employment and are registered in unemployment in the local labor and social security department. http: //www.stats.gov.cn/tjsj/zbjs/201310/t20131029_449543.html.

and pragmatically. It is generally believed that China has a vast number of surplus labor force in agriculture, meaning that there is an insufficient utilization of the agricultural labor force. However, since most farmers still keep a certain area of the contracted land, the utilization of agricultural labor is relatively crude or inadequate but still greatly different from the connotation of unemployment in a strict sense. In addition, in the statistics of the agricultural unemployment rate, the time series data will also face some operational difficulties that are hard to overcome. In the alternative method, it is assumed that no agricultural labor unemployment exists and the urban unemployment rate is independently estimated on this basis. The alternative method may be a more operable method with less error,[17] compared with the method considering the agricultural and urban sectors.

Second, the number of urban unemployed does not take into account the increase in the number of laid-off workers after the 1990s. Thus, it is proper to make some adjustments against this, and regard the laid-off workers as unemployment population in the calculation of unemployment rate and form alternative indicator data of the unemployment rate. The general indicator for the international unemployment rate refers to the surveyed unemployment rate according to the definition of unemployment recommended by the International Labor Organization (ILO),[18] which can largely overcome the foregoing problems.[19] It is understood that time series data have not been published systematically, even though the concept of employment recommended by the ILO has been adopted by

[17]Cai Fang: Consistency of China's Statistics on Employment: Stylized Facts and Implications to Public Policies, *Chinese Journal of Population Science*, 2004 (3), pp. 4–12+81.

[18]According to ILO standards, the population of different age groups may fall into one of the three states, namely, employed people, unemployed people and non-economically active population. Employed people are those who have worked in the past week for at least one hour with income or temporarily left the job; unemployed people are those who are not working but are actively looking for work with capacity of work immediately; the non-economically active population refers to the people who do not work and meet the ILO unemployment criteria (Zhang Chewei: International Comparison of the Definition of Unemployment Rate and Urban Unemployment Rate in China, *The Journal of World Economy*, 2003 (5), pp. 47–54+80.).

[19]Zhang Chewei: International Comparison of the Definition of Unemployment Rate and Urban Unemployment Rate in China, *The Journal of World Economy*, 2003 (5), pp. 47–54+80.

relevant departments to investigate the surveyed unemployment rate and leaders have mentioned relevant data on a few occasions.[20]

This chapter provides three adjusted indicators of the unemployment rate based on the registered urban unemployment rate officially announced. First, for the numerator of the unemployment rate, the number of laid-off workers is added based on the registered urban unemployment officially announced. Second, for the denominator of the unemployment rate, two methods are used to calculate the economically active urban population: economically active urban population 1 = officially announced unemployment/announced unemployment rate; economically active urban population 2 = urban employment + urban unemployment + the number of laid-off workers. As a result, the following three unemployment indicators with different calibers are available: Unemployment rate 1 = official registered urban unemployment rate = registered unemployment/ economically active urban population 1; unemployment rate 2 = (registered unemployment + the number of laid-off workers)/economically active urban population 1; unemployment rate 3 = (registered unemployment + the number of laid-off workers)/economically active urban population 2. Thus, the problem that the official registered unemployment rate does not reflect the real employment situation is expected to be overcome to a considerable extent.

The difference between the adjusted indicator of the unemployment rate and the surveyed indicator of the unemployment rate in this chapter may be mainly attributable to the following two aspects. First, some urban non-agricultural employees without local household registration are not included in the statistical scope of the existing unemployment rate. Second, there are differences between the two methods for registering unemployment and investigating unemployment. The surveyed unemployment rate may be significantly different from the absolute level of the

---

[20] In September 2013, Premier Li Keqiang published a signed article in the *Financial Times*, revealing that the unemployment rate was about 5% in the first half of the year. In June 2014, when Premier Li Keqiang gave a talk on the economic situation for the academicians of the Chinese Academy of Sciences and the Chinese Academy of Engineering at the academician congress, and once again mentioned that the unemployment rate in China was 5.17%, 5.15% and 5.07% in March, April and May, respectively. http: //money.163.com/14/0611/17/9UFPN2DF00252G50.html.

current registered unemployment rate; however, there is a small difference in the variation trend. It is reasonable to speculate that the conclusions are likely to have no essential differences using different indicators of the unemployment rate to test the applicability of the standard Okun model in China. Undoubtedly, the lack of long-term surveyed unemployment rate data is a limitation on the relevant literature and the conclusions of this chapter. In case sufficient data are available in the future, it is apparently necessary to re-test the applicability of the standard Okun model.

Figure 5.7 shows three kinds of unemployment rates including the registered urban unemployment rate. The first official unemployment rate and the second adjusted unemployment rate with laid-off workers included are determined by the time limit for the availability of the data about laid-off workers, which overlap in the early (1978–1991) and later (2007–2012) periods. In the third estimation method, the unemployment rate denominator has been adjusted and thus is different from the official

Figure 5.7. China's unemployment rate (1978–2012).

Source: The China Statistical Yearbook over the years, estimated by the author.

unemployment rate statistics. The data show that the two high unemployment rates in China take place at the start of economic reform and the turn
of the century, due to the large-scale return of educated youth to cities and
the breakthrough in the reform of state-owned enterprises accompanied by
the surge of urban unemployment in a short period of time.[21] The urban
unemployment rates are aimed at a low level in the years other than the
two peak periods. It can be concluded that the difficulty in solving the
traditional urban employment problem within an environment of rapid
economic growth is how to better respond to the unemployment pressure
released by institutional transformation, and to address the challenge of
long-term transfer of labor from a more fundamental perspective. The
statistics regarding the unemployment rate have no apparent cyclical characteristics. Therefore, it is hard to explain the true correlation between
macroeconomic fluctuation and the change in the labor market just by
using the unemployment rate to estimate the Okun relationship.

3. Estimation of the Okun relationship model in China

Based on the generalized Okun model (1), the rate of the transfer of agricultural labor represented by m and three unemployment rate indicators
are used for a regression analysis. Since this chapter uses long-term time
series data, it is appropriate to first consider the stability of the data before
the regression analysis. For this reason, the Augmented Dickey–Fuller
unit-root test was conducted and the specific process is as follows:
(1) First determine the lag terms according to FPE, AIC, HQIC, SBIC and
other information criteria, including constant term and trend term;
(2) Perform the unit-root test according to the determined lag items.
According to the specific test results detailed in Table 5.1, the change in
the economic growth rate, the rate of the transfer of labor (m), and the two
unemployment rate indicators (unemployment rate 2 and unemployment
rate 3) constructed in this chapter passed the unit-root test at the 1% significance level with no unit root, indicating that the data are steady; the
change in the rate of the transfer of labor (migrant workers) and the

---

[21] At that time, the unemployed people were called "job-waiting people" and "laid-off workers".

Table 5.1. ADF Unit-Root Test Results of the Main Regression Variable of the Generalized Okun's Law in China.

Test variables	Lag terms determined according to information criteria	Test statistics	P-value	1% critical value	5% critical value	10% critical value
Economic growth rate	5	−4.066***	0.007	−4.334	−3.580	−3.228
Rate of the transfer of labor (*m*)	5	−4.107***	0.006	−4.352	−3.588	−3.233
Rate of the transfer of labor (migrant workers)	1	−3.334*	0.061	−4.371	−3.596	−3.238
Change in unemployment rate 1	0	−3.251*	0.075	−4.306	−3.568	−3.221
Change in unemployment rate 2	0	−6.430***	0.000	−4.306	−3.568	−3.221
Change in unemployment rate 3	0	−6.625***	0.000	−4.306	−3.568	−3.221

Note: The original data were extracted from the CEInet Statistics Database; the data in the table were estimated by the author. The symbols of ***, ** and * represent significant levels at 1%, 5% and 10%, respectively.

unemployment rate 1 (registered urban unemployment rate) also passed the unit-root test at the 10% significance level.

Table 5.2 sets forth the results of the estimation of the generalized Okun model, with the main findings as follows: (1) The coefficient *m* is significant and stable, and the *m* variation of 1 percentage point is accompanied by a GDP growth rate of 2.1–2.2 percentage points in the same direction. (2) The estimated variation coefficient of any one of the three unemployment rates with different calibers is not significant at the 5% significance level, and only unemployment rate 3 is significant at the 10% significance level, indicating that the indicator of the unemployment rate cannot well reflect the Okun relationship in China. (3) The estimated coefficient of the constant term is 7.5%–7.6%, roughly explained as the potential growth rate of the Chinese economy in the absence of a large-scale transfer of agricultural labor.

In the context of China's particular system, the historical form of the migrant workers is prevalent in the transfer of agricultural labor and the

Table 5.2. Regression Results of the Generalized Okun's Law in China.

	Model 1	Model 2	Model 3	Model 4
Rate of the transfer of	2.093***	2.096***	2.158***	2.183***
labor (*m*)	(0.335)	(0.346)	(0.332)	(0.334)
Change in	—	0.225	—	—
unemployment rate 1	—	(1.165)	—	—
Change in	—	—	−0.318	—
unemployment rate 2	—	—	(0.195)	—
Change in	—	—	—	−0.414*
unemployment rate 3	—	—	—	(0.239)
Constant term	7.598***	7.603***	7.516***	7.474***
	(0.517)	(0.523)	(0.509)	(0.512)
	0.506	0.507	0.521	0.522
Time quantum	1979–2012	1979–2012	1979–2012	1979–2012

Note: The original data were extracted from the CEInet Statistics Database; the data in the table were estimated by the author. The symbols of ***, ** and * represent significant levels at 1%, 5% and 10%, respectively.

migrant worker data provide a measure of the transfer of agricultural labor. According to the regression results of the generalized Okun relationship using the indicator for the transfer of migrant workers in Table 5.3, the speed variable of the transfer of labor measured by migrant worker data is also highly significant, and its coefficient estimate is slightly higher than that of the coefficient *m* in Table 5.2. The constant term has its coefficient estimate close to the level of significance. Al of the unemployment rates with three different calibers are not significant. However, the model fitting degree is lower than the *m* estimation model in Table 5.2 due to differences in the sample period for the data and the definition of the indicator.

The results of the regression analysis show that the changes in the unemployment rate do not well reflect the correlation between the labor market and the macroeconomic cycle in the transition stage of reform and opening-up in China, while different variables of the transfer of agricultural labor show significant macro periodicity and highlight the structural characteristics of the Okun relationship in China, and more importantly, indicate the limitation of the existing standard Okun's law model in the explanation of

Table 5.3.   Regression Results of the Generalized Okun's Law in China (Indicator of the Transfer of Migrant Workers).

	Model 1	Model 2	Model 3	Model 4
Rate of the transfer of	2.594***	2.517***	2.629***	2.622***
labor (migrant	(0.777)	(0.799)	(0.803)	(0.796)
workers)				
Change in	—	−1.982	—	—
unemployment rate 1	—	(2.029)	—	—
Change in	—	—	0.123	—
unemployment rate 2	—	—	(0.174)	—
Change in	—	—	—	0.183
unemployment rate 3	—	—	—	(0.218)
Constant term	7.182***	7.427***	7.136***	7.149***
	(0.975)	(1.073)	(1.024)	(1.014)
	0.313	0.336	0.316	0.317
Time quantum	1986–2012	1986–2012	1986–2012	1986–2012

Note: The original data were extracted from the CEInet Statistics Database; the data in the table were estimated by the author. The symbols of ***, ** and * represent significant levels at 1%, 5% and 10%, respectively.

China's experience. However, due to the limited unemployment rate data, the results of the research remain to be further discussed in combination with the surveyed unemployment rate data that may be published in the future.

IV. Test with Multinational Data

The generalized Okun's law considers that the correlation between the labor market and macroeconomic fluctuation is not only determined by the indicator of the unemployment rate emphasized by the standard textbook model but is also subject to the characteristics of the stage of development of different countries and the relative importance of the transfer of agricultural labor to economic growth. In this section, the generalized Okun's law is preliminarily tested from the perspective of international experience. First of all, based on the panel data of more than 100 sample countries, the international empirical general formula of the generalized Okun model is estimated, and the generalized Okun's law is tested by observing whether the variable of the transfer of labor is significant. Then, according to the proportion of agricultural labor, the sample countries are divided into two groups, i.e., transition countries and mature countries, to estimate the generalized Okun equation, and the generalized Okun's law is tested by observing the difference in the significance of the coefficient estimate of the transfer of agricultural labor and unemployment variables.

1. General formula of the generalized Okun model

The data on economic growth and the labor market for the countries from 1980 to 2012 can be found in the World Bank WDI Database. Time series data about the economic growth rate, the unemployment rate,[22] the proportion of agricultural labor, the transfer of agricultural labor and other indicators are summarized for 104 countries, of which the indicator of the speed of the transfer of labor *m* is established in the same manner as that in the previous section. Finally, the non-equilibrium panel data of 104 countries (or regions) are obtained. Table 5.4 shows the statistics of transnational data of major regression variables used for the regression analysis.

First of all, the standard Okun model and the generalized Okun model are estimated, and the generalized Okun's law is preliminarily tested by observing whether the coefficient estimate of the variable of the transfer

---

[22]The unemployment rate in the World Bank WDI Database is defined as "the proportion of total unemployment in the total labor; unemployment refers to the number of people who are currently unemployed but are able to work and are seeking work." At the same time, the Database reveals that "the definitions of labor and unemployment vary from country to country." As for the empirical analysis based on international experience, it is ideal to adopt the unemployment rate data completely consistent with the definition caliber of theoretical analysis. However, the definitions of labor force and unemployment vary from country to country as indicated by the WDI Database, so it is impossible to acquire the optimal and completely consistent data for the unemployment indicator in reality, and thus, we can only choose the suboptimal and relatively reasonable indicators for empirical analysis. The focus of regression analysis is the change in unemployment rate rather than the level of unemployment. As long as the indicator is consistent in time during the survey period, its change can reflect the change in the unemployment situation on the labor market. Therefore, the detailed differences in the indicators of the unemployment rate of a country are supposed to not exert a great impact on the basic reliability of the conclusions of the analysis.

Table 5.4.   Statistics of Regression Variables of the Generalized Okun Model (1981–2012).

Variable	Observed value	Mean	Median	Standard deviation	Minimum	Maximum
GDP growth rate (%)	1575	3.54	3.65	4.12	−17.96	34.50
Unemployment rate (%)	1575	8.58	7.60	5.11	0.10	37.30
Change in unemployment rate (%)	1575	−0.01	−0.10	1.49	−12.00	10.80
Proportion of agricultural employment (%)	1575	15.10	9.50	14.52	0.00	70.20
Rate of the transfer of labor m (%)	1575	0.33	0.20	1.37	−7.69	13.82

Note: World Bank WDI Database, estimated by the author. The data are shown in Appendix 1 of Lu Feng's literature (2014, Vol. 1, p. 469, Figure 1).

of agricultural labor has a significant positive correlation. Due to the non-equilibrium panel data, two regression methods, namely, OLS (ordinary least square) and FE (fixed effects), which control the annual validity, are used for regression in order to maximize the use of sample information and ensure the quality of the regression results.

Table 5.5 shows the regression results. The estimated results obtained from the two regression methods have a certain degree of consistency, indicating robust regression conclusions. The indicator of change in the unemployment rate is significantly negative and steady in both the standard Okun model and the generalized Okun model. In the generalized Okun model, the indicator of the speed of the transfer of labor is significantly positive and stable. The regression results in Table 5.5 show that both the change in unemployment rate and the transfer of agricultural labor are important variables related to the macroeconomic cycle and changes in the labor market. Thus, it is necessary to consider the variable of the transfer of agricultural labor in the analysis of the Okun relationship and relevant employment policies.

Considering that the proportion of agricultural employment is a key variable in measuring a country's labor transition, it may affect the correlation between the variable of the structure of the labor market and the economic growth rate. The cross-term among the proportion of

Table 5.5.   Benchmark Regression of the Generalized Okun Model.

Variable	Model 1: Standard Okun model		Model 2: Generalized Okun model	
	OLS	FE	OLS	FE
Change in unemployment rate	−1.102***	−1.041***	−1.170***	−1.093***
	(0.0886)	(0.121)	(0.0875)	(0.119)
Rate of the transfer of labor	—	—	0.469***	0.322***
	—	—	(0.0803)	(0.0780)
Constant term	3.564***	3.820***	3.054***	3.433***
	(0.507)	(0.460)	(0.509)	(0.462)
Vintage effect	Yes	Yes	Yes	Yes
Number of observed value	1,575	1,575	1,575	1,575
R^2	0.327	0.408	0.350	0.420
Number of individuals	104	104	104	104

Note: The symbols of ***, ** and * represent significant levels at 1%, 5% and 10%, respectively.

agricultural employment, the change in the unemployment rate and the speed of the transfer of labor is incorporated in the estimating equation in order to explore whether a country's proportion of agricultural employment can strengthen or weaken the correlation of the change in the unemployment rate and the speed of the transfer of labor with the economic growth rate.

The regression results with a consideration of the cross-term in Table 5.6 show that the cross-term between the change in the unemployment rate and the proportion of agricultural employment is significantly positive, indicating the higher the agricultural employment proportion, the weaker the negative correlation between the change in the unemployment rate and the economic growth rate. Thus, it can be concluded that in a country with labor transition, the impacts of the macroeconomic cycle are reflected in the job market in part, thus weakening the correlation with the unemployment rate. Since the speed of the transfer of labor reflects the characteristics of labor transition, the cross-term between it and the proportion of agricultural employment is not significant. In addition, the coefficient of the proportion of agricultural employment itself is also significantly positive in OLS regression, indicating that the countries with

Table 5.6. Extended Regression of the Generalized Okun Model.

Variable	Model 3: Extended generalized Okun model	
	OLS	FE
Change in the unemployment rate	−1.364***	−1.349***
	(0.115)	(0.149)
Labor transfer rate	0.387***	0.296**
	(0.135)	(0.117)
Agricultural employment proportion	0.0565***	−0.00269
	(0.00731)	(0.0449)
Change in the unemployment rate × agricultural employment proportion	0.0160**	0.0175**
	(0.00723)	(0.00677)
Rate of the transfer of labor × proportion of agricultural employment	−0.00165	−0.000363
	(0.00461)	(0.00433)
Constant term	2.235***	3.495***
	(0.511)	(0.912)
Vintage effect	Yes	Yes
Number of observed value	1,575	1,575
R^2	0.390	0.427
Number of individuals	104	104

Note: The symbols of ***, ** and * represent significant levels at 1%, 5% and 10%, respectively.

a more backward economic developmental stage have a higher economic growth rate, revealing the convergence effect of economic growth. On the contrary, the coefficient of the proportion of agricultural employment is not significant in the fixed-effect regression, which is possibly because the fixed-effect regression has restrained the convergence effect by control of the individual effect.

2. Analysis of the subtype regression of sampling countries

According to a proportion of a certain level of agricultural employment in the sample period, the sample countries are divided into two groups of subsamples, namely, transition countries and mature countries, to conduct a regression analysis. The generalized Okun's law is further tested by observing the relative significance and importance of the transfer of labor and unemployment variables in the regression equation of subsamples. In this chapter, with the boundary of 10%, the countries with an average proportion of agricultural employment higher than 10% in the sample period are regarded as transition countries, while those with one that is lower than 10% are regarded as mature countries, for the purpose of the regression analysis of the generalized Okun model.[23] In view of the significant impact of the cross-term on the overall sample analysis, the cross-term variable is also considered in the regression analysis for subsamples.

The regression results in Table 5.7 show that both the change in the unemployment rate and the speed of the transfer of labor are very significant in the Okun model of countries in transition. In the Okun model of mature countries, the indicator of the unemployment rate is highly significant but the indicator of the speed of the transfer of labor is the contrary, showing a high level of consistency with the theoretical expectation contained in the generalized Okun's law. The regression equation of the countries in transition also shows that both the proportion of agricultural employment and its cross-term with the change in the unemployment rate are highly significant, also showing a high level of consistency with the benchmark regression in Table 5.5. In the regression equation of mature countries, both the indicator of the speed of the transfer of labor and the cross-term of the proportion of primary industry employment are not significant, only the indicator of the unemployment rate is highly significant, and the value of the regression coefficient greatly increases. Thus, it can be concluded that the specific form of implementation of the generalized Okun equation in different countries is closely linked with the structural variable of labor transition. For countries in transition with a continuous transfer of agricultural labor, either the change in the unemployment rate or the speed of the transfer of labor is a basic variable of

---

[23] With the initial level (10%) of the proportion of agricultural employment as the boundary, the samples are divided into two groups of subsamples, namely, transition countries and mature countries, to conduct the regression analysis of the generalized Okun model. The results obtained are basically consistent with those obtained by the method adopted in this section and thus are not repeated.

Table 5.7.   Subtype Regression of the Generalized Okun Model Sampling Countries.

Variables	Transition country		Mature country	
	OLS	FE	OLS	FE
Change in the unemployment rate	−1.689***	−1.677***	−1.179***	−1.256***
	(0.199)	(0.289)	(0.188)	(0.222)
Rate of the transfer of labor	0.580**	0.577***	0.0955	0.0777
	(0.230)	(0.204)	(0.225)	(0.158)
Proportion of agricultural employment	0.0649***	0.0617	−0.0269	0.0439
	(0.0116)	(0.0570)	(0.0351)	(0.168)
Change in the unemployment rate × proportion of agricultural employment	0.0282***	0.0294***	0.000504	0.0273
	(0.00928)	(0.00970)	(0.0290)	(0.0350)
Rate of the transfer of labor × proportion of agricultural employment	−0.00704	−0.00731	0.0365	0.0108
	(0.00611)	(0.00552)	(0.0290)	(0.0269)
Constant term	1.739	1.833	2.665***	2.498**
	(1.072)	(2.168)	(0.614)	(1.041)
Vintage effect	Yes	Yes	Yes	Yes
Number of observed value	773	773	802	802
R^2	0.392	0.423	0.382	0.483
Number of individuals	59	59	45	45

Note: The original data were extracted from World Bank WDI Database, estimated by the author. The symbols of ***, ** and * represent significant levels at 1%, 5% and 10%, respectively.

the Okun relationship. However, with the end of the transfer of agricultural labor, the indicator of the speed of that transfer loses its significance, and the generalized Okun relationship shifts to a form of the standard model.

The previous results of the estimation of the generalized Okun equation in China show that the variable coefficient of the transfer of agricultural labor is highly significant, which has provided some empirical experience in the correlation between China's labor market and the macroeconomic cycle, namely, the essential correlation of the Okun's law, from the perspective of the generalized theory of Okun's law, thus solving the riddle of the standard Okun's law not being suitable to explain the correlation between macroeconomics and the labor market. However, the indicator of the unemployment rate is not significant and deviates from the estimated result of the unemployment rate variable in the multi-country model of any transition and developing country. In this regard, we observe and discuss some characteristics of the stage of China's system and policy of labor employment during the period of reform and opening-up.

First, subject to the dual system of the urban–rural divide in the planned economy period, the special system and regulation policy favorable for urban residents to the disadvantage of farmers is still implemented in terms of household registration and labor force to varying degrees. Consequently, the employment of the laborers with urban household registration has a shielding effect on the macroeconomic fluctuation to varying degrees, which may greatly reduce the sensitivity of the indicator of the unemployment rate responding to macroeconomic fluctuations.

Second, under the above system, the agricultural labor group flexibly shifts between outside employment and return to one's home village for agricultural work, which is reflected by the popular term "migrant workers", a seemingly logical but contradictory term. As a result, the transferring agricultural labor can serve as a "buffer" or "reservoir" to regulate the overall supply and demand of labor. The fluctuation of the macroeconomic cycle actively responds to the transfer of labor, which objectively weakens the significance of the response of the unemployment rate variable.

Third, two important shocks leading to a surge of the urban unemployment rate took place during the reform period of China, i.e., the return of educated youth to cities in the early stages of the reform and the breakthrough in the reform of state-owned enterprises at the end of the previous century. The two institutional and policy changes that aggravate the urban unemployment pressure are relatively independent of the short-term macroeconomic fluctuations highly concerned by the Okun relationship and would also hinder the unemployment rate from showing a significant impact consistent with the theoretical speculations in the Okun relationship.

Last but not least, the incomplete statistical indicators of the unemployment rate cannot better reflect the actual employment situation, which may also be one of the reasons why the indicator of the unemployment rate is not significant.

V. Conclusions

In view of the inapplicability of the standard model of Okun's law in China's empirical data, this chapter proposes the generalized Okun's law by introducing the variable of the transfer of agricultural labor, and empirically tests the generalized Okun's law with China's empirical data and transnational panel data containing more than 100 sampling countries.

The generalized Okun's law considers that the correlation between the labor market and the macroeconomic fluctuation is not only determined by the indicator of the unemployment rate emphasized by the standard textbook model but also subject to the characteristics of the stage of development of different countries and the relative importance of the transfer of agricultural labor to economic growth. The Okun model, which only includes the unemployment rate variable, is applicable to the developed countries that have completed the transfer of labor. In contrast, the Okun model applicable to the vast economies in transition is supposed to include the transfer of agricultural labor, a key structural variable. Thus, the standard textbook model can be regarded as a special case of the generalized Okun's law.

With the panel data of more than 100 sampling countries, this chapter preliminarily tests the generalized Okun model and obtains the following results. First, the significance of the unemployment rate variable is verified by the regression of the generalized Okun relationship with all the samples. Besides, the indicator of the speed of the transfer of labor is significantly positive and relatively stable, indicating either a change in the unemployment rate or that the transfer of agricultural labor is a key variable associated with the macroeconomic cycle and the labor market. Second, the cross-term among the proportion of agricultural employment, the change in the unemployment rate and speed of the transfer of labor is incorporated in the equation for the estimation of the generalized Okun relationship for the purpose of regression, with the results proving the importance of the transfer of labor. Finally, with the proportion of agricultural employment as a criterion, the sample countries are divided into transition and developing countries and economically developed countries to carry out regression analysis, and the regression analysis suggests that the estimated difference of the transfer of labor and the unemployment variables of the two groups of subsamples are consistent with the hypothesis of Okun's law.

The equation for China's estimated Okun relationship based on the generalized Okun's law reveals that a significant correlation does exist between the transfer of agricultural labor relative to its trend of change and the fluctuation of the macroeconomic cycle. The estimate of the transfer of labor is fairly stable and highly significant in the estimating equation established with different data regarding the transfer of labor and the unemployment rate. The generalized Okun's law raises a theoretical hypothesis that there is a significant correlation between the transfer of labor and the macroeconomic cycle, which has been supported by relevant empirical data in China. Thus, the generalized Okun's law solves the riddle of the inapplicability of the model of the standard Okun's law in revealing the correlation between the macroeconomic cycle and the change in the labor market. Compared with the estimating equation of the Okun relationship in developing countries, the indicator of the unemployment rate is varied in the estimating equation in China, which may be explained from the background to China's special system and policy for labor employment in the transition period.

This chapter expands the general understanding of the correlation between the labor market and macroeconomic cyclical fluctuation. The exploration of some important characteristics and phenomena in China's transition period provides us with an opportunity to go beyond the basic assumptions of the traditional standard textbook model and deepen our understanding of the correlation between certain macroeconomic variables in the modern economic environment. Furthermore, according to the empirical analysis of the Okun relationship in China, some characteristic attributes of the change in China's unemployment rate and the transfer of labor are made clear under the environment of a specific system and policy. The estimation results of the Okun relationship in China provides an empirical reference or benchmark for discussing and evaluating the internal relations and laws between the labor market and the macroeconomic fluctuation in different periods.

Chapter 6

The Policy Implications of the Transfer of Agricultural Labor

I. Conclusions and Policy Recommendations

This book primarily presents the three basic characteristics of China's economic development. First, since the reform and opening-up, China has maintained an extremely high rate of investment, but the rate of capital return has kept rising over the past two decades. Second, since the reform and opening-up, China's national rate of saving has been on the rise steadily. Especially in the 21st century, the rate has grown at a faster rate but recently it has fallen slightly. Third, no significant inverse relationship exists between China's GDP growth rate and the existing data regarding the unemployment rate as described by Okun's law, indicating a lack of a necessary correlation between China's macroeconomic cycle and the changes in the labor market. On this basis, this book explains these three characteristics of China's economic development from the perspective of the transfer of agricultural labor, draws some basic conclusions and puts forward policy recommendations.

First, this book re-examines China's economic structural transformation from an endogenous angle. Considering the transfer of agricultural labor and the effect of the technology spillover are stressed, an extended dual economic model is established to explain the coexistence of a high investment rate and a rising rate of return in China. The extended model relaxes the unit elasticity hypothesis of the "knowledge spillover model" on the technology spillover effect, and proposes the "strong condition" and "weak condition" required by an economy at different stages of development to maintain the same or growing rate of return on capital. The findings of the theoretical study show that factors of the transfer of labor result in a reduction from the strong condition to the weak condition required by the rising capital return on the technology spillover effect, and the combination of the transfer of labor and the technology spillover effect is the key to explaining the continuous rise of return on capital in China. According to the empirical analysis, China's technology spillover effect not only fulfills the weak condition but also backs up the rising rate of return on capital together with the continuous transfer of labor.

Second, this book discusses the reasons for the rise in the rate of household saving and the rate of national saving in China from the perspective of the transfer of agricultural labor under the dual economic framework. A general equilibrium model is constructed to analyze the households' decisions regarding consumption and savings, and to divide the total rate of saving into three groups, namely, the rate of saving of urban residents, that of migrant workers and that of farmers. The migrant workers have a higher tendency toward marginal saving than farmers and urban residents due to the difference in the levels of social security and of income. In the process of the continuous transfer of agricultural labor to the non-agricultural sector, the group of migrant workers expands continuously with the capital accumulation of the non-agricultural sector, and their behavior of a high degree of saving also contributes to the rise in the rate of household saving and the national rate of saving.

Third, based on the empirical observation of the relationship between China's macroeconomic cycle and the transformation of the labor market, this book proposes the concept of Okun's law considering the transfer of agricultural labor in a broad sense, and explains the inapplicability of Okun's law in China with the empirical data. The applicable form of the generalized Okun's law is related to the stage of economic development. The textbook Okun model, which only includes the variable of the unemployment rate, is applicable to developed countries that have completed the transfer of labor, and Okun's relationship that applies to more economies in transition is supposed to also include the variable of the transfer of agricultural labor. China's unique institutional environment results in a lack of a significant link between the urban unemployment rate and macro-cyclical changes. The transnational panel data are also used to carry out the preliminary test to the generalized Okun's law.

The results of the research of this book can be used for reference to understand the characteristics of the stage of China's economic development and its future evolutionary trend. First, the rising rate of return on capital and the sustained high economic growth in China in recent years are attributable to the technology spillover effect in the process of investment and production on the one hand, and are supported by the transfer of agricultural labor on the other hand. Now, the ratio of the agricultural labor force in China still exceeds 30%. Compared with the steady level of less than 10% in developed countries, China's agricultural labor force still has a great potential of transfer in the coming 20 years. However, the report on the monitoring survey on migrant workers in recent years shows that the transfer of agricultural labor has slowed down. The research in this book indicates that China's technology spillover effect only meets the weak condition, and therefore is solely unable to support the rise or maintenance of the rate of return on capital. As the tide of labor migration fades, China needs to create new growth mechanisms to ensure the high rate of return on capital. Therefore, there is a great deal of room for further improvement of policies. Currently, we should actively implement policies to promote the transfer of agricultural labor, give full play to the combined effect of the transfer of labor and technology spillover in the promotion of capital return, and continue the period of rapid economic growth. Besides, we should formulate and put into practice policies to promote technological innovation, raise the level of the technology spillover effect, and make preparations for meeting the strong condition of capital return in the future.

Second, China's excessively high rate of saving has led to a serious imbalance in the internal and external structure of China, and has even led to global structural imbalance to some extent, further resulting in a housing price bubble and a financial crisis. This book explains the reasons for China's high rate of saving from the perspective of household savings, and thus provides ideas for alleviating structural imbalances. The research in this book suggests that narrowing the urban–rural gap in the level of social medical security will be an effective measure to improve the level of consumption and reduce the rate of saving. The reason why the transfer of labor force has pushed up the household rate of saving is that, in spite of a significant increase in income, the level of social medical security accessible to the migrant workers still has a great deal of room for further improvement, so that the migrant workers have a high tendency to precautionary saving and do not convert their increased income into effective consumption. Therefore, establishing a unified system of social medical security can help improve the level of social medical security accessible to the migrant workers, promote the consumption of farmers, especially migrant workers, and reduce the rate of household saving, thus contributing to a decline in the national rate of saving. Moreover, an improvement in the level of social medical security of the migrant workers can also help increase the labor costs of enterprises, thus reducing the surplus profits of enterprises and the rate of saving of enterprises and further lead to a decline in the national rate of saving. From the perspective of sociology, a unified system of social medical security is essential for achieving social equity. The citizens with equal rights are supposed to enjoy equal interests in their social medical security. In the context of the increasing urban–rural income gap, narrowing the urban–rural gap in the level of social medical security will also help narrow the real urban–rural income gap. In addition to a unified system of social medical security, reducing the transfer costs of agricultural labor is also an effective measure to reduce the rate of saving. The research in this book reveals that the greater the cost of the transfer of labor in urban and rural areas, the greater the labor remuneration gap between migrant workers and farmers. In the process of the transfer of labor, the migrant workers make a greater contribution to the growth rate of the total social savings than the growth rate of the total labor remuneration, thus resulting in the rise of the total rate of social saving. This means that reducing the cost of the transfer of agricultural labor can facilitate the transfer of labor, support the development of the non-agricultural sector, narrow the labor remuneration gap between migrant workers and farmers, and reduce the rising rate of saving brought about by the transfer of labor. In terms of the policy level, the government can effectively reduce the cost of the transfer of labor by strengthening the construction of infrastructure that is conducive to the transfer of labor, safeguarding the rights and interests of migrant workers in cities, etc.

Third, in view of the fact that the standard model of Okun's law is not applicable to China's empirical data, this book proposes the concept of generalizing Okun's law by introducing the variable of the transfer of agricultural labor, and conducts an empirical test of Okun's law by using China's empirical data and transnational panel data containing more than 100 samples of countries. The generalized Okun's law holds that, for a country, the correlation between the labor market and macroeconomic fluctuation not only depends on the indicator of the unemployment rate emphasized by the standard textbook model but is also subject to the characteristics of different stages of development and the relative importance of the transfer of agricultural labor to economic growth. The textbook Okun model, which only includes the variable of the unemployment rate, is applicable to developed countries that have completed the transfer of labor. The Okun model applicable to most economies in transition should include the key structural variable of the transfer of agricultural labor. Therefore, the standard textbook model can be regarded as a special case of the generalized Okun's law. The research in this book helps to broaden the understanding of the general form of the relationship between the labor market and macroeconomic cycle fluctuation. The exploration of some important characteristics and phenomena in China's transition period may go beyond the limitations in the basic assumptions of the traditional standard textbook model and deepen the understanding of some macroeconomic relations. Furthermore, the empirical analysis of China's Okun relationship highlights some characteristics of the change in China's unemployment rate and the transfer of labor under a specific system and policy environment. The results of the equation to obtain an estimation for China's Okun relationship provide an empirical reference or benchmark for discussing and evaluating the internal relations and laws between the labor market and macroeconomic fluctuation in different periods.

Fourth, the agricultural labor force still has a huge potential for transfer, and the potential "transition dividend" will continue to bring about a huge growth effect in the long run. It is not pessimistic about whether China can successfully get out of the middle-income trap. For instance, improving the level of the construction of infrastructure is a powerful measure to promote the transfer of agricultural labor, as well as a crucial material basis for industrialization and urbanization. Although the scale of infrastructure in China has been growing rapidly in recent years, the level of infrastructure remains to be further improved in terms of international comparison. In the event of a macroeconomic downturn, the government may take an opportunity to strengthen the construction of infrastructure and increase the investment in infrastructure that is conducive to improving economic efficiency and effectively promoting the transfer of agricultural labor. In a short run, investment in infrastructure, as a means of the government's expansionary fiscal policy, can boost the domestic demand and prevent excessive economic decline under the current economic slowdown. In a medium to long run, the expansion of infrastructure can raise the efficiency of economic operations, facilitate the transfer of agricultural labor, narrow the urban–rural income gap, and create favorable conditions for a smooth economic transformation, thus laying a solid foundation for China's urbanization and modernization. Undoubtedly, we should give importance to optimizing the direction and structure of government-led investment in infrastructure, and appropriately encourage the introduction of some private capital in the specific process of implementation, so as to play the role of infrastructure in the improvement of production efficiency and the income distribution of residents.

Fifth, China's economy has been at a crucial stage of the optimization of the economic growth rate and structural adjustment after more than 30 years of rapid economic growth. On the one hand, China still has a large number of the members of the agricultural labor force to be transferred. In 2013, the ratio of the agricultural labor force exceeded over 30%. On the other hand, the developed provinces along the east coast have frequently suffered "labor shortage" in recent years: despite the rapid rise in labor wages, many enterprises still face a labor shortage, which has become an important factor in the declining international competitiveness of Chinese enterprises. Therefore, we should continue to promote the fundamental role of the transfer of agricultural labor in China's rapid economic growth, and pay a great amount of attention to the following two aspects in the future. First, it is important to boost agricultural labor productivity and give full play to its supporting role. Due to the transformation of the reform and opening-up system, China's economy has grown at an average annual rate of about 10% over the past 30 years, and with the rapid transformation of China's economic structure toward industrialization and urbanization, China has shifted from the poorest country in the international comparison and has initially entered the ranks of middle-income countries. All this has been achieved on the basis of the rapid evolution of the function of agricultural production and the upward trend of the capacity of agricultural production. In the future, China's smooth economic transformation is still bound to depend on the upward trend of agricultural productivity. Second, the driving factors of the transfer of agricultural labor continue to actively promote the transfer of labor. The research in this book shows that a variety of measures can significantly contribute to the transfer of labor, such as improving the level of infrastructure and return on capital, promoting economic growth, reducing the proportion of state-owned enterprises or facilitating the development of the private sector, correcting the current biased financial development and public education expenditure, etc.

II. The Directions of Future Research

This book analyzes China's economy from the perspective of the transfer of agricultural labor, explains the three basic characteristics of China's economic development, and makes some achievements in understanding China's mechanism of economic development. However, due to limited knowledge and objective conditions such as data availability, this book still has the following shortcomings needing to be further improved, which are also the directions of the future research of this book.

First, the research in this book remains to be further improved in the comprehensive and systematic understanding of China's mechanism of economic development. The theoretical model and empirical analysis in this book indeed explain some aspects of China's economy, but many important issues are still not analyzed profoundly. For example, although this book involves the transformation of the industrial structure, and focuses on the analysis of the decline in the proportion of agriculture, the transformation of the industrial structure has richer meanings to be explored. Especially, the rise of the proportion of the service industry is not analyzed in this book, which is exactly the direction that needs to be further studied in-depth in the future. In addition, this book takes the transfer of agricultural labor as a starting point to analyze several major aspects of economic development, but the links among them are not closely analyzed, and therefore need to be considered in this book in the future.

Second, the object of research in this book is a large closed economy, without considering China's external sectors. However, as the second largest trading country and the third largest outward foreign direct investment (OFDI) country in the world, China has a strong interaction with the world in terms of economy. With full realization of the importance of the external sector, the author has analyzed the relationship between China's OFDI and trade in a special article. Unfortunately, the author has not succeeded in properly introducing it into this book, which is a key aspect that needs to be improved in the future.

Third, due to the limitation of data availability or other conditions, some problems are not addressed temporarily in this book, and need to be further discussed if the objective conditions permit in the future. For example, based on the logic of theoretical analysis, the generalized Okun model is estimated by using multinational data and Chinese data, respectively, in Chapter 5. The data of many countries show that the transfer of agricultural labor and the unemployment rate coincide well with the predictions of the theoretical model, which supports the theoretical extrapolation of the generalized Okun's law. However, the results of the estimation of China's model of the Okun relationship show that the results of the estimation of China's unemployment rate variable are still not significant, though a significant positive correction exists between the transfer of agricultural labor and macroeconomic fluctuations, consistent with theoretical predictions. One of the four explanations given in this book is the possible impact of incomplete unemployment data in China. China's insignificant unemployment indicator is worth discussing. However, in view of the unavailable historical data of the survey of the unemployment rate at the national level, this book cannot verify this conjecture, which greatly limits the research conclusions of this book. With the release of the surveyed unemployment data by the National Bureau of Statistics, it will be possible to further improve the research regarding this aspect in this book.

In summary, the research in this book still remains at a primary stage, and therefore, needs to be further improved. Besides, there is also a great deal of room for improvement in the style of writing. It is a pity that the author is not so talented, so the author is willing to discuss and draw out further criticism from all of the people who read this book.

Appendix A: Proof of Lemma in Chapter 4

I. Proof of Lemma 3

(1) According to $\beta > \varphi(\theta)$, $W(K) \geqslant 0$, $L \geqslant 0$ we can obtain $F(K) \geqslant 0$.

Besides, since $F(K)$ is continuous in the whole space, we can obtain $\lim_{K \to 0} F(K) \geqslant 0$ by the limit number theorem.

(2) If $K \in (0, K_0)$, no transfer of labor exists, thus,

$$F'(K) = \frac{\beta - \varphi(\overline{\theta})}{1 + \beta} W_u'(K) L_u + \frac{\beta - \varphi(\theta)}{1 + \beta} W_a'(K) L_a, \qquad (29)$$

where

$$W_u'(K) = \frac{1 - \alpha}{1 + \varphi(\overline{\theta})} \alpha K^{\alpha - 1} \left(A_u L_u \right)^{-\alpha} A_u, \qquad (30)$$

$$W_a'(K) = 0. \qquad (31)$$

Obviously, $F'(K) > 0$.

162   *Appendix A*

If $K \in (K_0, \infty)$,

$$F'(K) = \frac{\beta - \varphi(\bar{\theta})}{1+\beta} W_u'(K)L_u + \frac{\beta - \varphi(\underline{\theta})}{1+\beta} W_m'(K)L_m(K) + \frac{\beta - \varphi(\theta)}{1+\beta},$$

$$W_m(K)L_m'(K) + \frac{\beta - \varphi(\theta)}{1+\beta} W_a'(K)L_a(K) + \frac{\beta - \varphi(\theta)}{1+\beta} W_a(K)L_a'(K),$$

where $W_u'(K) > 0$, $W_m'(K) > 0$, $W_a'(K) > 0$, $L_m'(K) > 0$ and

$$L_a'(K) = -L_m'(K).$$

After sorting out,

$$F'(K) = \frac{\beta - \varphi(\bar{\theta})}{1+\beta} W_u'(K)L_u + \frac{\beta - \varphi(\theta)}{1+\beta} W_m'(K)L_m(K) + \frac{\beta - \varphi(\theta)}{1+\beta}.$$

$$W_a'(K)L_a(K) + \left[\frac{\beta - \varphi(\theta)}{1+\beta} W_m(K) - \frac{\beta - \varphi(\theta)}{1+\beta} W_a(K) \right] L_m'(K) \qquad (32)$$

and if $\tau > 1$, we can obtain $W_m(K) > W_a(K)$, so $F'(K) > 01$.

(3) $\lim\limits_{K \to 0} F'(K) = \infty$, $\lim\limits_{K \to \infty} F'(K) = 0$.

According to (2), if $K \to 0$, then $F'(K) \to \infty$.
If $K \to \infty$, the limit for Eq. (18) is solved to obtain

$$\lim\limits_{K \to \infty} L_m(K) = N_a$$

and

$$\lim\limits_{K \to \infty} F(K) = \infty$$

and

$$\lim\limits_{K \to \infty} \frac{W_a(K)}{K} = \lim\limits_{K \to \infty} \frac{W_m(K)}{K} = \lim\limits_{K \to \infty} \frac{W_u(K)}{K} = 0.$$

According to L'Hospital's rule,

$$\lim_{K \to \infty} F'(K) = \lim_{K \to \infty} \frac{F(K)}{K} = 0.$$

II. Proof of Theorem 1

According to the proof process of A1 (3), we can obtain $\lim\limits_{K \to \infty} \frac{F(K)}{K} = 0$.

There is $\overline{K} > 0$ according to the limit number theorem. If $K > \overline{K}$, $\frac{F(K)}{K} < 1$, that is, $F(K) < K$.

But $F(0) \geqslant 0$, due to the continuity of function, we can obtain $\overline{\overline{K}} > 0$, thus $F(\overline{\overline{K}}) = \overline{\overline{K}}$ and there is an interval $(\overline{\overline{K}} - \varepsilon, K + \varepsilon)$. If $K \in (\overline{\overline{K}} - \varepsilon, \overline{\overline{K}})$, $F(K) > K$, but if $K \in (\overline{\overline{K}}, \overline{\overline{K}} + \varepsilon)$, $F(K) < K$, this means that the equilibrium is stable and balanced.

III. Proof of Theorem 2

It is only necessary to prove that the steady-state equilibrium $\widetilde{K} > 0$ in the absence of transfer of labor will at least stay in the original equilibrium when transfer of labor is permitted, or it may climb to a new higher equilibrium, that is, proof $F(\widetilde{K}) \geqslant \widetilde{K}$.

To prove

$$\frac{\beta - \varphi(\theta)}{1 + \beta} W_m(\widetilde{K}) L_m(\widetilde{K}) + \frac{\beta - \varphi(\theta)}{1 + \beta} W_a(\widetilde{K}) L_a(\widetilde{K}) \geqslant \frac{\beta - \varphi(\theta)}{1 + \beta} W_a(\widetilde{K}) L_a.$$

Thus,

$$W_m(\widetilde{K}) \geqslant W_a(\widetilde{K})$$

$\tau > 1$, thus showing the completion of the proof of the theorem.

Appendix B: Driving Factors and Spillover Effects of the Transfer of Agricultural Labor

I. Introduction

The transfer of agricultural labor to the non-agricultural sector is a key issue of development economics. In the Lewis dual economy model, the agricultural labor force continues to transfer to the non-agricultural sector with the development of the non-agricultural sector, and that transfer depends on the demand of the non-agricultural sector for the agricultural labor force. The demand is directly affected by the marginal labor productivity of the non-agricultural sector. The higher marginal labor productivity of the non-agricultural sector makes enterprises have more incentive to hire more labor force, thus leading to the higher degree of transfer of labor.[1] Therefore, the marginal labor productivity–wage return of the non-agricultural sector constitutes the main determining force of the transfer of labor.

---

[1]Lewis, W. A.: Economic Development with Unlimited Supplies of Labour, *Manchester School*, 1954 (22) (2), pp. 139–191; Harris, J. R. and M. P. Todar: Migration, Unemployment and Development: A Two-Sector Analysis, *American Economic Review*, 1970 (60) (1), pp. 126–142.

The Lewis model has laid a basic analytical framework for the study of the transfer of labor in developing economies and guided the theoretical research to enrich and improve the dual structure model in combination with the actual situation. Harris–Todaro pioneered the study of cross-sectoral transfer of labor. Grinols, Chandra and Khan divided the industrial sector into formal and informal sectors. A labor migration model was established under the premise that the unemployed people of the urban formal sector are completely absorbed by the informal sector. Gupta expanded the model of Chandra and Khan by introducing the migration cost, and formed the CKG framework[2] for research on the transfer of labor.

In reality, on the one hand, scholars have observed the prevalent phenomenon of "semi-urbanization" in Latin America and other regions and directly related it to the informal employment issue.[3] This phenomenon has also obviously been reflected and manifested with different forms in the non-agricultural process of China's labor population. The term, "migrant worker", reflects the contradictions between the identity and lifestyle of most transferred workers and the industrialization input of labor factors, which can be regarded as a special phenomenon of "semi-urbanization".[4] This means that the transfer of labor will encounter various obstacles in reality, including move-in, move-out and mobility barriers, and thus face the impact of transfer costs. On the other hand, with the slowdown of the transfer of labor in recent years, the wages of China's

---

[2]Harris, J. R. and M. P. Todar: Migration, Unemployment and Development: A Two-Sector Analysis, *American Economic Review*, 1970 (60) (1), pp. 126–140. Grinols, Earl L.: Unemployment and Foreign Capital: The Relative Opportunity Costs of Domestic Labour and Welfare, *Economica*, 1991 (58), pp. 107–121. Chandra, V. and M. Khan: Foreign Investment in the Presence of an Informal Sector, *Economica*, 1993 (60), pp. 79–103. Gupta, M. R.: Foreign Capital and the Informal Sector: Comments on Chandra and Khan, *Economica*, 1997 (64) (254), pp. 353–363. Chandra, V. and M. Khan: Foreign Investment in the Presence of an Informal Sector, *Economica*, 1993 (60), pp. 79–103.
[3]Jacoby, Erich H.: The Coming Backlash of Semi-Urbanization, *Ceres* (*FAO Review*), 1970 (3) (6), pp. 48–51.
[4]Wei Houkai: China's Urbanization Strategy for the 21st Century, *Management World*, 1998 (1), pp. 191–196; Wang Chunguang: A Study of Floating Rural People's "Semi-Urbanization", *Sociological Studies*, 2006 (5), pp. 111–126+248.

migrant workers have been rising continuously, thus leading to a coexistence between "sustained and rapid growth of wages of migrant workers" and "a large number of surplus labor in rural areas".[5] Thus, the Lewis model assumes that the non-farm sector can maintain the infinite labor supply under the same level of wages, which means that the marginal labor productivity–wage return of the non-agricultural sector can remain unchanged and continue to absorb the transfer of rural labor, and that the agricultural labor force can achieve free and permanent transfer between the rural and urban areas without costs, neglecting the existence and importance of transfer costs. Therefore, many difficulties are bound to arise in the direct use of the "original" conclusion of the Lewis model to analyze and explain the reality of China, so that serious differences or even misjudgments exist in the issue whether the "Lewis turning point" has come.[6]

So far, China's economic development and experience in transfer of labor has been the successful model of practice of development economics, and its more complex and rich connotations have also constituted the difficulty in expansion and growth point of the theory of development economics. China has transferred more than 270 million migrant workers to the non-agricultural sector over the past 30 years since the reform and opening-up. Such a great number of migrant workers constitutes an important supporting force for China's economic growth, which is conducive to expanding the size of the labor market and improving the total factor productivity of the urban economy.[7] The key to China's long-term and rapid economic growth is to promote the continuous transfer of surplus labor, which can bring huge potential benefits to

---

[5]Li Hongbin and Li Lei: Reducing the Transfer Cost of Migrant Workers and Promoting the Equalization Policy of Welfare, *Chinese Social Sciences Today*, Column 014, August 23, 2011; Lu Feng: Wage Trends among Chinese Migrant Workers: 1979–2010, *Social Sciences in China*, 2012 (7), pp. 48–68+205.
[6]Cai Fang: Growth and Structural Changes in Employment in Transitional China, *Economic Research Journal*, 2007 (7), pp. 5–15+23.
[7]Du Yang, Cai Fang, Qu Xiaobo and Cheng Jie: Sustain the China Miracle: Reaping the Dividends from Hukou Reforms, *Economic Research Journal*, 2014 (8), pp. 4–13+78.

China's economy.[8] With 30 years of rapid economic growth, China's economy has entered a critical stage of optimizing the economic growth rate and structural adjustment. On the one hand, the agricultural labor force mostly still stays in rural areas and China's current agricultural labor force accounts for more than 30%; on the other hand, the developed provinces along the east coast have frequently suffered a "labor shortage" in recent years: despite the rapid rise in labor wages, many enterprises still face a shortage of labor, which has become an important factor in the declining international competitiveness of Chinese enterprises. Against this background, how to promote the transfer of agricultural surplus labor has become an important and urgent task to be addressed.

To solve this practical problem, it is necessary to further clarify the determinants of the transfer of labor theoretically. Why did rural labor transfer on a large scale and show an extremely obvious characteristic of spatial agglomeration in the past 30 years or so? What factors influence this process to present a change in turning point? How does urban–rural productivity difference form and apply to the transfer of labor? Are there more specific factors that affect China's transfer of labor apart from the urban–rural productivity differences? We can truly grasp the internal laws of the historical process of the transfer of labor in China only by clarifying these general and special factors, thus providing targeted countermeasures for further promoting the transfer of labor, the reform of the labor factor market and economic growth in the next stage.

It is further noted that the government sector is not incorporated into the traditional dual structure-transfer of labor model, which is crucial for developing countries. The "Big Push" balanced strategy of development, the "take-off" leading industry and unbalanced growth theory, the flying geese model of the newly industrialized economies, the successful experience of the East Asia model and its underlying unsustainability all show

---

[8]Li Yang and Yin Jianfeng: High Savings, High Investment, and China's Economic Growth in the Process of the Transfer of Labor, *Economic Research Journal*, 2005 (2), pp. 4–15+25; Du Yang, Cai Fang, Qu Xiaobo and Cheng Jie: Sustain the China Miracle: Reaping the Dividends from Hukou Reforms, *Economic Research Journal*, 2014 (8), pp. 4–13+78.

that the strategy of development and industrial policy are lingering shadows, and the government that develops and implements the strategic policy is key to success or failure.[9] As we all know, the government departments and their patterns of behavior are the primary factors that cannot be avoided in the process of China's economic development. The government-led system of mobilizing resource allocation and the invest-ment-driven economic growth model have become the consensus descrip-tion. When it comes to the issue of the transfer of labor, the dual distribution of population–labor force is actually formed in the context of the urban–rural household registration system compulsively established by the government and the difference in welfare security. Such structural evolution can only be investigated in the process of government-led economic development. For this reason, during the analysis of the driving factors of the transfer of agricultural labor, this section develops a trans-formation model of the dual economic structure of endogenous growth by introducing the infrastructure of government productive expenditure capi-talization based on the classic dual economic model, so as to explore the transfer of labor under the dual economic structure evolution, and carry out the empirical analysis of China's provincial panel data, thus providing empirical evidence for theoretical analysis.

This chapter is organized as follows: The second section describes the process of China's transfer of labor by a theoretical model in the context

---

[9]Roodman, D.: A Note on the Theme of Too Many Instruments, *Oxford Bulletin of Economics and Statistics*, 2009 (71) (1), pp. 135– 158. Rosenstein-Rodan, P. N.: The Problem of Industrialization of Eastern and South-Eastern Europe, *Economic Journal*, 1943 (53) (210– 211), pp. 202–211; Murphy, Kevin M., Andrei Shleifer and Robert W. Vishny: Industrialization and the Big Push, *Journal of Political Economy*, 1989 (97) (5), pp. 1003–1026; Rostow, W. W.: The Take-Off into Self-Sustained Growth, *Economic Journal*, 1956 (66) (261), pp. 25–48; Acemoglu, Daron and Veronica Guerrieri: Capital Deepening and Nonbalanced Economic Growth, *Journal of Political Economy*, 2008 (116) (3), pp. 467–498; Krugman, Paul: The Myth of Asia's Miracle, *Foreign Affairs*, 1994 (73) (6), pp. 62– 78; Kojima, K.: The "Flying Geese" Model of Asian Economic Development: Origin, Theoretical Extensions, and Regional Policy Implications, *Journal of Asian Economics*, 2000 (11) (4), pp. 375–401; Lin Yifu and Ren Ruoen: East Asian Miracle Debate Revisited, *Economic Research Journal*, 2007 (8), pp. 6–14+59.

of dual economic transformation, and discusses the spillover effect and its impact on economic development in this process.

II. Theoretical Model

This section first constructs a model of partial equilibrium analysis to analyze the process of the transfer of agricultural labor and highlight the relationship between infrastructure and the transfer of labor. The infrastructure and the costs of the transfer of labor are introduced under the dual economic framework, and the spillover effects caused by the differences in production efficiency among sectors are mainly investigated, as well as the effects of the improvement of the efficiency of infrastructure production and the reduction of transfer costs on the transfer of labor, so as to make an in-depth analysis of the role of public infrastructure in the development of a dual economy.

1. *Model specification*

It is assumed that an economy consists of two production sectors, i.e., agricultural sector a, and non-agricultural sector b. The initial labor force of the two sectors is N_a and N_b, respectively. The total labor force is $N = N_a + N_b$. To simplify the analysis, this chapter assumes that the total labor force remains unchanged. $u_1 = N_b/N$, which is the non-agricultural (urbanization) ratio of the labor force to represent the absolute level of the transfer of labor; $u_2 = N_b/N_a$, which is the ratio between urban and rural areas to represent the relative level of the transfer of labor. For the sake of simplicity, semi-urbanization is not considered here.

Non-agricultural sectors employ the N_b unit labor and K unit capital for production, and the production function is expressed as follows:

$$Y_b = \hat{A}(g)K^\alpha g^{1-\alpha} N_b^{1-\alpha}, \tag{1}$$

where $0 < \alpha < 1$ is the elasticity of the private capital output of the non-agricultural sector; g is the level of public infrastructure, which has two basic functions under the setting of this function. One is to directly enter the production function as productive capital,[10] and the other is to have a spillover effect on the technical level.[11] Meanwhile, it is assumed that the financing of infrastructure comes from capital tax, i.e., $g = \tau K$, where τ is the capital tax rate;[12] $\hat{A}$ is the level of production technology of the non-agricultural sector, affected by the spillover effect of public infrastructure, that is, $\hat{A}$, $(g) > 0$; besides, make $A = \tau^{1-a}\hat{A}$, where A and $\hat{A}$ are equivalent in meaning, thus leading to $A'(g) > 0$. Therefore, the production function is converted into the following:

$$Y_b = \hat{A}(g)\tau^{1-a}KN_b^{1-a} = A(g)KN_b^{1-a}. \tag{2}$$

　　Apparently, it is an endogenous economy of increasing returns to scale from government capitalization of productive expenditure. In this section, the difference between the production function setting of the non-agricultural sector and the standard dual economic model is that endogenous capital deepening and endogenous technological progress represented by public infrastructure are added to the model. Therefore, the model in this chapter is the dual economic model of the endogenous growth of modern sectors.

---

[10]When it is entered into the production function as productive capital, the elasticity of output is assumed to be $1 - \alpha$ to simplify the following calculations. It can be proved that this simplified assumption will not materially affect the conclusions of this section.

[11]Barro, R.: Government Spending in a Simple Model of Endogenous Growth, *Journal of Political Economy*, 1990 (98), pp. 103–125. Alesina, Alberto and Dani Rodrik: Distributive Politics and Economic Growth, *Quarterly Journal of Economics*, 1994 (109), pp. 465–490. Hulten, R., E. Bennathan and S. Srinivasan: Infrastructure, Externalities, and Economic Development: A Study of the Indian Manufacturing Industry, *World Bank Economic Review*, 2006 (20) (2), pp. 291–308.

[12]Here, infrastructure financing will not be discussed, and the capital tax rate is directly assumed to be a constant. The improvement of the level of infrastructure can, on the one hand, raise capital marginal output and promote capital accumulation, and on the other hand, reduce the real rate of return on capital and restrict capital accumulation, because infrastructure financing comes from capital tax. Thus, it can be argued that there is an optimal capital tax rate that enables the economy to grow at the highest rate. Due to limited space, the derivation process will not be described in detail here, and the discussion on the optimal capital tax rate is also beyond the scope of this section. Readers who are interested in it may contact the author to request the derivation results.

Agricultural sectors use N_a unit labor for production:

$$Y_a = N_a^\gamma = (N - N_b)^\gamma, \tag{3}$$

where $0 < \gamma < 1$ is the elasticity of the labor output of the agricultural sector.

As the non-agricultural sector develops, the distribution of the transferred labor force is subject to the supply of non-transferred labor force, and the wage rate is maintained at the marginal productivity level, so that the non-agricultural sector has more surplus shares for additional capital accumulation, thus accelerating economic industrialization (non-agriculturization). The demand for the corresponding labor will increase with the accumulation of capitals, and the production efficiency of the transfer of labor will also increase with the deepening of capitals and the improvement of technical conditions. As a result, its marginal product-wage return rises accordingly, and the agricultural labor constantly shifts from the agricultural sector to the urban non-agricultural sector until the transfer process ends completely. In this process, two issues remain to be confirmed, namely, $\lim_{N_b \to \infty} u_1 = 1$ and $\lim_{N_b \to \infty} u_2 = \infty$. However, due to various obstacles in reality, the transfer of labor is insufficient, despite a higher wage level in the non-agricultural sector than in the agricultural sector. This chapter summarizes the obstacles leading to the insufficient transfer of agricultural labor as the existence of transfer costs.

(1) *Balance*

According to the foregoing model specification, both the agricultural sector and non-agricultural sector select the optimal number of labor and capital to maximize output. The first-order condition meets the following:

$$W_a = \gamma(N - N_b)^{\gamma-1}. \tag{4}$$

$$W_b = (1 - \alpha)A(g)KN_b^{-\alpha}. \tag{5}$$

$$R_b = A(g)N_b^{1-\alpha}. \tag{6}$$

W_a and W_b are the wage levels of the agricultural sector and non-agricultural sector, respectively, and R_b is the rate of return on capital of the non-agricultural sector.

In the presence of transfer costs, when the transfer of labor is balanced, the relationship between the wages of the two sectors is determined by the following formula:

$$W_b = (1+\theta)W_a, \tag{7}$$

where $\theta > 0$ is the discount factor reflecting the transfer costs. According to Eqs. (4), (5) and (7), we can obtain the following:

$$(1-\alpha)A(g)KN_b^{-\alpha} = (1+\theta)\gamma(N-N_b)^{\gamma-1}. \tag{8}$$

Therefore, theorems 1 and 2 are given in this chapter:

Theorem 1: The transfer of labor depends on the difference of factor productivity between the two sectors and the transfer costs.

After the expansion and sorting out of the foregoing formula, we get

$$N_b = \left[\frac{(1+\theta)\gamma}{(1-\alpha)}\right]^{-\left(\frac{1}{\alpha}\right)}\left[\frac{N_a^{\gamma}}{A(g)KN_a^{[(1-\alpha)+\alpha]}}\right]^{-\left(\frac{1}{\alpha}\right)} = N_a\left[\frac{(1-\alpha)}{(1+\theta)\gamma}\right]^{\frac{1}{\alpha}}\left[\frac{A(g)KN_a^{(1-\alpha)}}{N_a^{\gamma}}\right]^{\frac{1}{\alpha}},$$

namely,

$$\frac{N_b}{N_a} = \left[\frac{(1-\alpha)}{(1+\theta)\gamma}\right]^{\frac{1}{\alpha}}\left[\frac{A(g)KN_a^{(1-\alpha)}}{N_a^{\gamma}}\right]^{\frac{1}{\alpha}}. \tag{9}$$

Apparently, the transfer of labor depends on the difference of labor productivity between the two sectors and the transfer costs, so theorem 1 is proved.

Theorem 2: Labor force is constantly transferred to the non-agricultural sector with the continuous accumulation of capitals in the non-agricultural sector.

The derivative of both sides of Eq. (8) with respect to K can be obtained as follows:

$$\frac{dN_b}{dK} = N_b^{-\alpha} \left[\frac{\alpha K}{N_b^{1+\alpha}} + \frac{(1+\theta)\gamma(1-\gamma)}{(1-\alpha)A(g)}(N-N_b)^{\gamma-2} \right]^{-1} > 0$$

$$\frac{dN_a}{dK} = \frac{d(N-N_b)}{dK} = -\frac{dN_b}{dK} < 0,$$

namely, with the continuous accumulation of capitals, non-agricultural employment keeps increasing while agricultural employment keeps decreasing, so theorem 2 is proved.

(3) *Labor mobility spillover*

The relationship between capital accumulation and the transfer of labor in the event of equilibrium is discussed above. Next, let us turn to the spillover effect of the flow of labor. For this, theorem 3 is proposed:

Theorem 3: The free migration of workers creates value.

For the proof of this theorem, the following three aspects are discussed: The direct value of free migration to production.

This chapter defines the product marginal rate of transformation (MRT)[13] of the two sectors as

$$\lambda \equiv -\frac{dY_b}{dY_a} = -\frac{dY_b / dN_a}{dY_a / dN_a}. \tag{10}$$

$$\frac{dY_b}{dN_a} = \frac{d\left[A(g)KN_b^{1-\alpha}\right]}{dN_a} = \frac{d\left[A(g)K\left(N-N_a\right)^{1-\alpha}\right]}{dN_a}$$

$$= -(1-\alpha)A(g)K(N-N_a)^{-\alpha} = -(1-\alpha)A(g)KN_b^{-\alpha} = -W_b$$

---

[13]The product marginal rate of transformation is also referred to as rate of product transformation or marginal rate of transformation, which indicates the output of product 2 to be abandoned for the increase of one unit product 1 under a given social resource condition, usually abbreviated as RPT1, 2. This means that a "transformation" relationship exists between the two products. This transformation relationship is known as "the MRT of product". In addition, the product MRT is the absolute value of the slope of the production possibility curve.

$$\frac{\mathrm{d}Y_a}{\mathrm{d}N_a} = \gamma N_a^{\gamma-1} = W_a.$$

Thus,

$$\lambda = \frac{W_b}{W_a}. \tag{11}$$

The MRT of the two-sector products is equal to the ratio of two-sector marginal outputs. According to the definition of product MRT, $\lambda > 1$ means that the increase of one unit of agricultural products needs to give up more than one unit of non-agricultural products, that is, a decrease of one unit of agricultural products can increase more than one unit of non-agricultural products. $\lambda < 1$ means that the increase of one unit of agricultural products requires the abandonment of less than one unit of non-agricultural products, that is, a decrease of one unit of agricultural products can increase less than one unit of non-agricultural products:

$$-\frac{\partial \lambda}{\partial N_b} = \frac{\partial \lambda}{\partial N_a} = \frac{\partial \left(\dfrac{(1-\alpha)AK(N-N_a)^{-\alpha}}{\gamma N_a^{\gamma-1}} \right)}{\partial N_a} = \frac{1-\alpha}{\gamma}$$

$$A(g)K(N-N_a)^{-\alpha} N_a^{1-\gamma} \left(\frac{\alpha}{N-N_a} + \frac{1-\gamma}{N_a} \right) > 0. \tag{12}$$

Therefore, with the transfer of agricultural labor, the number of agricultural labor is decreasing, while that of the non-agricultural labor is increasing, thus leading to a decline in the product rate of transformation.

In Figure A.1 in the Appendix, the λ curve reflects the variation of the MRT of the two-sector products with the number of non-agricultural labor. The area below the λ curve and above the $\lambda = 1$ curve indicates the increase in the total output of the agricultural labor that has been transferred to the non-agricultural sector, that is, the "spillover effect". The black area indicates the increase in total output due to the spillover effect when the number of non-agricultural labor increases from N_{b1} to N_{b2}. As long as $\lambda > 1$, the transfer of labor can create a spillover effect.

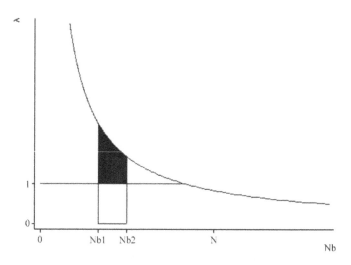

Figure A.1. MRT and the number of non-agricultural labor.

Due to the existence of transfer costs, the wages of the two sectors are determined by Eq. (13):

$$W_b = (1 + \theta)W_a. \tag{13}$$

$\theta > 0$ is the discount factor reflecting the transfer cost, thus,

$$\lambda = \frac{W_b}{W_a} = 1 + \theta > 1. \tag{14}$$

Therefore, with the transfer of agricultural labor to the non-agricultural sector, the total output of the two sectors will increase, reflecting that the transfer of agricultural labor to the non-agricultural sector creates an efficiency spillover.

Even when the transfer of agricultural labor reaches an equilibrium, $\lambda = (1 + \theta) > 1$, transfer of labor still has a "potential spillover effect" until $\lambda = 1$. At this time, if the transfer cost θ can be reduced, the transfer of labor will continue to occur, during which the potential spillover effect will be converted into the actual spillover effect. This process is also a process of the internalization of transfer costs. In view of the fact that the infrastructure can contribute to the reduction in the costs of the transfer of labor, this section presents the following propositions:

1. Infrastructure can increase efficiency spillovers by reducing transfer cost and facilitating the transfer of labor.
2. Free migration can make contributions to the output of capital accumulation.

The contribution of free migration of labor to the output of capital accumulation can be expressed as

$$\frac{\partial \lambda}{\partial K} = \frac{\partial \left(\dfrac{(1-\alpha)AK(N-N_a)^{-\alpha}}{\gamma N_a^{\gamma-1}} \right)}{\partial K} = \frac{(1-\alpha)A(g)(N-N_a)^{-\alpha}}{\gamma N_a^{\gamma-1}} \equiv S_K^* > 0, \quad (15)$$

where S_K^* is the efficiency spillover of capital, which reflects the increase in capital return.

(4) *Free migration and technology spillover*

The free migration of labor can also bring about technology spillovers:

$$\frac{\partial \lambda}{\partial A} = \frac{\partial \left(\dfrac{(1-\alpha)AK(N-N_a)^{-\alpha}}{\gamma N_a^{\gamma-1}} \right)}{\partial A} = \frac{(1-\alpha)K(N-N_a)^{-\alpha}}{\gamma N_a^{\gamma-1}} \equiv S_A^* > 0, \quad (16)$$

where S_A^* is the contribution spillover of technological progress. It can be seen that the transfer of labor not only improves its own efficiency but also enhances the contribution of capital and technology to output. The improvement of efficiency of the two factors only benefits from the positive spillover of the scale effect rather than depending on whether the efficiency of the transferred labor has increased. Focusing only on technology spillovers indeed underestimates the total effect of the transfer of labor on the factor efficiency.

This chapter further discusses the issue of liquidity spillover in infrastructure. From Eq. (16), this chapter introduces the contribution of technological progress caused by the public infrastructure, so the infrastructure has an efficiency spillover, namely,

$$\frac{\partial \lambda}{\partial g} = \frac{\partial \lambda}{\partial A(g)} \frac{\mathrm{d}A(g)}{\mathrm{d}g} = S_A^* A'(g) > 0, \tag{17}$$

where $S_A^* A'(g)$ is the contribution spillover of technological progress caused by public infrastructure; due to the public goods attribute, it is fully reflected in the positive spillover of returns to other factors, and the neutrality, capital bias or labor bias of the technological progress.

From another perspective, this chapter can decompose the MRT, namely,

$$\lambda = \frac{W_b}{W_a} = \frac{(1-\alpha)A(g)KN_b^{-\alpha}}{\gamma(N-N_b)^{\gamma-1}} = \frac{(1-\alpha)AKN_b^{-\alpha}}{\gamma(N-N_b)^{\gamma-1}} + \frac{(1-\alpha)[A(g)-A]KN_b^{-\alpha}}{\gamma(N-N_b)^{\gamma-1}} = 1 + \theta. \tag{18}$$

If $\frac{(1-\alpha)AKN_b^{-\alpha}}{\gamma(N-N_b)^{\gamma-1}} = 1$ and $A = 1$ (i.e., initial marginal wage equivalent), $\frac{(1-\alpha)[A(g)-A]KN_b^{-\alpha}}{\gamma(N-N_b)^{\gamma-1}} = \theta \geqslant 0$. In other words, the technological advancement of the public infrastructure and the deepening effect of capitals together constitute the internalization of the cost of transfer.

Thus, the transfer of labor from the agricultural sector to the modern sector has produced productivity spillovers. This efficiency spillover originates from the differences in production conditions between the traditional agricultural sector and the modern sector, especially the capital deepening and technological improvements resulting from investment in public infrastructures. Conversely, in case there is no increase in wages due to the efficiency spillover, the internalization of the costs of the transfer of labor will not be achieved, and thus it will be impossible to carry out transfer with welfare improvements.

In general, as the productivity of the modern sector is promoted by infrastructure both directly and indirectly, infrastructure and transfer of labor will have a positive relationship, so Theorem 4 is generated:

Theorem 4: An increase in the level of infrastructure will facilitate the transfer of labor from the agricultural sector to the non-agricultural sector under a given capital stock K.

The partial derivative with respect to g from the two sides of Eq. (8) is solved thus:

$$\frac{\partial N_b}{\partial g} = \left(\frac{A'(g)}{A(g)} \right) \Big/ \left(\frac{1-\gamma}{N-N_b} + \frac{\alpha}{N_b} \right) > 0. \tag{19}$$

Therefore,

$$\frac{\partial u}{\partial g} = \frac{1}{N} \frac{\partial N_b}{\partial g} > 0. \tag{20}$$

Theorem 4 is proved.

The effect of the reduction of the cost of transfer brought about by public infrastructure is discussed above, as well as the spillover of the transfer of labor caused by technological progress and the capital deepening effect. On the balanced path, the improvement of level of infrastructure will promote the transfer of labor, thus boosting economic growth. In addition, the unbalanced situation can also be discussed: Suppose that the economy initially strictly controls the transfer of labor, causing a separated development of the agricultural sector and the non-agricultural sector, the capital accumulation and technical progress of the non-agricultural sector will make its marginal labor productivity increase significantly. As long as the two effects are strong enough, the MRT will be $\lambda > 1 + \theta$. In this case, if the free transfer of labor is allowed, the transfer of labor will bring about the improvement of the overall welfare on the unbalanced path.

The static model analysis does not take into account the dynamic process of investment accumulation in an economy. However, it can be proved that, in the dynamic model considering household utility maximization and capital accumulation, infrastructure can bring about constant production externalities in the long term and thus further promote the transfer of labor, even though it may squeeze some productive capital accumulation in the short term. Intuitively, instead of instant contribution to the transfer of labor, the expansion of the short-term investment in infrastructure squeezes out productive capital and makes the transfer of labor retrograde temporarily. However, in the long run, as the higher level of infrastructure is put into use, the total factor productivity will be further improved, the cost of the transfer of labor will be further reduced, and a larger scale of labor will be invested in the non-agricultural sector for production, so that the amount of capital of the economy will converge to a desirable higher level. This process not only advances the transfer of labor but also further deepens the capital accumulation and the development of the economy at a higher level.[14]

---

[14]Due to limited space, the dynamic model will not be expanded here. If you are interested, please contact the author for the specific derivation process.

Table A.1. Analysis of the Robustness of the Regression of the Transfer of Agricultural Labor.

Explanatory variable: Transfer of agricultural labor	Spatial autoregressive model (SAR)			Spatial error model (SEM)		
	(1)	(2)	(3)	(4)	(5)	(6)
Urban–rural income gap	0.399***	0.919***	0.854***	0.524***	0.943***	0.868***
	(0.133)	(0.168)	(0.166)	(0.149)	(0.177)	(0.174)
GDP growth rate	3.147***	3.469***	3.321***	3.301**	3.011***	2.985***
	(1.193)	(0.986)	(0.993)	(1.278)	(1.050)	(1.043)
Highway density (logarithm)	0.500***	0.549***	0.543***	0.518***	0.547***	0.534***
	(0.049)	(0.048)	(0.048)	(0.052)	(0.050)	(0.050)
Total factor productivity (logarithm)	-0.580***	-0.620***	-1.019***	-0.643***	-0.631***	-1.033***
	(0.202)	(0.176)	(0.193)	(0.206)	(0.176)	(0.194)
Agricultural labor productivity (logarithm)	-0.462***	-0.289***	-0.348***	-0.549***	-0.345***	-0.398***
	(0.075)	(0.068)	(0.068)	(0.084)	(0.071)	(0.071)
FDI / GDP	—	-9.683***	-8.778***	—	-10.23***	-9.318***
	—	(1.480)	(1.475)	—	(1.517)	(1.504)
Total imports and exports/GDP	—	-0.018	-0.216	—	0.060	-0.134
	—	(0.155)	(0.156)	—	(0.154)	(0.156)
Proportion of state-owned enterprises	—	-1.511***	-1.458***	—	-1.852***	-1.791***
	—	(0.256)	(0.252)	—	(0.281)	(0.282)
Loans/GDP	—	-1.116***	-0.842***	—	-1.023***	-0.803***
	—	(0.185)	(0.188)	—	(0.189)	(0.189)

(Continued)

Table A.1. (*Continued*)

Explanatory variable: Transfer of agricultural labor	Spatial autoregressive model			Spatial error model		
	(1)	(2)	(3)	(4)	(5)	(6)
Loans/deposits	—	0.453*	0.172	—	0.321	0.142
		(0.257)	(0.259)		(0.261)	(0.259)
Public education expenditure level	—	-0.118***	-0.136***	—	-0.133***	-0.142***
		(0.024)	(0.024)		(0.026)	(0.025)
Changes in surveyed urban unemployment rate (%)	—	—	0.068	—	—	0.064
			(0.041)			(0.041)
Rate of return on capital	—	—	3.503***	—	—	3.452***
			(0.730)			(0.723)
CPI (%)	—	—	0.006	—	—	0.003
			(0.007)			(0.008)
ρ	0.230***	0.114***	0.095**	/	/	/
	(0.045)	(0.041)	(0.041)			
λ	/	/	/	0.257***	0.217***	0.194***
				(0.051)	(0.049)	(0.052)
Moran's I	0.248***	0.217***	0.171***	0.253***	0.229***	0.191***
R^2	0.891	0.885	0.892	0.890	0.883	0.890
Adjusted R^2	0.884	0.877	0.884	0.883	0.874	0.881
Log-likelihood	-721.7	-616.9	-602.3	-722.3	-611.7	-598.5
Number of observations	589	589	589	589	589	589

Note: ***, ** and * represent significance at the significance level of 0.01, 0.05 and 0.1, respectively. Moran's I is the spatial correlation test result. ρ or λ is the spatial correlation coefficient of the spatial autoregressive model (SAR) or the spatial error model (SEM), respectively. R^2, adjusted R^2 and log-likelihood are the likelihood of fit.

Appendix C: Estimation of China's Agricultural Labor Productivity

I. Introduction

Over the past 30 years and more, China has made remarkable achievements in economic development. An indispensable basic condition is the transformation of China's agricultural production structure and the continuous improvement of its efficiency. Since China is a populous country, agriculture is of particularly important significance as a foundation of the entire national economy. The issue of food security has always been a great concern of scholars and policymakers. Since the reform and opening-up, China's agricultural labor has kept transferring to the non-agricultural sector, and the ratio of agricultural labor in the total labor has been declining at an annual rate of more than 1 percentage point. China can successfully achieve economic transformation only if the agricultural labor productivity reaches a high level and more agricultural products can be obtained with less labor consumption. In this way, more agricultural labor can be transferred to the non-agricultural sector, thus powerfully backing up the development of the non-agricultural sector and the transformation of economy and society.

The reason why agriculture is an essential condition for the development of a large country is extremely simple: For an economy as large as China with a population of more than one billion, its growth and transformation must be supported by the improvement in the efficiency of traditional agricultural production, especially the corresponding increase in agricultural labor productivity. Otherwise, the law of primary demand derivation for food will fundamentally restrain the process of economic growth or indirectly restrict the process by agricultural price rise beyond the acceptable range (especially for economies in the process of the transfer of agricultural labor). Marx always pointed out that agricultural labor productivity that exceeds the individual needs of workers is the foundation of all societies.[1] Further, modern development economics considers the growth of agricultural labor productivity as a prerequisite for economic development, because the food and raw materials produced by the agricultural sector constitute the condition for basic material security that meets the needs of human existence and development. Only when the agricultural output of unit labor increases, is it possible for social economy to deepen its efficiency through the division of labor and to promote the development of material civilization. The practice of economic development in many countries, especially large countries, provides the support of extensive international experience and verification of the above basic laws.

Therefore, considering the global characteristics of the rapid and profound structural transformation of China's contemporary economy, it is reasonable to speculate from the point of view of economic common sense that the structure and the level of efficiency of China's agricultural system must have undergone a revolutionary change. For this reason, measuring and interpreting China's contemporary agricultural productivity, especially the growth of labor productivity, are the simplest and most basic ways to understand the agricultural revolution. Besides, exploring the economic and institutional roots in productivity change by observation of the trajectory of agricultural labor productivity is an important issue of agricultural economics, an approach to observing how China, historically known as a "famine country", solves its problems regarding food security, and an indispensable element to understanding the basic preconditions for the

---

[1] *Capital*, vol. 3, People's Publishing House, 1974, p. 885.

overall transformation of China's giant economy. How has the level of the quantity of agricultural labor productivity changed in China over the 60-year history of the development of the People's Republic of China, especially since the reform and opening-up? What characteristic does the fluctuation trend of labor productivity have for different periods and different varieties? For the labor productivity measured by different indicators, is it comparable or what is the difference? In the context of cross-sectoral transfer of labor and the interactive development of the two sectors in China, what is the changing situation of the productivity of marginal agricultural labor? Systematically measuring agricultural labor productivity is of great significance for a quantitative description of the improvement of the efficiency of agricultural production and for an understanding of the stage success of China's economic transformation and growth.

In the domestic academic community, there have been many studies on the analysis of agricultural labor productivity. However, the existing studies still face some problems, such as different orientations and a lack of a systematic and pertinent understanding of China's agricultural labor productivity. In the period of a planned economy, some literature paid attention to exploring the analysis method of agricultural labor productivity, including in-depth discussions on how to measure labor input in the design of statistical indicators and other detailed problems.[2] Later, there was also some literature that focused on the research and application of agricultural production functions.[3] In recent years, lots of studies have given importance to investigating the agricultural labor productivity in specific regions, and the differences and convergence of agricultural labor productivity in different regions.[4] The rough literature review reveals that

---

[2]Zhang Minru: Discussion on Several Issues in the Calculation of Agricultural Labor Productivity, *Economic Research Journal*, 1962(8), pp. 43–50; Li Yuxian and Zhu Daohua: Calculation of Direct Labor Time in Agricultural Labor Productivity Statistics, *Economic Research Journal*, 1963 (10), pp. 42–43.

[3]Li Xiangyin and Shen Dazun: Several Problems in the Research and Application of Agricultural Production Functions, *Journal of Agrotechnical Economics*, 1995 (1), pp. 19–22.

[4]Tian Weiming: Comparative Study on Agricultural Labor Productivity in Different Provinces and Cities in China, *Journal of Agrotechnical Economics*, 1987 (1), pp. 18–21; Xu Xiuli: Estimation of Grain Production and Agricultural Labor Productivity in Modern

many studies have examined China's situation of agricultural production from different perspectives. However, the basic and systematic measurement for agricultural labor productivity over a long period of time is relatively scarce, especially the measurement of marginal labor productivity.

Thus, this chapter attempts to systematically estimate the changes of agricultural labor productivity by different methods based on the results of the existing research. Through the estimation and analysis of the trend of agricultural labor productivity in more than 60 years since the founding of New China, this chapter provides a realistic basis for the sustainable and stable transfer of agricultural labor in China and examines whether the continuous large-scale transfer of agricultural labor to the urban sector has affected food security in China. To be specific, this section uses two sets of data, namely, the value of the agricultural sector and the physical quantity of national agricultural product cost-benefit survey under the national economic accounting system, to systematically estimate the evolutionary trend of the average and marginal value of labor productivity of the agricultural sector in China from 1952 to 2011 from different perspectives. The details of the estimated results may vary with different estimation methods, but they together form a basic conclusion, that is, compared with the long-term stagnation of or even decline in agricultural labor productivity in the period of planned economy, the agricultural sector achieved a revolution in labor productivity in the period of reform and opening-up, thus playing a fundamental role in supporting the continuous and rapid

North China Plain, *2000 Youth Academic Forum of the Institute of Modern History CASS*, pp. 163-186; Chen Lai and Yang Wenju: The Effect of Output Growth Rate and the Labor Transfer on the Agricultural Labor Productivity Convergence of Our Country, *Industrial Economics Research*, 2005 (2), pp. 15–20; Xin Xiangfei and Liu Xiaoyun: Regional Disparity of Factor Endowments and Agricultural Labor Productivity in China, *World Economic Papers*, 2007 (5), pp. 5–22; Zhao Lei, Yang Xiangyang, and Wang Huaiming: Analysis on the Convergence of China's Provincial Agricultural Productivity since the Reform and Opening-Up, *Nankai Economic Studies*, 2007 (1), pp. 107–116; Gao Fan: Structural Transformation, Capital Deepening and Agricultural Labor Productivity Improvement — A Case Study of Shanghai, *Economic Theory and Business Management*, 2010 (2), pp. 68–75; Yu Kang, Guo Ping and Zhang Li: Determinants of the Dynamic Evolution of Regional Differences in Agricultural Labor Productivity in China — Disaggregate Approach Based on Stochastic Frontier Model, *Economic Science*, 2011 (2), pp. 44–55.

advancement of industrialization and urbanization, and the transformation of the contemporary economy in China.

This chapter is organized as follows: The second section discusses the ideas of estimation. The third section estimates the growth of average agricultural labor productivity under the two indicator systems, namely, value and physical quantity. The fourth section uses the value data of the agricultural sector to estimate and observe the indicator of the changes in marginal agricultural labor productivity. The fifth section estimates and observes the changes in marginal agricultural labor productivity by using the survey data on costs and benefits of national agricultural products, and specifically analyzes the changes in the productivity of grain and 10 major agricultural products. The sixth section shows conclusions and policy recommendations.

II. Ideas of Estimation of Agricultural Labor Productivity

Agricultural labor productivity is generally defined as the agricultural output brought by unit agricultural labor input, which is one of the basic indicators to measure the level of the efficiency of agricultural production. It is possible to directly calculate the average labor productivity based on output and labor input. However, the general analytical framework for the quantitative measurement of marginal labor productivity needs to be based on the agricultural production function. A properly constructed agricultural production function with good statistical experience can provide the elasticity value of input of labor and other factors to the output, and marginal labor productivity can be obtained by multiplying the value with the average labor productivity. Thus, on the basis of the conventional production function, mathematical formulas are made available to express the average and marginal labor productivity, and then the empirical expression of the agricultural production function can be estimated to obtain the elasticity of labor output. Finally, the estimated value of the elasticity of labor output is multiplied by the average labor productivity to estimate the marginal labor productivity.

The international academic community usually adopts the form of the Cobb–Douglas production function to estimate and analyze the empirical expression of the agricultural production function.[5] The general form of the Cobb–Douglas production function is $Y = A \prod_{i=1}^{n} X_i^{\alpha_i}$, where Y is the agricultural output, X_i is the input i, α_i is the output elasticity of input i and A is the technical level. Domestic scholars also widely use the Cobb–Douglas function to estimate the agricultural production in China. The agricultural production function estimated by Zhang Fengbo by using the data of 29 provinces and cities in 1985 shows that labor output has the largest elasticity, followed by chemical fertilizers and machinery, and by contrast, land does not make a significant contribution. This means that the agricultural production in China at that time was still at a lower level, the growth of output still relied heavily on the labor force, and partially on technological progress factors such as chemical fertilizers and machinery.[6] By analyzing the agricultural output and input data of 28 provinces in Mainland China from 1970 to 1987, Lin found that the growth of the agricultural output from 1978 to 1984 was largely attributable to the reform of the rural land system and the increase in the use of fertilizers, but the growth of agricultural output from 1984 to 1987 slowed down, which was mainly caused by the decline in the growth rate of fertilizer use and the accelerated transfer of rural labor, in addition to the full release of the effect of the reform of the land system.[7] By simulating the rice production function according to data on rice yield, labor and fertilizer input from 202 peasant households in three provinces and four counties during the period 1986–1991, Huang Jikun *et al.* discovered that both labor and

---

[5]Heady, E. O.: Production Functions from a Random Sample of Farms, *Journal of Farm Economics*, 1946 (28) (4), pp. 989–1004. Griliches, Z.: The Sources of Measured Productivity Growth: United States Agriculture 1940–60, *The Journal of Political Economy*, 1963 (71) (4), pp. 331–346. Griliches, Z.: Research Expenditures, Education, and the Aggregate Agricultural Production Function, *The American Economic Review*, 1964 (54) (6), pp. 961–974. Bardhan, P. K.: Size, Productivity, and Returns to Scale: An Analysis of Farm-level Data in Indian Agriculture, *The Journal of Political Economy*, 1973, pp. 1370–1386. Rosine, J. and Helmberger, P.: A Neoclassical Analysis of the US Farm Sector: 1948–1970, *American Journal of Agricultural Economics*, 1974 (56) (4), pp. 717–729.
[6]Zhang Fengbo: Analysis of Agricultural Production Functions, *Productivity Research*, 1987 (3), pp. 27–29.
[7]Lin, J. Y.: Rural Reforms and Agricultural Growth in China, *The American Economic Review*, 1992, pp. 34–51.

fertilizer input significantly affected rice yield, but the former played a less important role.[8] By analyzing the factors affecting rice yield according to the survey data of 106 peasant households in Qianjiang City of Hubei Province and Ji'an County of Jiangxi Province in 2003, Liao Hongle found that the planting area had a positive impact on rice yield, while the labor and fertilizer input did not significantly affect rice yield. The returns to scale of production factors varied from place to place, and the aging of agricultural workers had a negative impact on rice production.[9] Wang Meiyan used the national agricultural product cost-benefit survey data to estimate the production function of japonica rice from the panel data of 14 provinces and cities from 1980 to 2009. The results showed that compared with the period from 1980 to 2004, either labor output elasticity or marginal labor productivity of japonica rice increased significantly from 2005 to 2009.[10]

In addition, different specific indicators may be used, depending on different units of measurement of input and output. Agricultural output can be measured either by the value of market transactions or by physical units such as weight and volume. Agricultural labor input can be measured by hour, man-day and other time units, and with a lack of the support from microscopic investigation data, tends to be measured approximately by the number of agricultural force. In the sense of comparison, it is a measure in time series and needs to be assumed that the length and intensity of agricultural labor input each year are roughly comparable.

The national economic accounting system and related statistical system implemented and gradually improved after the reform and opening-up in China provide the time series and data of agricultural added value and

---

[8]Huang Jikun, Chen Qinggen and Wang Qiaojun: Discussing the Rational Application Structure and Countermeasures of Chemical Fertilizers in China — Analysis of the Rice Production Function Model, *Journal of Agrotechnical Economics*, 1994 (5), pp. 36–40.
[9]Liao Hongle: Estimation of the Rice Production Function of Peasant Households in the Southern China Rice Cultivation Area, *Chinese Rural Economy*, 2005 (6), pp. 13–20.
[10]Chow, G.: Capital Formation and Economic Growth in China, *Quarterly Journal of Economics*, 1993 (108) (3), pp. 809–842; Wang Meiyan: Can Migrant Workers Return to Agriculture? — Analysis of the National Agricultural Product Cost-Benefit Survey Data, *China Rural Survey*, 2011 (1), pp. 22–32+98.

agricultural labor force in different provinces and regions. By using the estimation results of agricultural capital stock by the academic community and the update of this section, this chapter can estimate and calculate the overall trend of change in the agricultural average and marginal labor productivity under the added value. According to the national agricultural product cost-benefit survey data conducted by relevant departments of the Chinese government, the long-term time series data with generally stable and comparable data indicators are made available, such as labor man-day input per unit area of land and capital investment, coupled with the panel data of major agricultural products of main producing provinces and regions in successive years, thus enabling this chapter to estimate the average and marginal labor productivity of major agricultural products measured by the physical quantity. As a strong supplement to the estimation of value, the agricultural product cost-benefit survey data have three advantages. First, the number of working days is used as a unit to measure the agricultural labor input, which helps to remove the uncertainties and errors in the annual per capita input of agricultural labor as a result of the length of the busy farming season and the slack farming season, etc. Second, the adoption of physical quantity statistics is conducive to eliminating the inter-period comparability problems commonly faced by the measurement of value. Even if the price indicator is used for adjustment to obtain the inter-period comparability data, there are still the quality problems of price data and the potential uncertain impacts on the statistical results. Third, the sampling survey data measured by the land unit of *mu* dynamically control the impact of land area changes, thus bringing convenience to the measurement and estimation of labor productivity.

With the existing relevant data, this section synthesizes two sets of measurement indicator systems, namely, value and physical quantity, to systematically estimate the evolution of the average and marginal value of agricultural labor productivity in China. The basic idea of econometric analysis in this section is: for a general Cobb–Douglas production function, average labor productivity is equal to the ratio of output to labor input, and marginal labor output is equal to the product of average labor productivity and labor output elasticity. Thus, it is more convenient to measure average labor productivity if output and labor input data in a specific period are available. Marginal labor productivity can be estimated if the empirical form of the production function and the elasticity of labor output can be measured by conventional measurement techniques. In view of this, this chapter uses the two sets of data, namely, the value of the agricultural sector and the physical quantity of national agricultural product cost-benefit surveys under the national economic accounting system, to systematically measure the agricultural average and marginal labor productivity in China. The results of the research in this section provide a reference for correctly understanding some important economic policy issues and academic issues such as the Lewis turning point.

III. Estimation of Average Agricultural Labor Productivity

Average labor productivity measures the output of unit labor, and its systematic measurement has a quantitative descriptive meaning for investigating the changes in labor productivity, and also provides data support for the subsequent estimate of marginal labor productivity. This section calculates the average agricultural labor productivity and its changes by using the output of different indicators such as value and physical quantity.

IV. Estimation of Agricultural Marginal Labor Productivity Measured by Value

The previous section systematically examines the trend of changes in average agricultural labor productivity since the founding of New China. In addition to average labor productivity, marginal labor productivity is also of paramount significance in economic analysis. In particular, in the current stage of labor market transformation in China, it provides an important reference for judging the situation of the transfer of agricultural labor and analyzing the macroeconomic situation of the two sectors. Therefore, this chapter uses different indicators and different estimation methods to estimate the empirical form of the function of agricultural production from different dimensions, and makes clear the elasticity of labor output, so that the marginal labor productivity of agriculture can be systematically estimated based on a defining relationship, that is, marginal labor productivity is equal to the product of average labor productivity and labor output elasticity.

1. Basic model of estimation of the function of agricultural production

In this chapter, the model of the Cobb–Douglas production function widely used in the academic community is adopted to estimate the form of agricultural production function. Specifically, with the simple form of the production function adopted by Wang Meiyan as a benchmark, this chapter gives different interpretations on whether to relax the assumption of constant returns to scale (CRS) and whether to add the land variable, etc., and sets up different econometric models with different details according to different data characteristics.[11] The production function adopted by Wang Meiyan is $Y = AK^{\alpha}L^{1-\alpha}$, where Y is the output, K is the capital input, L is the labor input, A is the technical level, and α and $1 - \alpha$ are the output elasticity of capital and labor, respectively. In other words, provided that the output growth is largely dependent on the growth of capital and labor input and the progress in technology, and the CRS hypothesis is fulfilled, then we can obtain the following econometric equation by solving the natural logarithm of both sides of the production function:

$$\ln \frac{Y}{L} = \ln A + \alpha \ln \frac{K}{L} + \varepsilon, \tag{1}$$

where ε is the error term. After the capital elasticity α is estimated according to Eq. (1), a statistical inference is carried out to obtain labor elasticity $\beta = 1 - \alpha$.

If the CRS hypothesis is relaxed, we can get the following regression equation:

$$\ln Y = \ln A + \alpha \ln K + \beta \ln L + \varepsilon. \tag{2}$$

---

[11]Wang Meiyan: Can Migrant Workers Return to Agriculture? — Analysis of National Agricultural Product Cost-Benefit Survey Data, *China Rural Survey*, 2011 (1), pp. 22–32+98..

Further, if the effect of the land variable (planting area) is taken into account, the regression model is constructed as follows:

$$\ln \frac{Y}{T} = \ln A + \alpha \ln \frac{K}{T} + \beta \ln \frac{L}{T} + \varepsilon, \tag{3}$$

$$\ln Y = \ln A + \alpha \ln K + \beta \ln L + \gamma \ln T + \varepsilon, \tag{4}$$

where T is the planting area and γ is the elasticity of output. Similar to Eqs. (1) and (2), a difference exists between Eqs. (3) and (4) as follows. Equation (3) has the CRS hypothesis $\alpha + \beta + \gamma = 1$, while Eq. (4) relaxes the CRS hypothesis.

In the estimation of the added value of the agricultural sector as an indicator to measure agricultural output, this chapter estimates the models (1)–(4), respectively, and further obtains four different production function expressions and labor elasticity values. This chapter only needs to estimate the models (1) and (2), because the impact of the planting area factor on production and labor productivity has been automatically controlled in the estimation model of the statistical survey on the agricultural cost-benefit data with the land unit of *mu*. Regardless of value estimation or physical quantity estimation, this chapter first performs a longer-term time series estimation and then a short-term panel estimation.

2. Estimation of agricultural capital stock

To estimate the form of the function of agricultural production measured by added value, it is necessary to first estimate the agricultural capital stock.[12] There have been some studies in the academic community to estimate the agricultural capital stock in China. The common practice is to adopt the perpetual inventory method, which generally consists of four basic steps. First, the comparable investment sequence is obtained according to the investment sequence and the investment price index; second, the appropriate capital depreciation rate is determined; third, the capital stock

---

[12]When the physical quantity productivity is estimated by agricultural cost-benefit data later, the material cost in the survey data can be directly used as an approximate measure of capital input.

of the base period is estimated; fourth, the capital stock series are estimated according to the formula for the perpetual inventory method. The formula for capital stock estimation by the perpetual inventory method is $K_t = (I_t / P_t) + (1 - \delta) \times K_{t-1}$, where K_t is the capital stock, I_t is the investment, P_t is the investment price index, δ is the depreciation rate and the subscript t is the period. The basic formula of the perpetual inventory method shows that to figure out the capital stock of the $t - 1$ period is conditional to the estimation of the capital stock of t period, so that it needs to be continuously iterated until the estimated capital stock, namely, initial capital stock, is known at a certain period. The basic iterative formula is as follows:

$$K_t = (I_t/P_t) + (1 - \delta) \times K_{t-1}$$

$$= (I_t/P_t) + (1 - \delta) \times (I_{t-1}/P_{t-1}) + (1 - \delta)^2 K_{t-2}$$

$$= \sum_{n=0}^{j-1} (1 - \delta)^n \times (I_{t-n}/P_{t-n}) + (1 - \delta)^j K_{t-j}, \forall 1 \leqslant j \leqslant t$$

$$= \sum_{n=0}^{t-1} (1 - \delta)^n \times (I_{t-n}/P_{t-n}) + (1 - \delta)^t K_0, j = t.$$

By means of continuous iteration forward, the actual investment data and initial capital stock over a longer historical period can be utilized, and the time series of capital stock can be estimated based on an appropriate depreciation rate. The difficulty normally lies in the estimation of initial capital stock. However, according to the aforementioned iterative formula, when the estimation period t is long, $(1 - \delta)^t$ tends to be 0, indicating that for any K_0, $(1 - \delta)^t K_0$ tends to be 0. The capital stock at the beginning of the period is depreciated and depleted in the long process. At this time, it exerts a very limited impact on the late capital stock, so that the error is controlled within a small range.

With the appropriate use of the results of the existing research, the estimation data of China's agricultural capital stock during the period 1952–2010 were obtained in this section. The data in 1952–1979 used

Chow's estimate of China's agricultural fixed capital stock during the period 1952–1985; the data for the period 1981–2004 came from the estimate of Wu Fangwei and Guo Yuqing. Both of them reflected the estimated agricultural fixed capital stock during the periods 1980–1997 and 1980–2004, respectively.[13] Through comparison, it is found that Chow shared consistent estimates of the Chinese agricultural capital stock series with Wu Fangwei and Guo Yuqing. Therefore, this section selects the year of 1980 as the combination point of the two pieces of literature from their research, and takes the average of the two years as the estimated value of capital stock in 1980. The data for the period 2005–2010 were obtained by the author using the perpetual inventory method based on the data of Guo Yuqing. In other words, those data were obtained at the depreciation rate of 5.42% estimated by Guo Yuqing using the agricultural fixed assets investment data for the years 2005–2010 with the year 2004 as the base period (adjusted by the fixed assets investment price index).[14] In line with the caliber of the agricultural value-added base period, all of the earlier capital stock data were adjusted by the fixed assets investment price index to the data series with the year 1978 as the base period.[15] In addition, this section also uses the perpetual inventory method and relevant data such as historical agricultural investment in fixed assets to independently estimate the agricultural capital stock series data of the years 1952–2010 in China. In general, the level of capital stock series independently estimated in this section is lower than that of the above-mentioned capital stock series estimated on the

---

[13] Wu Fangwei: Estimation of China's Agricultural Capital Stock, *Journal of Agrotechnical Economics*, 1999 (6), pp. 34–38; Guo Yuqing: Positive Research on the Optimal Scale of Fiscal Agriculture Input of China, *Research on Financial and Economic Issues*, 2006 (5), pp. 68–72.

[14] The depreciation rate used may vary from paper to paper. Hu Yongtai (1998) used a depreciation rate of 5%, Hall and Jones (1999) and Young (2003) a depreciation rate of 6%. Wu Fangwei (1999) and Guo Yuqing (2006) estimated a comprehensive depreciation rate of 5.42%, close to the above depreciation rates. To achieve consistent estimation results, this section also uses the depreciation rate of 5.42% to estimate the agricultural capital stock in the period 2005–2010.

[15] Due to the lack of a fixed assets investment price index in the early stage, the early data are adjusted by the agricultural production price index for the purpose of approximation.

Appendix C

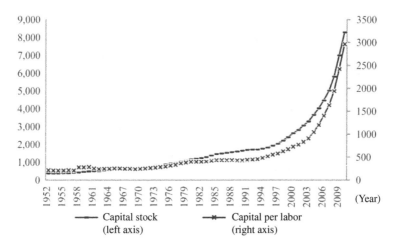

Figure C.1. China's agricultural capital stock and capital per labor (1952–2010, price in 1978, 100 million, yuan/person).

Source: Capital stock data from Chow (1993), Wu Fangwei (1999) and Guo Yuqing (2006) and the author's estimates.

basis of estimation by previous scholars, but the change of their direction is highly consistent. In view of this, the agricultural capital stock data obtained on the basis of the results of the existing research are used later.

Figure C.1 shows the estimates of China's agricultural capital stock and per capita capital of agricultural labor. Calculated at the constant price of 1978, China's agricultural capital stock increased from RMB 36.4 billion in 1952 to RMB 96.6 billion in 1977 on the eve of the reform, an increase of 1.65 times over 26 years and an average annual growth rate of 3.97%. During the period of reform and opening-up, investments grew faster, and agricultural capital accumulation also accelerated, reaching up to RMB 828.13 billion in 2010, an increase of 7.3 times over 33 years and an average annual growth rate of 6.62%. As the agricultural labor force witnessed a trend of rising first and then falling, the above changes in the two periods presented a more obvious contrast when they were measured by the index of capital stock per labor. The data set forth in Figure C.1 show that the capital stock per labor increased from RMB 210.2 in 1952 to RMB 329.8 in 1977 on the eve of the reform, an increase of 56.9% over 26 years and an average annual growth rate of 1.82%. During the period of reform and opening-up, both the rate of investment growth and capital deepening accelerated. By 2010, it had increased to RMB 2,965.0, an increase of 7.2 times over 33 years and an average annual growth rate of 6.57%, 3.6 times as fast as that before the reform.

3. Estimation of the marginal labor productivity of time series agricultural value added

This section uses the aforesaid four basic models, namely, models (1)–(4), to estimate the agricultural production functions measured by value.

Table C.1. Results of the Estimation of the Agricultural Production Function Measured by Value (1952–2010).

	Model (1)	Model (2)	Model (3)	Model (4)	Model (1) adopted
Capital elasticity	0.585***	0.688***	0.695***	0.584***	0.679***
	(0.113)	(0.0286)	(0.0290)	(0.0356)	(0.0387)
Labor elasticity	0.415***	0.309***	0.267**	0.475***	0.321***
	(0.113)	(0.114)	(0.111)	(0.119)	(0.0387)
Land elasticity	—	—	0.039	2.594***	—
	—	—	(0.0965)	(0.497)	—
Constant term	−0.852***	−0.825	−0.894***	−32.67***	−0.864***
	(0.0817)	(1.056)	(0.147)	(6.363)	(0.104)
Period	1952–2010	1952–2010	1952–2010	1952–2010	1978–2010
CRS	Yes	No	Yes	No	Yes
Land	No	No	Yes	Yes	No
R^2	0.914	0.954	0.951	0.965	0.912
F value	663.82	559.92	491.48	493.49	307.11
Observed value N	59	59	59	59	33

Note: For the estimated coefficient, the numbers in parentheses are stable standard errors; ***, ** and * are significant at the level of 0.01, 0.05 and 0.1, respectively. In model (1), the estimate of labor elasticity is the Wald statistic constructed according to an equation; the estimate of land elasticity in model (3) is the Wald statistic constructed according to an equation.

Source: Estimates of the author.

Table C.1 sets out the empirical form of the agricultural production function estimated by the four models. Model (1) gives the estimated results of national time series data over the past 60 years since the founding of New China under the assumption of CRS. The results show that the capital and labor elasticity are 0.585 and 0.415, respectively, with a significant estimated coefficient, and the fitting value of R^2 is 0.914, indicating that the estimation model has a strong explanatory power. In estimation model (2) with relaxed CRS hypothesis limitation, the estimated results of capital and labor elasticity are almost the same as those of model (1), indicating that the CRS hypothesis is reasonable. Considering that the land variable may have an impact on agricultural marginal labor productivity, both models (3) and (4) estimate the form of production function including a planting area, and respectively adopt the form with and without CRS hypothesis. The results show that both models (3) and (4) have significant labor elasticity, but they are slightly different in numerical value. In model (3), the estimated results of capital and labor elasticity are 0.695 and 0.267, respectively, which are close to the estimated results of models (1) and (2). The elasticity coefficient of the planting area is very small and insignificant, only 0.039. The estimated results of model (4) show that the labor elasticity rises to 0.475 and the capital elasticity is 0.584, while the elasticity coefficient of the planting area is as high as 2.594, meaning that if the planting area increases by 10% with no change in other conditions, the output will increase by about 26%, that is, the overall production function has a large-scale economic effect on land input. The last column of the table shows the estimation equation of model (1), which is used to estimate the agricultural production function since the reform and opening-up in a segmented manner. The results suggest that the estimated values of capital and labor elasticity are 0.679 and 0.321, respectively, close to the estimated results of the whole period since the founding of New China. In general, the four estimation models and piecewise estimations come to relatively consistent estimates of capital and labor elasticity, with R^2 above 0.9, indicating that the model has a good explanatory power and the estimation results are relatively steady.

According to the estimates of labor elasticity in the foregoing four models, and combined with the average labor productivity data previously reported, Figure C.2 sets out the estimates of agricultural marginal labor productivity measured by added value since the founding of New China. As

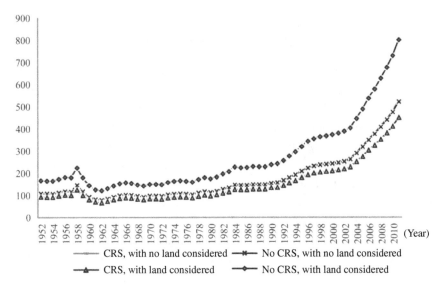

Figure C.2. Estimation of China's agricultural marginal labor productivity (1952–2011, price in 1978, yuan/person).

Source: Estimates of the author.

shown in Figure C.2, the marginal labor productivity calculated from the elasticity value estimated by model (1) and model (2) is the same and centered. Calculated at the constant price of 1978, China' agricultural marginal labor productivity fluctuated around RMB 110, without a trend of growth basically, during the planning system and the period of a people's commune. However, during the period of reform and opening-up, marginal labor productivity showed a sustained and accelerated growth trend, which increased to RMB 527 in 2011, with an average annual growth rate of nearly 5%. A great difference exists in the marginal labor productivity calculated from the elasticity estimates of models (3) and (4). Model (4) without CRS restriction gives a higher estimated value of labor elasticity, and a larger marginal labor productivity accordingly. As measured by the constant price in 1978, it reached RMB 800 in 2011, 53% higher than the estimation result of model (2). Model (3) with CRS restriction gives a smaller estimated marginal labor productivity, which was RMB 450 in 2011, 14% lower than that of model (1). In addition, China's agricultural marginal labor productivity experienced three periods of rapid growth (1978–1984, 1990–1997 and 2003–2011) after the reform and opening-up.

4. *Marginal labor productivity estimated by using the panel data of different provinces and regions*

In addition to the national time series estimation, marginal labor productivity can be estimated by sorting out the panel data of different provinces and regions and using three panel data models. The key constraint to this research intention lies in the estimation of the agricultural capital stock of each province and region. As stated earlier, the key to estimating capital stock by the perpetual inventory method is to acquire the data of agricultural fixed assets investment, initial capital stock and the depreciation rate. As the data of investments in agricultural fixed assets of different provinces and regions have been available from 1996, the panel data of agricultural capital stock of different provinces and regions from 1995 can be obtained by estimating the capital stock and depreciation rate of different provinces and regions in 1995 based on the results of the existing research. Therefore, the period that the data cover used for estimation in this section is the period of 1995–2010.

The estimation models are still classified according to the two basic dimensions, namely, the adoption of a CRS hypothesis and the introduction of the land variable. For each estimation model, two regression methods, namely, ordinary least squares (OLS) and fixed effect (FE), are adopted, respectively. Compared with OLS, FE can control both the vintage effect and the province effect.

Table C.2 sets out the estimated results without the land variable, while Table C.2 sets out the estimated results including the land variable. In each table, columns (1) and (3) show the estimated results with a CRS hypothesis; columns (2) and (4) show the estimated results without the CRS hypothesis. In Table C.2, the estimates of labor elasticity as provided in columns (1) and (3) are the Wald statistics constructed based on the equation $\beta = 1 - \alpha$; in Table C.2, the estimates of land elasticity as provided in columns (1) and (3) are the Wald statistics constructed according to the equation $\gamma = 1 - \alpha - \beta$.

According to the estimated results in Table C.2, the estimated values of labor elasticity are significantly positive. OLS regression estimates of labor elasticity with and without the CRS hypothesis are very close to each other, which are 0.775 and 0.763, respectively. In the FE regression,

Table C.2. Estimation of the Agricultural Production Function Measured by Value According to the Panel Data of Different Provinces and Regions (1995–2010, excluding the land variable).

	OLS		Fixed effect	
	(1)	(2)	(1)	(2)
Capital elasticity α	0.225***	0.141*	0.225***	0.141*
	(0.0638)	(0.0734)	(0.0638)	(0.0734)
Labor elasticity β	0.775***	0.763***	0.775***	0.763***
	(0.064)	(0.0423)	(0.064)	(0.0423)
Constant term	−0.567***	−0.0902	−0.567***	−0.0902
	(0.109)	(0.204)	(0.109)	(0.204)
CRS restriction	Yes	No	Yes	No
Provincial effect	No	No	No	No
Vintage effect	Yes	Yes	Yes	Yes
R^2	0.298	0.808	0.298	0.808
F value	8.47	134.82	8.47	134.82
Observed value	496	496	496	496

Note: The labor elasticity estimates as provided in columns (1) and (3) are the Wald statistics constructed according to the equation $\beta = 1 - \alpha$. For the estimated coefficient, the numbers in parentheses are stable standard errors; ***, ** and * are significant at the level of 0.01, 0.05 and 0.1, respectively.

Source: Estimates of the author.

the estimated values of labor elasticity with and without the CRS hypothesis are 0.955 and 0.342, respectively, which are quite different from each other. Based on the estimated value of labor elasticity in Table C.2, and combined with the annual average labor productivity data previously reported, the estimated results of the marginal agricultural labor productivity measured by added value over the past half century in New China are set forth in Figure C.3.

Table C.3 sets out the panel estimation results including the land variable (planting area). Similarly, OLS regression estimates of labor elasticity with and without the CRS hypothesis are very close to each other, which are 0.371 and 0.377, respectively. In the FE regression, the

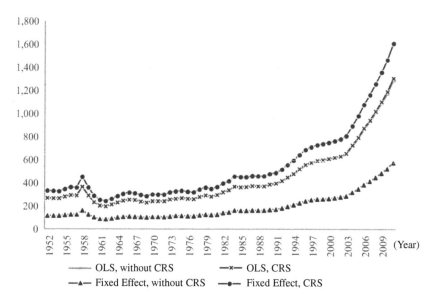

Figure C.3.   Estimation of China's marginal agricultural labor productivity (1952–2011, price in 1978, yuan/person; with no land considered).

Source: Estimates of the author.

estimated values of labor elasticity with and without the CRS hypothesis are 0.519 and 0.269, respectively, which are quite different from each other, but are smaller than those in Table C.3. In terms of regression results, the estimated value of land elasticity is significant and relatively stable, close to the value of labor elasticity, indicating that land area has an important impact on the value of agricultural output, and its important degree is equivalent to that of labor input. Compared with Table C.2, Table C.3 shows more stable estimated values of labor elasticity generally, ranging from 0.269 to 0.519, which are close to the estimated results of the time series for a longer period nationwide. According to the estimated values in Table C.3 and combined with the previously reported average labor productivity data, Figure C.4 gives the four groups of marginal labor productivity data obtained by using the estimated coefficient of labor elasticity in Table C.3. The maximum estimated result 0.519 of labor elasticity gives a higher marginal labor productivity, reaching up to RMB 876 in 2011 measured by the constant

Table C.3. Estimation of the Agricultural Production Function Measured by Value According to the Panel Data of Different Provinces and Regions (1995–2010, including the land variable).

	OLS		Fixed effect	
	(1)	(2)	(1)	(2)
Capital elasticity α	0.178***	0.112**	0.178***	0.112**
	(0.0519)	(0.0561)	(0.0519)	(0.0561)
Labor elasticity β	0.371***	0.377***	0.371***	0.377***
	(0.0484)	(0.0466)	(0.0484)	(0.0466)
Land elasticity γ	0.451***	0.433***	0.451***	0.433***
	(0.057)	(0.0508)	(0.057)	(0.0508)
Constant term	−1.369***	−0.952***	−1.369***	−0.952***
	(0.153)	(0.179)	(0.153)	(0.179)
CRS restriction	Yes	No	Yes	No
Provincial effect	No	No	No	No
Vintage effect	Yes	Yes	Yes	Yes
R^2	0.331	0.831	0.331	0.831
F value	10.86	179.54	87.97	300.14
Observed value	496	496	496	496

Note: The labor elasticity estimates as provided in columns (1) and (3) are the Wald statistics constructed according to the equation $\beta = 1 - \alpha$. For the estimated coefficient, the numbers in parentheses are stable standard errors; ***, ** and * are significant at the level of 0.01, 0.05 and 0.1, respectively.

Source: Estimates of the author.

price of 1978. The minimum estimated result 0.269 of labor elasticity gives a lower marginal labor productivity, reaching up to RMB 454 in 2011.

5. Summary of the results of the marginal labor productivity estimation by different methods

According to the estimation results of the above methods, we can draw two basic conclusions. First, before the reform and opening-up, China's

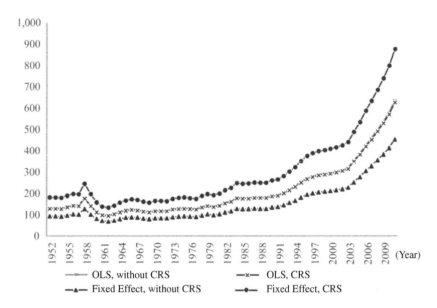

Figure C.4. Estimation of China's marginal agricultural labor productivity (1952–2011, Price in 1978, yuan/person; with land considered).
Source: Estimates of the author.

marginal agricultural labor productivity was kept at a low level and its development basically stagnated. Since the reform and opening-up, marginal agricultural labor productivity has been developing rapidly, especially from 2003. Second, different estimation methods lead to different estimation results. As shown in Figure C.4, the maximum estimate is nearly twice that of the minimum estimate by different estimation methods. Therefore, to use the estimation results in this section, it is important to determine the appropriate production function estimation method and model according to the different research purposes and understanding of agricultural production.

V. Estimation of Marginal Agricultural Labor Productivity Measured by Physical Quantity

In this section, the national agricultural product cost-benefit survey data are used to estimate the marginal labor productivity of several varieties of the main agricultural products. The national agricultural cost-benefit data of some major agricultural products began in 1953. Therefore, this chapter first of all estimates the national time series of agricultural products with long-term time series data, with the estimated interval from 1953 to 2010.[16] These agricultural products include grain, cotton, flue-cured tobacco, wheat, peanuts and corn. In addition, according to the distribution of various varieties of agricultural products in the main producing provinces and regions, this section sorts out and obtains the panel data from the period 1975–2010 of different provinces and regions, and estimates the panel data model of several main products. The selected major agricultural products are mainly determined by the scope of agricultural cost-benefit data surveys, with consideration of the length of the continuous period of relevant data. As a result, ten products, including cotton, flue-cured tobacco, wheat, peanuts, corn, japonica rice, soybean, rapeseed, sugar beet and pigs, were selected.

For crops (or pigs), the indicators of agricultural cost-benefit data survey basically use the input and output per *mu* (or per piece) as the basic statistical unit. Therefore, to use the estimation model of surveyed agricultural cost-benefit data based on the land unit of *mu*, this chapter only needs to estimate models (1) and (2), because the impact of the land area factor on production and labor productivity has been controlled.

$$\ln \frac{Y}{L} = \ln A + \alpha \ln \frac{K}{L} + \varepsilon, \tag{5}$$

$$\ln Y = \ln A + \alpha \ln K + \beta \ln L + \varepsilon, \tag{6}$$

where Y is the yield per *mu* (or per piece), K is the material cost per *mu* (or per piece), L is the number of laborers per *mu* (or per piece) and ε is the error term. After 1998, the caliber of "material cost" changes to "material and service cost", but they have no great difference and the ratio is generally steady. In the time series regression, this section adds the dummy variable of year to the period 1999–2010; in the panel

[16]In fact, it refers to the periods 1953–1965 and 1975–2010, and the statistics for the period 1966–1974 are interrupted due to the Cultural Revolution.

Table C.4. Estimation Results of Time Series Data Production Function of Major Agricultural Products by Variety.

Variety	Sample period	Capital elasticity	Labor elasticity	Constant term	Adjusted R^2	F value
Grain	1953–2010	0.524*** (0.0511)	0.476*** (0.051)	2.413*** (0.0529)	0.880	134.56
	1975–2010	0.850*** (0.0280)	0.150*** (0.028)	2.130*** (0.0185)	0.977	1008.9
Cotton	1953–2010	0.370*** (0.0644)	0.630*** (0.0644)	0.168*** (0.0360)	0.827	122.36
	1975–2010	0.784*** (0.0847)	0.216*** (0.0847)	0.0544 (0.0399)	0.916	192.38
Flue-cured tobacco	1953–2010	0.349*** (0.0418)	0.651*** (0.042)	0.811*** (0.0196)	0.865	174.13
	1975–2010	0.449*** (0.0200)	0.551*** (0.02)	0.775*** (0.0148)	0.949	455.02
Wheat	1953–2010	0.679*** (0.0539)	0.321*** (0.0539)	2.062*** (0.0645)	0.899	151.58
	1975–2010	0.965*** (0.0383)	0.035 (0.0383)	1.746*** (0.0370)	0.969	496.82
Peanuts	1953–2010	0.334*** (0.0735)	0.666*** (0.0735)	1.675*** (0.0638)	0.737	80.92
	1975–2010	0.813*** (0.0340)	0.187*** (0.034)	1.340*** (0.0214)	0.982	922.27
Corn	1953–2010	0.524*** (0.0582)	0.476*** (0.0582)	2.564*** (0.0483)	0.865	119.94
	1975–2010	0.930*** (0.0322)	0.07** (0.0322)	2.296*** (0.0123)	0.977	1093.00

Note: For the estimated coefficient, the numbers in parentheses are stable standard errors; ***, ** and * are significant at the level of 0.01, 0.05 and 0.1, respectively. The estimate of labor elasticity is statistically inferred from the Wald statistics constructed according to the equation $\beta = 1 - \alpha$.

Source: Estimates of the author.

Table C.4, and combined with the average labor productivity data of each variety, the marginal labor productivity of each variety can be calculated, as shown in Figure C.6. The marginal labor productivity calculated from the estimated elasticity value of the whole period and the segmented

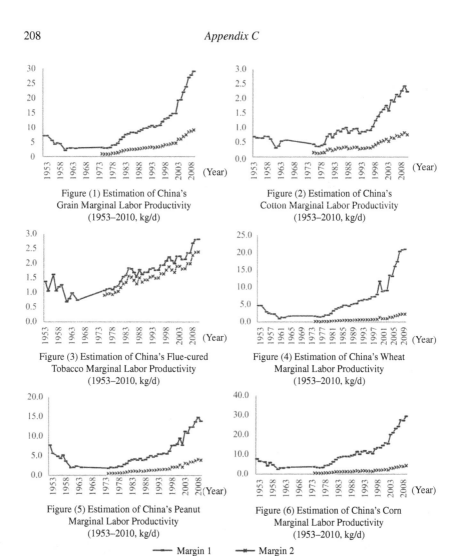

Figure C.6. Estimation of the marginal labor productivity of agricultural products in China (time series estimation).

Source: Estimates of the author.

period is marked as "margin 1" and "margin 2", respectively. Figure C.6 shows the marginal labor productivity of grain. The results show that during the planned economy period, China's grain marginal labor productivity decreased from 7.21 kg/d in 1953 to 3.16 kg/d in 1978, a decrease

Table C.5. Estimation Results of the Production Function of Major Agricultural Products by Variety According to the Panel Data.

Variety	Method	Capital elasticity	Labor elasticity	Constant term	R^2	n	N
Cotton	OLS	0.651*** (0.0319)	0.349*** (0.032)	−0.0567 (0.0729)	0.861	468	15
	FE	0.554*** (0.0958)	0.446*** (0.096)	−0.0802* (0.0447)	0.891	468	15
Flue-cured tobacco	OLS	0.646*** (0.0368)	0.354*** (0.037)	0.784*** (0.0873)	0.707	520	17
	FE	0.526*** (0.0629)	0.474*** (0.063)	0.737*** (0.0694)	0.815	520	17
Wheat	OLS	0.897*** (0.0129)	0.103*** (0.013)	1.839*** (0.0785)	0.956	604	20
	FE	0.918*** (0.0385)	0.082*** (0.039)	1.802*** (0.0686)	0.956	604	20
Soybeans	OLS	0.747*** (0.0321)	0.253*** (0.032)	1.962*** (0.0615)	0.849	392	13
	FE	0.620*** (0.0527)	0.380*** (0.053)	1.885*** (0.0956)	0.871	392	13
Japonica rice	OLS	0.777*** (0.0195)	0.223*** (0.02)	2.192*** (0.0655)	0.948	414	14
	FE	0.734*** (0.0508)	0.266*** (0.051)	2.181*** (0.0753)	0.961	414	14
Peanuts	OLS	0.588*** (0.0437)	0.412*** (0.044)	1.254*** (0.124)	0.891	332	11
	FE	0.560*** (0.0791)	0.440*** (0.079)	1.273*** (0.115)	0.930	332	11
Corn	OLS	0.946*** (0.0251)	0.054** (0.025)	2.429*** (0.0850)	0.901	640	21
	FE	0.632*** (0.0554)	0.368*** (0.055)	2.330*** (0.0754)	0.919	640	21

(Continued)

of more than half. Since the reform and opening-up, marginal labor productivity has been on the rise, reaching 29.1 kg/d in 2010, an increase of 8.2 times. In contrast, the estimated level of productivity by segmented

Table C.5. *(Continued)*

Variety	Method	Capital elasticity	Labor elasticity	Constant term	R^2	n	N
Sugar beets	OLS	0.738*** (0.0779)	0.262*** (0.078)	3.715*** (0.231)	0.861	148	10
	FE	0.473** (0.176)	0.527** (0.176)	3.726*** (0.265)	0.864	148	10
Rapeseed	OLS	0.725*** (0.0378)	0.275*** (0.038)	0.986*** (0.098)	0.839	517	29
	FE	0.492*** (0.0843)	0.508*** (0.084)	0.895*** (0.149)	0.891	517	29
Pork	OLS	0.884*** (0.0132)	0.116*** (0.013)	0.143*** (0.0434)	0.962	703	30
	FE	0.879*** (0.0285)	0.121*** (0.029)	0.186*** (0.0510)	0.968	703	30

Note: The estimate of labor elasticity is the Wald statistics constructed according to the equation $\beta = 1 - \alpha$. For the estimated coefficient, the numbers in parentheses are stable standard errors; ***, ** and * are significant at the level of 0.01, 0.05 and 0.1, respectively. n is the number of observed values, and N represents the number of provinces and cities.

Source: Estimates of the author.

manner is lower, an increase from 1 kg/d in 1978 to 9.17 kg/d in 2010. The other varieties of agricultural products have a similar trend and are not repeated here.

2. Marginal labor productivity estimation by the panel data method

This section uses the panel data of the period 1975–2010 of the main producing provinces and regions to estimate the agricultural production function and marginal labor productivity of each major agricultural product. For each agricultural product, two regression methods, namely, OLS and FE, have been adopted with a CRS hypothesis. Table C.5 shows the specific estimation results.

Further, according to the elasticity estimation as provided in Table C.5, and combined with the national average labor productivity data of each

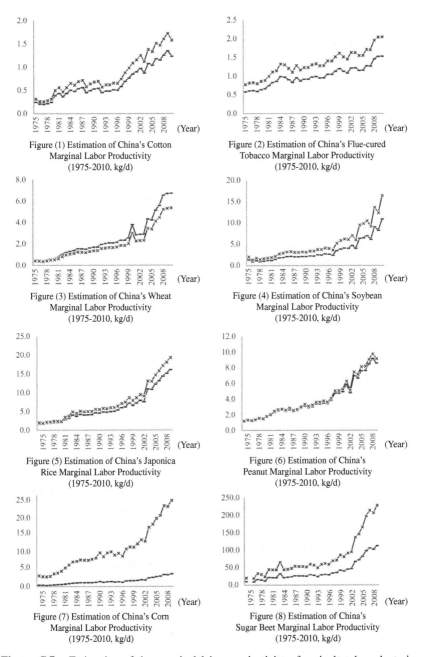

Figure (1) Estimation of China's Cotton
Marginal Labor Productivity
(1975-2010, kg/d)

Figure (2) Estimation of China's Flue-cured
Tobacco Marginal Labor Productivity
(1975-2010, kg/d)

Figure (3) Estimation of China's Wheat
Marginal Labor Productivity
(1975-2010, kg/d)

Figure (4) Estimation of China's Soybean
Marginal Labor Productivity
(1975-2010, kg/d)

Figure (5) Estimation of China's Japonica
Rice Marginal Labor Productivity
(1975-2010, kg/d)

Figure (6) Estimation of China's
Peanut Marginal Labor Productivity
(1975-2010, kg/d)

Figure (7) Estimation of China's Corn
Marginal Labor Productivity
(1975-2010, kg/d)

Figure (8) Estimation of China's
Sugar Beet Marginal Labor Productivity
(1975-2010, kg/d)

Figure C.7. Estimation of the marginal labor productivity of agricultural products in China (panel estimation).

Source: Estimates of the author.

variety, the marginal labor productivity of each variety can be calculated, as shown in Figure C.7. The marginal labor productivity calculated from the OLS estimation results is indicated as "margin 1" in the following figure, while that calculated from the FE estimation results is indicated as "margin 2". Figure C.7 clearly indicates the level of marginal labor productivity and the trend of change of 10 agricultural products from 1975 to 2010. Due to space limitations, they are not analyzed and interpreted in detail here.

3. Summary of the results of the marginal labor productivity estimation by different methods

It is possible to come to three basic conclusions according to the estimation results of major agricultural products by different methods. First, with the reform and opening-up as the demarcation point, China's agricultural marginal labor productivity has shown a trend of falling first and then rising. Second, different estimation methods lead to different estimation results, but except for corn, sugar beets and rapeseed, the estimation results measured by physical quantity are quite consistent and close, especially for wheat, japonica rice, peanuts and pork. Similarly, to use the estimation results in this section, it is necessary to determine different production function models according to the research purpose and the understanding of agricultural production. Third, labor elasticity varies with different varieties of agricultural products. For example, wheat, corn and pork have less labor elasticity, while cotton, flue-cured tobacco, soybeans and peanuts have greater labor flexibility. This means that the production of different agricultural products in China is different not only for the elasticity of labor demand but also for comparative advantages in international agricultural trade, and in addition, the difference in comparative advantage changes with the transfer of labor and the transformation of the labor market in China.

VI. Conclusions

This section uses two sets of data under the national economic accounting system, namely, the value of the agricultural sector and the physical quantity of the national agricultural product cost-benefit survey, and uses different econometric models and methods to systematically estimate the evolutionary trend of the average and marginal value of agricultural labor productivity in China from 1952 to 2011 from different dimensions. With the output and relative price factors taken into account, the method of measuring the value can reflect the value meaning of agricultural economic development in the national economy. The physical quantity estimation method can eliminate the influence of price factors and explore the improvement of the efficiency of the production of agricultural products. The long-term time series estimation shows the basic developmental track of the agricultural sector since the establishment of the People's Republic of China, while the medium and short-term panel estimation is conducive to the comparative analysis with different measurement methods. The overall estimation reveals the change in the overall level of efficiency of the agricultural sector, while the estimation of 10 major agricultural products by variety can explore the different developments and changes in the productivity of different crops in the agricultural sector.

According to the systematic estimation results of the evolution of the average and marginal labor productivity of China's agricultural sector from 1952 to 2011 in this section, the efficiency of China's agricultural production has made great progress after the reform and opening-up, even called an agricultural revolution. Since China is a populous country, agricultural development, as a foundation of the entire national economy, is of a particularly important significance. The improvement in agricultural labor productivity not only solves the issue of food security that has haunted China for a long time but also fundamentally improves the dietary structure of the people. In addition, as such an agricultural revolution takes place in the context of the transformation of China's economic structure and the transfer of labor, it not only increases farmers' income but also provides preconditions for the development of the non-agricultural sector in terms of raw material, land and labor force, thus backing up the rapid growth of the contemporary economy.

The understanding of the improvement in agricultural labor productivity can provide a reference for understanding some important economic policies and academic problems. Limited by the monotonous and constant input of traditional agricultural factors and the slow formation of technological progress, it is one-sidedly believed that agriculture is a weak industry and much attention is paid to the government's administrative intervention and control of agricultural production, circulation and land, causing serious distortion and meaningless losses to the development of agriculture. With land as an example, the meaning of marginal change of the land area on sustainable growth may be exaggerated due to an unclear understanding of the nature and law in the possibility of structural change of the agricultural production function. The unprecedented regulation of intensity on land is bound to be derived in China, where the traditional thought of "a problem needs regulation and a super problem needs super regulation" is deeply rooted. Thus, this section can greatly help to recognize the measurement of productivity, especially the agricultural cost-benefit data that controls the change of land area. When the author studied China's food economy and policy more than 10 years ago, he pointed out that the traditional agricultural mechanism described by the concept of the "Malthus Trap" and the food problem traditionally characterized by scarcity, had already undergone substantial changes.[18] The results of agricultural average and marginal labor productivity measured systematically in this section show that contemporary agricultural labor productivity needs to be considered from a positive perspective.

In addition, the results of the research of this section can also be used for a reference to correctly understand the Lewis turning point. Recently, the paradigm of the Lewis turning point is prevalent. As a descriptive concept, the Lewis turning point has positive cognitive value on how to understand the relationship between China's labor market and the staged characteristics of long-term growth and even short-term macroeconomic changes in recent years. However, the theoretical framework of the Lewis turning point has been established on the basis of constant marginal output, and its economic meaning is based on the premise of ignoring the agricultural growth at that time. Therefore, it is obviously necessary to discuss whether it is valid from today's theoretical height. One of the challenges that the paradigm faces at the level of theoretical logic is how to be

---

[18]Lu Feng: Food Marketization Reform: The Prerequisites for Recognition of Rethinking, *China Rural Survey*, 1997 (3), pp. 9–18; Lu Feng: Realistic Understanding of the Problem of Food Surplus — Question the View of "No Food Surplus", *Management World*, 1999 (3), pp. 168–175.

compatible with the empirical experience of productivity estimation. In the classic *Transforming Traditional Agriculture*, Schultz criticized the hypothesis of zero marginal agricultural labor productivity, and brought forward that marginal labor productivity should be directly estimated.[19] The systematic estimates for China's marginal agricultural labor productivity in this section are conducive to better judging the applicability of Lewis's theory in China.

Besides, combined with the theory and the observation of the actual situation of China's agriculture, it is not hard to understand the root causes of the agricultural revolution in China. Through deviation according to the previous definition of labor productivity, it can be simply concluded that agricultural average and marginal labor productivity are first of all affected by the level of agricultural technology and capital input per labor (capital deepening).[20] The higher the technical level, or the higher the capital per labor (and more broadly, the input of other factors per labor), the higher the labor productivity. Meanwhile, labor productivity is also affected by labor output elasticity. In particular, marginal labor productivity is greatly affected by labor output elasticity. Some scholars such as Gao Fan, have discovered through logic analysis and empirical research that structural transformation and capital deepening are the basic approaches to improving agricultural labor productivity in China.[21]

Marx and Engels gave great importance to the development of agriculture and put forward their own views on the factors affecting the improvement of agricultural labor productivity. They divided the factors affecting the improvement of agricultural labor productivity into three categories. The first category refers to the individual factors of laborers, including talent, skills, physical strength and intelligence, etc. The popularization of education and vocational training are associated with these factors,

---

[19]Schultz, T. W.: *Transforming Traditional Agriculture*, New Haven and London: Yale University Press, 1964.

[20]Through simple derivation according to the simple Cobb–Douglas production function and the definition of labor productivity, the average labor productivity is $APL = \frac{Y}{L} = \frac{AK^\alpha L^{1-\alpha}}{L} = A\left(\frac{K}{L}\right)^\alpha$; the marginal labor productivity is $MPL = \alpha * APL = \alpha A\left(\frac{K}{L}\right)^\alpha$.

[21]Gao Fan: Structural Transformation, Capital Deepening and Agricultural Labor Productivity Improvement — A Case Study of Shanghai, *Economic Theory and Business Management*, 2010 (2), pp. 68–75.

and can improve the production skills and average proficiency of laborers. The second category refers to the natural conditions of labor, such as land fertility, climate and light condition, which determine the natural productivity of labor. The third category refers to the improvements in social conditions of labor, specifically including large-scale production, capital concentration, combination of labor, division of labor, application of machines, improvement of production methods, level of the development of science and its application in crafts, the increase in and improvement of agricultural infrastructures such as transportation means and water conservation and irrigation facilities, legal protection of property rights and transaction, etc., which affect the social productivity of labor.[22] The aforementioned ideas are endowed with the meaning of public policy, clearly pointing out the direction for the formulation of agricultural policies.

In light of China's reality, the root causes of China's agricultural revolution can be mainly attributed to the following three factors. First, the institutional and policy environment has improved. Since the reform and opening-up, China has implemented the household contracted responsibility system, greatly mobilizing the farmers' initiative for production. Since then, through the market-oriented reform of agricultural prices, the control of circulation links has been reduced to encourage agricultural production and sales. In addition, the permission and encouragement of the transfer of agricultural labor has helped reduce the surplus rural labor and improve agricultural labor productivity. Second, the modern physical capital input increases, including operational input and capital input. Since the reform and opening-up, one of the characteristics in agricultural development is that capital replaces labor to promote the rapid growth of agricultural labor productivity. The increase in modern physical capital input has greatly improved the efficiency of agricultural production. For example, inputs such as pesticides and fertilizers have significantly increased the agricultural output, while inputs such as machines have greatly shortened the labor time. The growth of these modern material inputs jointly boosts the rapid increase in agricultural labor productivity.

---

[22]For details, refer to the *Wages, Price and Profit*, the *Capital*, the *Economic Manuscript (1861–1863)* and other works.

Third, the transformation of the volume and structure of the total trade makes the agricultural adjustment adapt to comparative advantages, thus improving the overall efficiency of production. For example, China's large importation of soybeans in recent years has, on the one hand, caused the replacement of the sectors with absolute and relatively low resource efficiency, and on the other hand, it has made it possible for animal products (such as pork, domestic poultry and fish) with sufficient feed support to grow.

Bibliography

Banerjee, A., X., Meng, and Nancy Qian, "The Life Cycle Model and Household Savings: Micro Evidence from Urban China", 2010, Unpublished Manuscript, Peking University.

Chivakul, Mali, W. Raphael Lam, Xiaoguang Liu, Wojciech Maliszewski and Alfred Schipke, Understanding Residential Real Estate in China, IMF Working Paper, No. 15/84, 2015.

Chow, G. C., "A Model of Chinese National Income Determination". *The Journal of Political Economy*, 1985, 93(4), 782–792.

Dessi, R., "*Household Saving and Wealth in China: Some Evidence from Survey Data*". Department of Applied Economics, University of Cambridge, 1991.

Feltenstein, A., D., Lebow, and S., Van Wijnbergen, "Savings, Commodity Market Rationing, and the Real Rate of Interest in China". *Journal of Money, Credit and Banking*, 1990, 22(2), 234–252.

Feng Lu, Guoqing Song, Jie Tang, Hongyan Zhao, and Liu Liu, "Profitability of China's Industrial Firms (1978–2006)". *China Economic Journal*, 2008, 1(1), pp. 1–31.

Fleisher, B. M., Y., Liu, and H., Li, "Financial Intermediation, Inflation, and Capital Formation in Rural China". *China Economic Review*, 1994, 5(1), 101-115.

Gou Qin, Huang Yiping and Liu Xiaoguang: "Is There Really Discrimination in Ownership of Bank Credit?" *Management World*, 2014 (1).

Hall, R. E., and Jones, C. I., "Why do some countries produce so much more output per worker than others?" *The Quarterly Journal of Economics*, 1999, 114(1), 83-116.

International Monetary Fund, 2015, *Adjusting to Lower Commodity Prices*, Washington D.C.: World Economic Outlook, pp. 1–2.

Jefferson, G. H., "The Impact of Economic Structure on the Fertility, Savings, and Retirement Behavior of Chinese Households". *Journal of Asian Economics*, 1990, 1(2), 205-223.

Kraay, A., "Household Saving in China". *The World Bank Economic Review*, 2000, 14(3), 545-570.

Lam, W. Raphael, Xiaoguang Liu and Alfred Schipke, China's Labor Market in the "New Normal", IMF Working Paper, No. 15/151, 2015.

Liu Xiaoguang and Lu Feng, "The Riddle of Rising Return on Capital in China". *China Economic Quarterly*, 2014 (13) (3).

Lu Feng, Liu Xiaoguang, Li Xin and Qiu Muyuan, China's Contemporary Agricultural Revolution — Systematic Estimation of the Agricultural Labor Productivity in New China (1952–2011), CCER Discussion Draft, No. C2014001.

Lu Feng, Liu Xiaoguang, Jiang Zhixiao and Zhang Jieping, "The Labor Market and China's Macro-Economic Cycles: With a Discussion of Okun's Law in China". *Social Sciences in China*, 2015 (12).

Ma, G., "Macroeconomic Disequilibrium, Structural Changes, and the Household Savings and Money Demand in China". *Journal of Development Economics*, 1993, 41(1), 115–136.

Pudney, S., "Income and Wealth Inequality and the Life Cycle: A Non-parametric Analysis for China" *Journal of Applied Econometrics*, 1993, 8(3), 249–276.

Qian, Y., "Urban and Rural Household Saving in China". International Monetary Fund Staff Papers, 1988, 35(4), 592–627.

Wang, Y., "Permanent Income and Wealth Accumulation: a Cross-sectional Study of Chinese Urban and Rural Households". *Economic Development and Cultural Change*, 1995, 43(3), 523–550.

Wang, Z., and J., Kinsey, "Consumption and Saving Behavior under Strict and Partial Rationing". *China Economic Review*, 1994, 5(1), 83–100.

Wang, Z., and W. S., Chern, "Effects of Rationing on the Consumption Behavior of Chinese Urban Households during 1981–1987". *Journal of Comparative Economics*, 1992, 16(1), 1–26.

Wong, R. Y. C., "Estimating and Interpreting Chinese Consumption Functions". Studies on Economic Reforms and Development in the People's Republic of China, 1993.

World Bank, "*China: Finance and Investment*". Washington: World Bank, 1988.

Xiaoguang, Liu, Zhang Xun and Fang Wenquan, "Effect of Urban and Rural Income Distribution for Infrastructure: Based on the Perspective of the Transfer of Labor". *The Journal of World Economy*, 2015 (3).

Xiaoguang, Liu, Qin Gou and Feng Lu, "Remedy or Poison: Impacts of China's Outward Direct Investment on Its Exports". *China & World Economy*, 2015 (23) (6), pp. 100–121.

Young, A., "Gold into Base Metals: Productivity Growth in the People's Republic of China during the Reform Period". *Journal of Political Economy*, 2003, 111, 1220–1261.

Zhang, Xun and Liu Xiaoguang (corresponding author), and Fan Gang, "Rural Labor Migration and the Rate of Household Savings: The Perspective of Discrepancy in Income and Social Security". *Economic Research Journal*, 2014 (4).

Index

CPSIA information can be obtained
at www.ICGtesting.com
Printed in the USA
LVHW011231230420
653775LV00004B/8